The World of the Polynesians

Potatau or Te Wherowhero

Principal Chief of all Waikato.

WHATA WHATA

The World
of the Polynesians

Seen through their myths and legends,
poetry and art.

Antony Alpers

Auckland
Oxford University Press
Melbourne Oxford New York

Oxford University Press

Oxford   New York   Toronto
Delhi   Bombay   Calcutta   Madras   Karachi
Petaling Jaya   Singapore   Hong Kong   Tokyo
Nairobi   Dar es Salaam   Cape Town
Melbourne   Auckland
and associated companies in
Beirut   Berlin   Ibadan   Nicosia

Oxford is a trade mark of Oxford University Press

First published in 1970 as *Legends of the South Seas*
First published in this edition 1987
©Antony Alpers 1970
Preface ©Antony Alpers 1987

ISBN 0 19 558142 3

Cover designed by John McNulty
Published by Oxford University Press
5 Ramsgate Street, Auckland 5, New Zealand

CONTENTS

HAWAIIAN ISLANDS

TONGAN GROUP

SAMOA

ATOLLS AND OUTLIERS

NEW ZEALAND AND THE CHATHAMS

'FROM DARKNESS TO LIGHT'

ACKNOWLEDGMENTS

COMPLETION of this book was made possible after 1966 by Queen's University at Kingston, Canada, to which I again express my gratitude. My thanks are also repeated here to all those institutions to which the illustrations are credited in the Notes.

Permission to use material quoted in the Introduction was kindly given by the following: Chatto and Windus Ltd. and Sir Moses Finley (*The World of Odysseus*); Cambridge University Press and the late Mrs Nora Chadwick (*The Growth of Literature*); Penguin Books Ltd. and Dr Claude Lévi-Strauss (*Structural Anthropology*). Dr Raymond Firth kindly allowed me to use his literal translation of a tale from Tikopia. Hare Hongi's translation of the 'Chant to Io' is used by permission of Roy Cowan.

NEW PREFACE, 1986

Science is the critique of myth. Without Genesis,
there would be no theory of evolution.

— W.B. Yeats

THIS book endeavours to put the oral literature of Polynesia before the reader as something to experience rather than be told about, and it continues to be the only book that does so for Polynesia as a whole. It was first published—under quite the wrong title, now removed—in 1970. In other words it was conceived and written during the sixties, just when modern techniques of archaeology, linguistics and anthropology were beginning to effect immense advances in our knowledge of the Polynesian past. Attention to the myths and legends was therefore firmly out of fashion, while digging was important. But the book was meant for non-professional readers, of two quite different kinds.

Beyond the Pacific, I had hoped it might make the pre-European world of the Polynesians better known and understood, entirely through their own creations and with as little interference from a Western mind as possible. Since theirs was one of the richest mythologies the world has known, that seemed to me worth attempting. We had heard a great deal from outsiders about their life and its beautiful environment, but what had the Polynesians made of it all themselves? And how could one suggest that?

At home in New Zealand I had dared to conceive another aim as well, which I thought best not to mention at the time. Thanks to a modern migration from the Islands the country was then in the process of acquiring the largest concentration of Polynesians that has ever existed, and the most varied: no such Polynesian mixture as New Zealand now accommodates had ever before assembled in one place. If it didn't read books its children someday might, as their Pakeha neighbours do. I hoped that this modest sampling might offer the newly evolving society a pan-Polynesian picture of the marvellous heritage that had been created in the adjacent ocean by the forbears of all these migrants. In private, I even dared to hope that it might be of help in the decades of adjustment that lay ahead.

So the book was written. I myself chose all the illustrations, and in 1970, superbly produced by John Murray—the same family firm that gave us Grey's *Polynesian Mythology* in 1855—it was published in London and New York, its main title then being *Legends of the South Seas.* The present title followed, as a sub-title only.

What happened next now seems, in retrospect, mere comedy. In the Northern Hemisphere the book all but vanished for lack of notice. Literary editors, on both sides of the Atlantic, seemed to spurn it rather as Horace Walpole spurned its earliest forbear and actual starting point, the *Voyages* of Captain Cook. As Walpole told the Countess of Ossory in 1777, he had neither read Cook's *Voyages* nor intended to:

> I have seen the prints—a parcel of ugly faces, with lubber lips and flat noses, dressed as unbecomingly as if both sexes were ladies of the first fashion; & rows of savages, with backgrounds of palm-trees. Indeed I shall not give five guineas—nay, they sell already for nine, for such uncouth lubbers; nor do I desire to know how unpolished the north or south poles have remained ever since Adam and Eve were just such mortals.

In fact this book won the National Book League's award for English book design in 1970, but it seems a book can be *too* handsome: review copies may simply be filched and never referred to in print. No major reviewing journal arranged for an assessment by someone qualified in the field. Enthusiastic things were said by non-experts in places where influence was least, and there was not one 'bad review', but of informed discussion, there was none. A semi-exception occurred in *Country Life*, where the poet Geoffrey Grigson said that unlike Andrew Lang I had made a truthful experiment with language—which worked, he surprisingly said. In New Zealand the *Journal of the Polynesian Society* dismissed its copy as 'received'. From readers themselves there was no response at all. I began to blame the title (imposed by publishing arrangements in America), but as clippings came in from around the world something else emerged: only two reviewers anywhere had referred to anything that was more than half way through the book. Then was it, as I now naturally ask myself, unreadable? To this point, I'll return.

The book's unapt relation to its time and to all the scientific advances in prehistory was an accident, as the tell-tale bibliography reveals (item 34a and the current material on page 3 of the Introduction were late additions). Its relation to those studies now is potentially quite different, and this preface to a brave reissue is my opportunity to state what I think it ought to be.

For more than a hundred years up to 1960 or thereabouts, all speculations as to Polynesia's past were dominated by the oral literature which the Polynesians had preserved with so much care: the myths and legends, poems and chants, and the tribal traditions of migration, along with the recited genealogies. But these things, like the vestiges left underground or in the languages, were not yet being arranged or read correctly. Essential distinctions between the categories were not being made: the nature of myth was not being investigated as it can be; so called traditions (including the myths!) were being read for their ostensible meanings only, and hence as a sort of 'history with mistakes'—which still occurs.

Pacific ethnology was not yet equipped to view those treasures as artefacts of the mind. What myth and symbol can reveal of a people's relation to the very distant past went unexamined, possibly out of embarrassment over Biblical myth. In regard to more recent tradition, the task was plagued by the enormous popular appeal of what used to be called 'The Whence of the Polynesians', and hence by the public's persistent love of being misled. Undoubtedly the 'Mystery of Easter Island' has a lot to answer for. Reaction had to follow, and in universities it did, in part.

From 1960 onwards a new breed of scholars began applying techniques that were capable of fixing events in time. Burials, middens, and finds of artefacts could be carbon-dated with a new precision. Sherds of pottery found on various western islands and belonging to the so-called Lapita People (*c.* 1500–500 B.C.) pointed to an assemblage of proto-Polynesians in the groups now called Samoa and Tonga. Modern linguistics, too, has its dating techniques, agreement was found between the disciplines, and confirmation now exists for the hypotheses briefly summarised on page 3.*

Although much more must await discovery, these fruitful investigations have since reached the stage of being reviewed in three authoritative books, all with the word prehistory in their titles. Peter Bellwood, an English archaeologist who worked on Polynesia from New Zealand, produced *The Polynesians: Prehistory of an Island People,* in 1978; in the following year a broad symposium by thirteen scholars, *The Prehistory of Polynesia,* edited by J.D. Jennings, came from Harvard; and in 1984 the New Zealand archaeologist Janet Davidson produced her own summation, *The Prehistory of New Zealand,* by no means a merely local study.

To one acquainted with the oral literature and the guesswork it once begot these books are a joy to read. They replace a muddled picture with an ordered one; they are models of science applied to man's comprehension of himself; and one conspicuous virtue of

---

*Some readers may notice in the Introduction various words and phrases which, ideally, should be revised after 16 years. 'Caucasoid' (page 3) is now an error; the kumara (page 7) has been accorded American origin; allusions to the book's original title remain, as well as an error of my own concerning chiefly assassinations (page 23), which did occur in Tonga. A modern technical problem, involving prohibitive cost, has ruled out the small revisions called for.

the various authors is the courtesy they show toward mistaken predecessors, and to each other in disagreement. I therefore hope very much that none of them will mind my saying that I find their disciplines guilty of a retreat into certitude, of a misplaced fear of the artefacts of the mind, and hence a narrowing of the field of view that will need correction in the next, more humanistic phase, by another new breed of scholars, who can read both kinds of record.

For the present situation is a little absurd. The Polynesians took extraordinary care to preserve in word and symbol the meaning of their past. 'Probably no race has ever held its history in greater esteem', says Nora Chadwick in a work of unique authority which is quoted on page 32; and we can add that as soon as they saw their cultural canoe being swamped they seized any chance of preservation for their narrative and poetic treasures, both the sacred and the secular. But now prehistory, as conceived by European and American minds after a century of cultural demolition, is based by choice on what was thrown away, mislaid, or lost, or placed in graves. It ignores the remarkable work of Mrs Chadwick; over-whelmingly, the evidence it respects is something physical or dis-carded; post holes, tools and fish-hooks, skeletons, moa bones, middens, even canine coprolites are made to yield undoubted facts—and how they do illuminate! That which lies *buried* in the languages—the vocabulary of Proto-Polynesian—has also been reconstructed with scrupulous ingenuity; but what the living lan-guages were used for—what made us respect the Polynesians in the first place—is pushed aside, though its quantity is vast, and its quality superb.

Once it was 'the missionaries' who avoided certain topics from embarrassment, and sometimes even cut bits off the human figures they sent to London, lest the ladies blush. Today the big sym-posium from Harvard, just referred to, displays the new embar-rassment. Since thirteen excellent contributors took part, its *total* avoidance of the literary hoard must reflect editorial direction.

The synthesis now called for may not be easily achieved, but prehistorians are surely mistaken in thinking it impossible or improper. Joseph Campbell's masterly study of world mythologies, which draws on all their disciplines and more, demonstrated that as long ago as 1959. Nora Chadwick's 1940 work is equally important. It functions by studying the forms employed—an approach not neglected in countless works on the other arts of Oceania.

If a new role exists for this book on its being reissued, it is a modest one: perhaps no more than to urge attempts upon the synthesis by a new breed of scholars, putting flesh back on the bones to which archaeology has given new meaning. No doubt it won't be possible to restore imaginings to the dried Maori heads which gather impious dust in our museums. But the Maoris did declare, along with Tokelauans and Hawaiians, that it was possible to return the spirit to a respected corpse. (You start at the feet, and you have to push; for a vivid description of the process from Hawaii, see page 266.) Whatever the method—and that of Joseph Campbell has been markedly successful—it has got to be attempted, so that that which *used* to be soul and body joined as one may yet seem so again. You do need to try to understand the nature of the Polynesian spirit, and of mythology itself; and you have to push. To the new breed then, good luck; and start with original texts, consulting manuscripts where possible.

The examples chosen for this book have nearly all been re-expressed, to a greater or lesser extent, from often difficult originals in English which no one reads, in the hope of making them agreeably accessible to a willing reader. Are they, nevertheless, as unreadable as it seems reviewers found them in 1970? I find them no more so than anthropology. But I should perhaps explain that the often experimental style resulted from aspersions cast at my previous collection (*Maori Myths and Tribal Legends,* 1964). I had humoured too much the Western reader, I was told, standing nearer to him than to the original narrators. So in this book I resolved to express my regard for the original narrators by trying to draw the reader in their direction, with a sometimes harsh result. The task is to stay in equilibrium between two strong magnetic fields.

To the ordinary reader now I would say: begin with that chilling masterpiece from the Chatham Islands, the story of Apukura's mourning for her son. With a shiver, then turn to the marvellous tropical riches of the legend of Rata (I myself cannot reread either without a stirring of the blood). Then move about from there, always surrendering to the *magic* of the Polynesian world. The lubricious improprieties ascribed to the Tuamotu tales may hold appeal. The second line of *Kae and the Whale* contains the most outrageous of the book's improper jokes.

Toward the back there is a fascinating dramatic piece, the libretto of a musical sketch composed on Mangaia about 1780: an authentic native comedy depicting the visit of Captain Cook to that island three years earlier (*their* view of *us*). It still awaits revival in New Zealand, with real Mangaians, now plentiful in Auckland. What a romp it would make! In 1970 its presence in this book went quite unnoticed, outside Glasgow.

With *Hine and Tu* (and its note) an attempt is made to rescue from disrepute, and restore to its rightful place in a widespread Polynesian tradition, what I think must be New Zealand's earliest piece of tourist trash, the 'Legend of Hinemoa'. Grey's sentimentalised version of 1855 is regrettable for what it started—the cheapening of the Maori in a popular tourist location. My own could doubtless be improved, but at least it stands for the second of my original good intentions: my wish that all of New Zealand's Polynesians, whether Maoris or Islanders, standing upright together might rediscover, through their shared new language, their shared traditions and their roots in a lost Havaiki, indeed in a world-wide heritage of myth.

ANTONY ALPERS

Christchurch
New Zealand
June 1986

INTRODUCTION

THE name Polynesia, meaning 'many islands', defines that part of the Pacific which lies inside a triangle made by drawing lines on the map to enclose Hawaii, Easter Island, and New Zealand. This triangle has Tahiti near its centre and Samoa and Tonga toward the west. It excludes Fiji, the Solomon Islands, the New Hebrides and other parts of Melanesia ('black islands') where the people in general have black skin and Negroid features, some frizzy hair, and innumerable languages. It also excludes a region to the north of Melanesia known as Micronesia, which comprises sprinklings of very small islands such as the Marshalls and the Gilberts. These regional distinctions, like the title chosen for this book, are a form of shorthand used for convenience.

The Melanesians have their mythology as well, but it is markedly different from that of the Polynesians, and not so lavishly developed. For some reason the Melanesians threw their talents into the plastic arts (with wonderful results, as can be seen by a glance at any book on the arts of the South Pacific) and did not magnify their gods and heroes by means of the literary art in which their Caucasoid neighbours to the east excelled. It is true that theirs are 'South Sea Islands', but it is also true that when a Westerner thinks of a South Sea Islander it is probably a Polynesian that he has in mind—most likely a Tahitian or Hawaiian. Hawaii of course is not in the south at all, but is north of the Equator. There is no escaping inexactness if we use the common terms.

The islands inhabited by Polynesians are not all tiny, they do not all have reefs and blue lagoons, and a few are distinctly cool. *Most* of them lie within the tropics, to be sure, but Easter Island does not, and New Zealand and the Chathams lie well to the south; they lie in a similar latitude to Spain. In stories from Easter Island, cooled by the Humboldt current, we hear of children sun-bathing after a swim; while in the Chatham Islands we actually hear of fog, and of chiefs who keep warm in sealskin cloaks.

Physically, the islands range from small atolls to the considerable land mass of New Zealand, which has high and ancient mountains, glaciers, inland lakes and live volcanoes. The dry ground of an

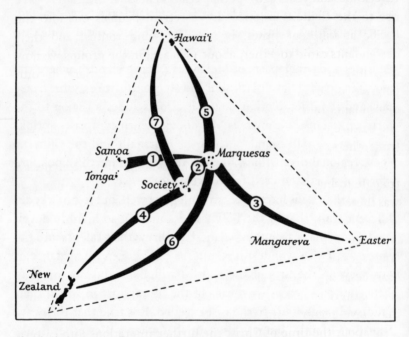

The shaded pointers, from one to seven, show the order in which the primary migrations are believed to have occurred, according to modern evidence. (After K. P. Emory and Y. H. Sinoto—see note on page 4.)

atoll is seldom higher than ten feet above sea-level or wider than a few hundred yards; but those Polynesians who some eighteen centuries ago migrated north to 'flaming Hawaii' found their lives in danger from the largest live volcano in the world. They evolved, in consequence, a set of volcano myths that are their own.

These people came, of course, from somewhere else. There is

no real controversy on the broad issue.* Their ancestors came from islands to the west and ultimately from the Asian mainland, their stock being strongly Caucasoid but with some Negroid and Mongoloid admixture. The ethnic strains, and a multitude of other facts, suggest that something that was happening in Asia about three thousand years ago—perhaps the events that ultimately gave rise to the Chinese empire—drove certain peoples out into the Pacific at different times, by various island routes; and their descendants came together, about 1500 B.C., in the groups we now call Samoa and Tonga. There, in the view of K. P. Emory, in comparative isolation and before east Polynesia was settled, their descendants took on the characteristics of appearance, language, and culture which the Polynesians now share in common and apart from others.

Samoa and Tonga, in short, were the first land in the Polynesian triangle to be occupied, and the source of all later settlements. It was there that the people we are speaking of became 'Polynesians', and there too, probably, that they became split into two main language groups, represented today by the West Polynesian languages of Tonga and Samoa, and the eastern languages of the Marquesas and Tahiti—New Zealand and Hawaii being offshoots of the eastern zone. Linguistic evidence suggests that this divergence may have begun about 300 B.C.

By about the time of Christ the further migrations into eastern Polynesia had probably begun. The more distant Marquesas, it seems, were settled first, and from them the Society Islands—both, according to strong suggestions in the archaeology, by well planned, purposive voyages. Then, as population pressures once again built up, there were further movements out from those areas (see map):

---

* The next three paragraphs attempt to summarize the present state of a complex scientific debate involving recent work in the fields of archaeology, ethnology, linguistics and physical anthropology. An accessible popular summary is R. C. Suggs's *The Island Civilizations of Polynesia* (1960), but I am mainly indebted here to K. P. Emory and to papers contributed by R. C. Green and Y. H. Sinoto to two recent symposia (items 21 and 34a in the list of References). The map on page 2 is from item 21, where it is acknowledged to an earlier source published by Emory and Sinoto, 1965.

Tamanu flower

south-east to Mangareva and Easter Island, from the Marquesas; south-west to New Zealand, first from the Marquesas and later from Tahiti; and northward to Hawaii (again from both). On present knowledge the whole dispersion process, from the West Polynesian base, may have run from about the time of Christ until the thirteenth century, with Easter Island paradoxically an early landfall.

The dates implied here are all much earlier than those that used to be accepted on the strength of traditions and genealogies. The traditions are now known to be highly inaccurate as to time-span; yet they do have a part to play at this point, by telling us something of the migrations that archaeology hardly can, though common sense certainly would: in the legends, migrations are usually connected with some sort of quarrel in the homeland just left, and the leaders are, by implication, defeated chiefs, who then become the great chiefs of the newly settled lands.

To my knowledge only one tradition—from a suspect source— contains an admission of being blown away by accident: the New Zealand story of Whatonga, as related by Te Matorohanga and published by S. P. Smith.* That Polynesians, given the choice, would rather admit defeat than admit being blown off-course seems most unlikely. The traditions on this score ring true—which may add somewhat to the case for purposive voyaging as the means of Polynesian dispersal. But there seems no point in denying that *some* landfalls of Polynesian voyagers may have been fortunate accidents, while others, and probably the most important ones, were the result of well planned expeditions carrying the essentials of women and food-plants and animals.

Be that as it may, the achievement of the Polynesians as sailors will hardly stand belittling. Long before the Vikings had made their crossing of the Atlantic, Polynesians were heading out across the largest and emptiest stretch of water on the globe. Nowhere

---

* 82(2): 97. Numbered references to sources begin on page 397. Future references in the introduction are located by a number in the text.

Vini, the Tahitian parakeet; and a maomao

else has one people occupied so great an area of the world's surface—or so little, if we speak of dry land only.

The culture they carried with them was that of a hunting and planting people—a fact that is reflected in their myths. Their important food plants were the coconut (which could not by itself have colonized the whole Pacific, since though it floats, it rots), with the breadfruit tree, the starchy root-crop known as taro, the yam, the sweet potato or kumara (which they may eventually have carried to Peru, since it is known as kumar in some localities there), and the gourd, which provided their bowls and flasks. They also had a kind of dog, though not like ours (it didn't bark), together with the pig, the jungle fowl, and a species of rat, which was eaten and enjoyed. They did at one time make pottery, for shards have been found in Samoa and Tonga and even in the Marquesas; but this craft they abandoned, whether for want of clay, or because gourd, coconut and wooden bowl sufficed. Their women practised finger-weaving, but did not have the loom. They had the bow and arrow, but as a plaything only—it was nowhere in use as a weapon or even for shooting birds, and no one seems to know why. The men also played with kites, and flew them very high, using precious cord which was made by rubbing coconut fibre on the thighs. Among pastimes they also had the string games we call 'cat's cradle', and children's spinning-tops; and in New Zealand there was a kind of marionette or jumping jack, worked with string. All these things their ancestors no doubt brought out with them from the Asian homelands.

They also brought, of course, not merely the gift of fire, and tools that were characteristic of their last continental home, including an adze not known elsewhere, but all that prior mental furniture which we call today mythology; and this was naturally drawn from the ancient stock of universal myth, its elements being ultimately traceable to a nuclear seedbed of the Neolithic Age, somewhere in what we call today the Near East. Joseph Campbell, with incomparable fusion of scholarship and insight,

has put the modern evidence before us in his *Primitive Mythology*—
the first book of his four-volume work *The Masks of God*—to which
the reader should certainly turn for the larger background to the
present collection.

Chaos, creation of the world, quarrels of the gods, the creation of
woman and man's first sin of incest; the phallic serpent, fire-theft,
ritual love-death (food-plant out of human head), realm of the
dead, resurrected hero, cannibal ogress—all these occur in some
form in the tales from Polynesia, and remind us that wherever
man took his hunting and planting ways, his tools and weapons,
he also took his myths.

In the oceanic environment, however, not only were there no

Tahitian fish called iri

metals to be unearthed but there were no land mammals of any
sort—with the single exception of the 'flying-fox', a fruit-eating bat
which is presumed to have found its own way there. Their 'hunting' therefore was mainly the catching of birds and fish. The pig,
dog and rat which the proto-Polynesians carried into the Pacific
gave their descendants their only knowledge of quadrupeds, and

this has had a restricting effect upon their language and imagery which is specially noticeable to us. For animal metaphors and symbols they always draw on fish and lizard, bird and insect—as if they somehow recognized that the imported animals were not a part of nature in their island home. There were also, incidentally, no snakes in Polynesia—a serious omission, one would think, from the symbolic point of view. But, as we shall see, the smooth-skinned eel was more than capable of taking up the serpent's role.

After about the eighth century A.D. there was evidently a vigorous and stimulating burst of further expansion, which lasted until about our thirteenth century—the approximate date that was formerly assigned to the migrations to New Zealand, Hawaii, and Easter Island, on the evidence of traditions. It would seem that the people flourished, multiplied, and throve intellectually as they adapted themselves to what obviously was one of the most *enjoyable* environments ever found by man. But they also soon reached the point, on many islands, at which some people must either die, if there was to be enough to eat, or go away. The probable pattern is that chiefs defeated in quarrels over land (or over women, which may often have amounted to the same thing) were continually being forced to build canoes and set off in search of new homes known or unknown—where eventually some of their descendants would repeat the pattern. Hawaii, New Zealand and Easter Island, the three points of the triangle, all have traditions that exemplify this trend. The chant from Mangareva on page 230 suggests what painful moments must have occurred between the members of a family at many such departures into the unknown sea.

After the thirteenth century, however, it seems that some sort of equilibrium was reached, for migration then appears to have stopped. The causes are unknown, but we are hardly entitled to ignore the possibility that the Polynesians simply knew there were no more islands to be found. Warfare itself is often mentioned as a form of population check. It obviously would be if many food-bearing trees and women and children were destroyed;

but the actual numbers of enemy killed in fighting, when they are recorded, are often rather small.

Once the period of expansion and occupation was completed to the limit of human habitability (that is, sometime before the European arrived on the scene in the sixteenth century), all Polynesia had one thing in common—that the people considered themselves as having come from a legendary homeland known to nearly all of them by the same name—'Havaiki'.

Seventy or eighty years ago it was considered very important to try to locate Havaiki, and at least two prominent amateur collectors of legends vitiated much of their life's work in the process. Today we can see more easily that 'Havaiki', when used geographically, is a relative term at best. But it also has another meaning, as the reader of this book will find. It sometimes means the World Below, the darker place of origin, a place whence lands themselves have been fished up or which such mobile demigods as Maui might visit from time to time.

In the geography of the upper world—the World of Being or the World of Light as it is sometimes called—Havaiki means approximately 'the place our ancestors came from'. Since that place was seldom known with any certainty, no one today should try too hard to locate Havaiki on the map. It is not necessarily Samoa, Tahiti, the Marquesas, or any of those dispersal points, yet it may be one or more of them. The name has been appropriated (in the local dialect) as a place-name for Savai'i, in Samoa, and of course for Hawaii. In the form Havai'i it was an old name for Ra'iatea, near Tahiti.

Polynesian Life

Descriptions of Polynesian society and village life are available in various popular or more specialized books—of which Margaret Mead's *Coming of Age in Samoa* is probably still the best known. Since it is one of my aims in this book to let Polynesia portray

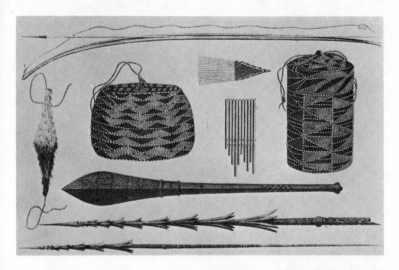

Tongan artifacts brought back by Cook

herself, I shall not attempt any systematic description here.
Instead, let me simply take up some points that may help the
reader to assemble a picture of his own, of tolerable completeness.

It will strike anyone soon enough that the life from which these
stories arose was *radically* different from our own. Attitudes to
life and death, to property, to relations between men and women,
to society as a whole, and especially to food, may seem so strange
as to make the stories actually difficult to read. Yet at the same time
there may be a feeling that all this is somehow familiar: 'just like
ourselves, essentially'; or at any rate like something heard before.

The causes of the major differences are plain enough: the absence
of mammals, for instance, of the seasons, and the constant presence
of the sea. But as to those many little similarities that flicker
like a fish beneath the surface as we read—do they simply betoken
man's 'universality', or have they come into our minds from somewhere nearer home?

I think a glance at the Greeks may answer this question. Between the society of the Polynesian 'savage' and the civilization of

the first Europeans there are some striking parallels, which show up plainly in M. I. Finley's *The World of Odysseus*, a book that might almost have been written to suit our purpose here. Let me take some examples directly from this excellent account of Greek society based on Homer's epics:

'There is no social conscience in these words,' Mr. Finley writes after quoting a speech of Hector's in the *Iliad*, '. . . no responsibility other than familial, no obligation to anyone or anything but one's own prowess and one's own drive to victory and power.' The comment might be applied without alteration to innumerable passages in Polynesian oral literature.

'The word "hero" is a class term for the whole aristocracy,' Mr. Finley says on the same page, 'and at times it even seems to embrace all the free men.' If for 'hero' we merely substitute 'chief', again the comment fits the Polynesian world.

'The profundity of the Greeks' kinship attachment, throughout their history, is immediately apparent from their passion for genealogies.' . . . 'The language had no word at all for the small family, in the sense in which one might say, "I want to go back to live with my family".' . . . 'And then there is the word "to love". That is how we render *philein*, but the question remains open as to what emotional quality, what overtones, the Greek verb really possessed.' . . . 'Where, in the many references to Odysseus's sad longing for his home and his wife, is there a passage in which sentiments and passions that the modern world calls "love" shine through?'

In all this Mr. Finley might just as easily have been speaking of Polynesia—where the word corresponding to *philein* would be 'aroha' ⋆ or one of its dialectal equivalents.

⋆ Defined by Stephen Savage in his Rarotongan dictionary (65) as 'Tender affection, deep solicitude, affectionate consideration . . .' and in a verbal sense, 'to love or cherish'. Savage adds: 'It is to be noted that it does not convey the meaning of "to be in love," as expressed by the English word.' To speak of that (or to say 'I love you') would require a different verb, *inangaro*. In short, *aroha* must always be translated 'according to the emotional context.'

A tattooed Marquesan chief

There is in Polynesia the 'endless feasting' that Mr. Finley discusses, and, not unrelated to this aspect of archaic economy, the practice which he terms 'gift-exchange'—it being a rule of both primitive and archaic society that 'no one ever gave anything, whether goods or services or honours, without proper recompense, real or wishful, immediate or years away, to himself or to his kin'. Again: 'there is no single word in either the *Iliad* or the *Odyssey* that is in fact a synonym for "merchant".'

Mr. Finley remarks that nowhere in Homer is there a rational discussion, 'a sustained, disciplined consideration of circumstances and their implications, of possible courses of action, their advantages and disadvantages'. There are indeed some long arguments; but they are 'quarrels, not discussions', and 'never was a dispute resolved by talk, but always by decision of the gods carried out through the prowess of the heroes'. We are still in Polynesia.

Lastly, Mr. Finley quotes Coleridge's observation that 'There is no subjectivity whatever in the Homeric poetry'. Indeed there is not—nor in the Polynesian, either; for the very notion of the individual as we have conceived it since the Renaissance had never emerged in those societies. Here let us turn from Mr. Finley to Jacob Burckhardt's *Civilisation of the Renaissance in Italy*. In the Middle Ages, Burckhardt has told us, both sides of the human consciousness, the inward and the outward, lay half awake beneath a common veil. The veil was woven of 'faith, illusion, and childish prepossession', and through it the world and history were seen in strange hues, while man was conscious of himself 'only as a member of a race, people, party, family or corporation—only through some general category'. In Italy, says Burckhardt, this veil melted, so that an *objective* view of the State and the world became possible; and with this went a corresponding assertion of the subjective side—'Man became a spiritual *individual*.' In pre-Christian Polynesia this never happened, of course.

Such parallels—which will not surprise anyone already familiar with the bases of archaic society—may explain what it is beneath

Tavake, the red-tailed tropic bird

the surface that persistently 'sounds familiar', in spite of all the strangeness, as we read a Polynesian saga. But there remain some important aspects of Polynesian life for which we find no counterparts—and for which, in two cases, we had no word at all until the Polynesians gave us one.

'Tapu', in the form 'taboo', has now come into common use with us. One of its earliest definitions is still useful: 'This singular Institution, which pervades the entire extent of Polynesia,' wrote the New Zealand missionary Richard Taylor in his book *Te Ika a Maui*, 'may perhaps be most correctly defined as *A religious observance, established for political purposes*. It consisted in making any person, place, or thing sacred for a longer or shorter period....' (A thing that was tapu was not to be touched in any way.)

Tapu produced real fear in the New Zealand Maori—though rather less, I think, in his tropical cousins, who seem to have had no Calvin in their past. It had the function of strongly reinforcing the authority of a chief or priest, and in one of its practical forms it was widely used, under the name 'rahui', as a conservation measure—for dwindling supplies of fish or coconuts, for instance. (The eradication of tapu by Europeans as a 'superstition' brought calamitous results to some islands that formerly had well-kept stocks of lagoon-fish.) In modern Honolulu, where it has the dialectal form 'kapu', the word has been degraded to a sign on private parking lots.

F. E. Maning's portrayal of tapu in his *Old New Zealand* (74) still conveys, as no objective description could, the intensity of *feeling* involved in Maori tapu; but it is far too long to be quoted here.

'Mana' is the other word adopted into European use—though only by specialists, outside the Pacific. From adding to the many elusive definitions of this complex cluster of ideas (which includes notions of personal ascendancy and the supernatural), I would like to be excused. But I have noticed that 'charisma', coming into use where 'mana' is unknown, covers part of mana's meaning. The legends of Tahaki and of Rata, in this book, show mana in action.

'Kura', meaning approximately the colour red—*including* the dull tone of red ochre, but meaning especially the brilliant gold or scarlet of the feathers of various birds of tropical Polynesia—is a good deal easier to define, even though it involves a visual experience now irretrievable by us, and indeed by the Polynesians too.

Captain Cook, with his sure eye for essentials, speaks in the journal of his second voyage of 'the extraordinary fondness the people of Otaheite showed for red feathers, which they call Oora and are as valuable as jewels are in Europe'. This was not some odd quirk of the Polynesians with a hidden ceremonial meaning. The explanation of it is soon obvious to anyone who visits Polynesia with his eyes open. The glamour of the tropic island in its natural state is composed (apart from the neutral tones of grasses, wood and sand) of three tiresomely insistent colours: blue, green and white. There are some red flowers, it is true—ephemeral things, which quickly wilt. Apart from these there is the sunset and the dawn—and there is blood. It is hardly surprising—whatever part may be played by some natural hunger of the human eye for the missing primary colour—that red or golden feathers, where they could be had, should have acquired a very powerful symbolic force and meaning for the Polynesians. Even where they were, relatively speaking, 'plentiful', they were hard to come by. In Hawaii the birds that yielded them were by no means always killed; the gorgeous capes that were made of mamo feathers were naturally the property of chiefs alone, and became, as it were, divine insignia. In Tahiti the famous maro 'ura, or Scarlet Girdle of the chiefs, was made from feathers taken from the head of a small bird, the vini. In the Marquesas, young men climbed steep cliffs at night to snatch the feathers of the red-tailed tropic bird. In New Zealand, nothing like the Hawaiian cloaks was made possible by the little parakeet, but there was abundance of red ochre in certain places, and sacred objects were coloured with that, the earth being mixed with shark-oil, to make a stinking but possibly rainproof paint. On Easter Island the quarry at Punapau yielded a red tufa that was used to make the 'hats' that surmounted the famous statues. The stories in this book of 'Tahaki kirikura', ('Tahaki of the Golden Skin') and 'Ahu ula', ('The First Feather Cloak') may convey something of the meaning that kura had for the Polynesians before Cook gave away his presents of red cloth, or French traders took to Tahiti the now widely used 'pareu' prints that give the paintings of Gauguin their wholly imported glamour. Kura, 'ura, ula, and Cook's Oora are of course all versions of the same Polynesian word. Gauguin and the airline calendar by now have fixed in our minds a picture of Polynesia in which the hunger for red is more than satisfied. But the reader of this book should try to imagine a scene of tiring blues and greens, and dazzling whiteness of the reef and coral-gravel paths. Then the feathers of the little vini will appear as they truly were—'as valuable as jewels are in Europe'.

Turning from red to what we are pleased to call 'white', some readers may not realize that the Polynesians were great fanciers of a pale skin long before the superior European came among them, and that they went to extraordinary lengths to achieve it in chiefly persons. Since a case of this was noticed with amazement in the very first hours of first European contact with the Polynesians, let us hear it described in Quiros's account (29) of Mendaña's discovery of the

Marquesan fan

Marquesas in 1595 (the italics are mine). Some seventy canoes swarmed out from Fatu Hiva to inspect the ship, paddled by extremely handsome natives who included some 'beautiful youths':

> Among them was a boy, who appeared to be about ten years of age. He came rowing in a canoe with two others. His eyes were fixed on the ship, and his countenance was like that of an angel, with an aspect and spirit that promised much, of a good colour, *not fair but white*; his locks like that of a lady who valued them much. He was all that has been said, so that I never in my life felt such pain as when I thought that so fair a creature should be left to go to perdition.

The practice of bleaching the skin turns up in the stories in this book in several ways, and the boy the Spaniards saw was probably a 'poea', like the one in the story 'Tahia the Fragrant Girl'. There is more on this subject in the Notes.

Polynesian sexual customs are another topic on which there may be a need to dispel misapprehension. A belief has had some currency that the healthy, uninhibited Polynesians were a blessed and fortunate people, wholly free of the deplorable taboos of our own society; that as to verbal expression they lived in a sort of Lawrentian Utopia where there were no rude thoughts or words, and all the women were enlightened Lady Chatterleys until the wicked missionaries came and made them cover up their breasts, and so on. This is an immature and misleading fantasy, though perhaps not surprising in a society which, so far from speaking clearly on the subject of its own taboos, did not have a word for them until it got one from the Polynesians.

The Polynesians were not without rude words. They had the same use as we for their releasing power, and possessed some word-taboos that seem to have been actually *more* violent than ours, only they were connected with the head and with food, not with the genitals and evacuation. Since this links up with the fact of cannibalism (which we will come to next), and also throws light on various references in the stories which otherwise might merely seem 'quaint savage customs', let us speak of it briefly.

First, there is much truth in the popular notion of Polynesian sexual freedom, though only before marriage. The delightful hospitality that was enjoyed by the first English sailors at Tahiti is not to be dismissed as merely equivalent to what greeted them on their own docks at home—though that point was worth making. But the great attention that has been paid to it, and to the professional conduct of the ariois of Tahiti, has tended to overshadow the modesties of Polynesian life, which were considerable, and especially in other parts of Polynesia.

On the remote little western outlier of Kapingamarangi, a charming reticence was the general rule. 'It was considered offensive', writes K. P. Emory in his report of an ethnological expedition to that island (139), 'to refer to sex organs or functions, as well as the excretory ones, by their own terms, at least in connexion with humans.' The direct names for these things did not appear in any of the songs or chants collected, and if old men were reciting chants with a sexual theme they would stop if a woman or boy came within hearing. Acceptable indirect terms were 'needle' for penis and 'thing' for vulva; and for the sexual act itself, 'to do the sacred thing'. The worst insult the island knew was 'vulva of your mother'. No obscene gestures were seen. All this may be no more typical of Polynesia as a whole than were the novelties of Stimson's Tuamotu stories (pages 83 and 107); but it was the case, and it was Polynesian.

And so to the awful fact of cannibalism—the eating, with undoubted relish, of the flesh of other persons, who may have been spoken to not long before. Again, not a universal Polynesian practice at the time of European contact, and regarded with clear horror by the people of some islands, including Tahitians. Not to be explained in dietetic terms, since it occurred where animal proteins were freely available, and was absent where these were often in short supply. A practice beset with paradox, but closely linked, I believe, with Polynesian notions of obscenity. The point is already discussed in the Preface to the American edition of my *Maori Myths*. In this place a briefer note must serve.

Certain Polynesian customs can more easily be understood by us if they are seen as a straight reversal of things we do ourselves. The Maori custom of weeping over friends or relatives when they *return*, rather than when they go away, is one example, which has a logic not impossible to grasp. A similar straight reversal is found in regard to food. The Polynesian notion of the lowest thing, the most *devoid* of sacredness, was cooked food: not what comes out of the body, but what goes into it. To grasp the logic here is a little harder: a deliberate effort of the imagination is required, and still may not succeed. But it is necessary, if numerous references in the stories that follow are not to seem absurd, or meaningless. Examples are the fire-god's complaint of Maui's dreadful treatment of him on page 100; Puna's degrading treatment of Rata's mother on page 141, and young Rata's revulsion on hearing of it; and the repeated references to the severed head of Tu whakararo as the 'left-over food of other warriors', in the bloody tale of Apukura. All these are instances of the Polynesian curse involving food—the strongest obscenity they had, and one of immense releasing power. If it seems meaningless to us, that is presumably because we are incapable of imagining the ultimate act itself—the eating of another person's flesh. That it had such force for the Polynesian was surely just because he *could* imagine doing that. That eating is pleasurable invalidates nothing: a moment's cogitation on our equivalent obscenities will perhaps bring home the point. The act of cannibalism, I am suggesting, was the ultimate obscenity for the Polynesian.

It has been stated that cannibalism was not practised at all in Hawaii—but certain legends of that group refer to it. In respect of Tonga, Gifford has said that there was little information but it was believed to be rare. The story of the Origin of Kava, given in this book, is based upon a child-eating incident. Cook's Tahitian passenger Hitihiti (actually from Porapora) was 'struck with horor at the sight' when some New Zealand Maoris obligingly ate human flesh on the very deck of the *Resolution* in Queen Charlotte Sound in 1773. He wept and scolded by turns, and 'told them to their faces that they were vile men', etc. But the story of the female cannibal known as Rona (p. 118) came from his homeland. There were evidently few if any places in Polynesia where people knew nothing of the custom, but some where it was out of fashion at the time of European contact. On Mangaia, according to Wyatt Gill, it had been forbidden, some time before the coming of the Gospel, by a beneficent chief of the eighteenth century named Mautara, of whom Gill heard nothing but good reports. If any one group of Polynesians is to be held innocent of cannibalism as a common practice, I believe the honour might go to the charming atoll peoples, whose normal diet was coconuts and fish. An atoll is one place on earth—if earth those fairy-rings of ocean can be called—where the brotherhood of man seems almost real.

There is one other respect in which (as we prepare to leave the subject of society and customs) a sign of grace is perhaps to be discerned in the native literature. Though warfare was a universal presence in Polynesia, and was a passion with the New Zealand Maori, some preaching against it was not unknown. One historic (legendary) instance of it is discussed in my *Maori Myths*: Houmai tawhiti's exhortation to his sons, as they left Havaiki, to 'live in peace' in the new land. And from Rarotonga, Wyatt Gill (60) records a mother's 'song in favour of peace', which ends with these words:

> Let there be peace, O son—let not war prevail.
> .   .   .   .
> Put down thy spear and leave it as a token—
> That thy posterity may behold it.
> Go to thy grandparent—to Auruia,
> That he may instruct thee in the korero.

Let there be no war; for a man of war can ne'er
   be satiated;
But let my son be instead a man of wisdom and
   learning,
A keeper of the traditions of his house.
Let there be no war.
Plant deeply the spirit of peace
That your rule may be known—the land of
   enforced peace.

Perhaps it is worth mentioning also that, except twice in Gill's Mangaian writings, I know of no reference to poisoning in the Polynesian literature of murder. A form of poison was widely used for catching fish: the grated nut of the utu (*Barringtonia speciosa*) when sprinkled on the lagoon caused fish to be paralysed, and Gill says in his *Jottings from the Pacific* (58) that three persons had been poisoned with this on Rarotonga—'since the introduction of Christianity'. On Mangaia, however, a shrub named reva (*Cerbera lactaria*) yielded a poison so virulent that it could not be used for catching fish, and Gill adds: 'This was the dreaded instrument of death used by sorcerers in the olden times.'

Assassination does not seem to have occurred to the Polynesians as a means of removing unpopular chiefs, or even popular ones. I know of no reference to anything resembling this Western practice.

European Contact, and Collection of the Myths

The first island with Polynesians on it to be seen by Europeans was, by an odd trick of Pacific history, one of the 'Polynesian outliers' located in Melanesian waters well outside the famous 'triangle'— the little atoll of Kapingamarangi, already mentioned. Fernao de Grijalvares, sent on a westward errand from Mexico by Cortez, passed close to it in 1536, saw men fishing and called it Dos Pescadores, but did not land. By an even odder chance, Kapingamarangi was the *last* Polynesian island to experience Western contact. Its first white man went ashore in 1877. Being well off trade routes it still had little contact, and when visited by Emory and others in 1947 its society had not been denatured.★

However, the classical date for the start of European contact with Polynesia is 1595—when Mendaña discovered the Marquesas, saw the astonishing spectacle of a 'poea' (the beautiful youth described by Quiros, above), landed on Tahu Ata, and departed after his arquebusiers had sent some two hundred Marquesans to perdition, apparently for the sport of it.

The other discoveries followed much later, and Cook made his first visit to Tahiti in 1769. The first London Missionaries landed there in 1797; the Gospel was carried to Tonga in the same year, to New Zealand in 1814, to Hawaii in 1820, and to Rarotonga in 1823. (It only reached Kapingamarangi, through a native pastor, in 1919.)

Generally speaking, it is from missionaries that we first hear of Polynesian myths in any satisfactory detail, but there is one outstanding exception to this—provided by Cook of course.

Cook, as the Notes explain, is the author of the first European references to Maui, the most famous of all Polynesian heroes; but he also recorded a Tahitian account of the Creation, in a scrap of manuscript that we can regard as the first record of Polynesian mythology ever made, and hence as the true starting-point for this book. We are told by Hugh Carrington (35), who saw the significance of the unpublished fragment and sent it to the *Journal of the Polynesian Society* in 1939, that it briefly gives the story of Maui separating sky and earth, and continues with 'Creation, original cause of things'. This is the passage we want to see. Its place in this book is not in the main text, though, for its interest is mainly historical. Let us have it here, with the minimum of respelling and repunctuation. The words in parenthesis are supplied by Cook. Those in square brackets are conjectured by the present author.

★ See also the Notes, page 389.

Creation origl. cause of things by many names:
Ta'aroa tahi tumu, 'Ta'aroa origl. stock'—most commonly
Ta'aroa or Te Tumu—existed before everything except of a rock
(Te Papa) which he compressed and begat a daughter (Ahuone)
that is Vegetable Mole.* After he begot the earth the sea fresh
water sun moon stars etc. and at last atuas, beings between himself and man and who afterwards begot mankind, [he] went to
heaven and left the world to his posterity.

O Ti'i the first [? man] was the son of Te Tumu and Ahuone
whenua, both atuas. He was born in shape of a round ball
which his father shaped as we now are and called him O Ti'i
(finished). O Ti'i lay with his mother, after many attempts, and
begot a daughter, Hina i 'ere'ere nonai, who when grown up
persuaded her father, with difficulty, to initiate her in the same
mysteries, whence sprang Hina i o wai, another daughter [on]
whom he begot Hina i ta'a ta'a, who he was then obliged to
impregnate and begot Hina rorohi, from who sprang Hina nui
ta'i te marama, who brought him a son Taha i te ra'i, who of his
mother begot a son 'Oro and a daughter Hina i pia, who together
begot Ana, another son. From these three men and the women
sprang all mankind.

O Ti'i is said to have lived in an island Havaiki to the northward, from which come hogs, dogs, fowls etc.

This account of Tangaroa and of Tiki the First Man will be found
to convey more after the Creation stories that follow have been
read, and there is a Note discussing it more fully on page 366.

After Cook, very few of the explorers have anything useful to tell
us about Polynesian myths or legends. They had not the *time* to
learn such things. We turn instead to a series of collectors who,

---

* Ahuone means 'earth heaped up'—a widespread name for the Polynesian first
woman. It sounds as if Cook also heard the term applied to the banks of humus and
rotting material on which taro is grown. In the English of his day this was known as
'vegetable mould'.

Marquesan bowl

spread over the next one hundred and seventy years, fall into four categories:

1. The Christian missionary, taking a humanistic interest in the mythology he has come to supplant. He has to learn the language thoroughly in order to translate the Scriptures for local use, and in doing so is inevitably exposed to the native religious thought.
2. The educated administrator or official, taking a more secular interest in the superstitions and customs of his subjects. He learns the language too, but less thoroughly than the missionary.
3. The amateur folklorist, active at the end of the nineteenth century and principally in Hawaii and New Zealand where there was a reading public for his work, which verges at times on journalism. His knowledge of the language is serviceable, but often unsophisticated.
4. The professional ethnographer or anthropologist of the twentieth century, who learns at least one dialect thoroughly, is aware of modern linguistics, and is trained in methods of observing and recording. He is equipped with comparative information before he starts.

Broadly, we can say that it is the missionaries and the ethnographers who have done the best work, and that they complement each other well. The missionaries suppressed and censored things, but they had a sense of wonder, and the language to convey religious thought; the ethnographers may lack both of these, but they do not suppress. The knowledge of the two can sometimes be combined. Most of the material in this book is owed to these two kinds of collector. Rather less is owed to the two intervening groups, but all have their part to play, and no group is without at least one member whose work is a good example to the rest:

J. M. Orsmond, for instance, who went to Tahiti for the London Missionary Society in 1817 when he was 31, taking a wife he had married in Sydney on the way. He came from Hampshire. Described as a 'man of ruddy appearance, with driving energy', he was also a turbulent spirit and in the end he was not at all happy about the way in which Tahiti had been 'converted'. He laboured for the L.M.S. on Mo'orea, Huahine, Ra'iatea and Porapora before settling finally on Tahiti in 1831, all the time collecting irreplaceable material from native priests and others, whose names he usually records. When the French took over in Tahiti, Orsmond opposed missionary incitements to the natives to resist them, and refused his principals' instruction to leave the island. For this he was dismissed by the L.M.S. in 1844. He completed the manuscript of his book and trustingly handed it to French officials for publication by the Government in Paris. They managed to lose it. It is believed to have been burned, about 1850. Orsmond died in 1856. However, there was a grand-daughter, Teuira Henry, who was a school-teacher in Tahiti and never married. She made it *her* life's work to recreate the book from Orsmond's notes, adding comparative material in Honolulu. She died in 1915, but after many delays her monument to Orsmond, *Ancient Tahiti*, was published by the Bishop Museum in 1928. It is one of our richest sources.

W. Wyatt Gill, another L.M.S. missionary, came from Bristol. After obtaining his B.A. he went to Mangaia at the age of 22, taking a wife in Sydney on the way, like Orsmond. On Mangaia he began as assistant to his predecessor William Gill, who was no relation;

the natives called them Gilli one and Gilli two. He was on Mangaia for twenty years and on Rarotonga for eight, and his several books, mostly published in London by the Religious Tract Society, are full of valuable things, especially the numerous pieces of dramatic poetry which the Mangaians created in such profusion. Gill unfortunately tells us little about his native informants, but the two principal Mangaian chiefs of his time were among them.

Of the class of collectors I have called administrators and officials, our best example would be Sir George Grey, the Governor of New Zealand, except that we have little of his work here because it is much drawn on in my *Maori Myths*. But we do have three tales, including that of 'Te Kanawa', which he evidently heard from the warrior chief Te Wherowhero, whose portrait by G. F. Angas is seen in the frontispiece. It is thanks to Grey that we possess the famous New Zealand version of the story of Maui (not in this book) which has been a subject of discussion by scholars ever since it was published in 1855.

Among the amateur collectors, pride of place here must go to Alexander Shand of the Chatham Islands, since his work, if brief, was by far the best in quality. The son of a Resident Magistrate on the Chathams, Shand had been a court interpreter there before he took up sheepfarming. The work he did in the 1860's in conjunction with the Moriori, Hirawanu Tapu, has some of the best qualities of modern professional recording. Better than that, Shand's English is exactly suited to his purpose. I have followed the style of his renderings closely.

To give Shand his proper credit is to thrust aside somewhat two energetic amateurs of New Zealand and Hawaii whose efforts were of great importance in those islands: S. Percy Smith, who was a surveyor, and Abraham Fornander, who was a Government official and a judge. Smith founded the Polynesian Society and its *Journal*, and our debt here is more to the *Journal* than to his own collecting, which is marred by some naïve dabbling in 'linguistics' and by his determined efforts to locate Havaiki somewhere in India. Fornander's immense *Collection* (111), though it has defects similar to those of Smith's work, has served Hawaii well in default of early mission collecting, which was lacking there. It is only drawn on incidentally in this book.

It is the ethnographers, finally, who have set the standards by which all previous work now has to be judged. E. S. C. Handy, on Hiva Oa in 1921, working in the evenings with Haapuane (the 'sorcerer' of Gauguin's painting of twenty years before), produced renderings which, though scrupulously exact, yet seem to let us hear the very voices and smell the perfumes of those enchanted islanders whom we find in the dream-world of Gauguin's art and in the early descriptions of Quiros. From the *Voyages of Quiros* to the tales of Haapuane hardly seems a leap of three centuries.

After Handy, Sir Peter Buck (Te Rangi Hiroa), the New Zealander—half-Maori, half-Irish, doctor and soldier also—who was able to bring his Polynesian intuition and considerable mana into play when he joined the team of ethnographers who, between the two World Wars, gradually worked over all the 'unspoiled' areas of Polynesia for the Bishop Museum, while there was yet time. We draw on Buck for pieces from Mangareva and Aitutaki, but indirectly in a hundred other ways as well. And then there is J. F. Stimson, of Ra'ivavae and Mo'orea—without much doubt the most 'colourful' of all our nesophiles. Stimson, according to his brother-in-law Van Wyck Brooks, went to Tahiti in 1912 after reading *Typee* and *Omoo*. He had been practising as an architect in San Francisco, but wished to see no more of the 'hell' America was creating for herself. He spent the rest of his life in the islands, married a French Tahitian, and graduated from amateur collecting to linguistically scrupulous work that was sponsored by the Bishop Museum. Lloyd Osbourne, Robert Flaherty and Henri Matisse all knew the hospitality of Stimson's roof on Mo'orea, and Charles Nordhoff, Edward Sapir and R. B. Dixon were among his friends. He once solved a chess problem by spiritualism. Without Frank Stimson this book would certainly lack its lightest moments.

To the devoted work of all of these and the fifteen or so others who are named in the Notes, a book of this kind entirely owes its being. Their work is honoured, and respectfully acknowledged.

Publication and Study of the Myths

We have seen that the first piece of Polynesian mythology to be collected—Cook's account of Tangaroa and Tiki—can be dated 1769. The last opportunity for the directed collection of unimpeachable material (for so I would call it) was in 1947—when Buck, Emory and Elbert visited Kapingamarangi. We therefore begin, most fittingly, with a Creation myth that is owed to Cook himself, and end (in point of time) with some idle tales from the first Polynesian island that Europeans saw—and the last one they invaded. This is a span of 178 years, but in fact our main collection period begins with Orsmond in 1822, and so is shorter by some fifty years. Compared, then, with the full ten centuries allowed to what we describe as 'Greek Mythology', Polynesia's literature was collected all at once, within the compass of a single historical moment (the moment of contact), and essentially from the members of only five generations. It is important to remember, also, that both the priestly and the secular arms of Polynesian society yielded their material very freely. All that we know of *some* ancient literatures (Sanskrit and Hebrew for instance) comes exclusively from the priests.

As can be seen from the References, the publication of Polynesian mythology was under way by the 1850s, with the missionary accounts and with Grey's and Richard Taylor's important books from New Zealand (both 1855). In the libraries of today, books from this period—their leather spines now cracking and their gilt worn dull—occupy the shelf for the first forty years; then come the bound volumes of 'JPS' from 1892 onward until the task is taken over by the fully professional publications of the Bishop Museum— the 'bulletins' as they are called. The Bishop Museum has also published numerous studies of special aspects of Polynesian oral literature, among which those of Katharine Luomala are important. Miss Martha Warren Beckwith's valuable work on *Hawaiian Mythology* also ranges all over Polynesia in its examination of comparative material.

It was not in Honolulu, though, that the first comprehensive survey of Polynesian oral literature was made. That was done in England—by a Cambridge scholar who, I believe, had never known the sickly smell of copra in the hold nor any of the standard discomforts of travel in the islands. Mrs. Nora Kershaw Chadwick's 227-page section on Polynesia in Volume III of *The Growth of Literature* (9), a joint work with her husband H. Munro Chadwick, was a remarkable achievement in any light.

The work as a whole surveys the ancient literatures of Europe; the Russian, Yugoslav, early Indian and early Hebrew oral literatures; and those of the Tatars, the Polynesians, the Sea Dyaks, and certain African peoples. It is a survey of 'literary types', of the forms and styles of early literature, and in no sense a study of *mythology* (its authors in fact seem remarkably impervious to the spiritual and sensual qualities of the work they discuss). A serious limitation with regard to Polynesia is that the study was made before the main output of the Bishop Museum was published, and is therefore unduly dependent on some of our 'amateur' collectors, who are superseded now by better work. But Mrs. Chadwick, uniquely, was in a position to make comparisons between the oral literature of the Polynesians and of the other peoples considered, and it is on her unmatched authority that we can accept such statements as these, made jointly with her collaborator:

'Polynesia offers a richer store of traditional learning and speculation regarding cosmogony and the creation of mankind and the universe than any other area known to us. . . .'

'Writing was unknown throughout the Pacific Islands. . . . It is all the more remarkable, therefore, that the standard and range of [the Polynesians'] oral literature shows a greater intellectual activity than that of any other people with whom we have been concerned. . . .'

Mrs. Chadwick avers that the little island of Mangaia, with its population of two thousand-odd which was at all times independent, 'was for many centuries probably the most literary community of its size in the world'. Her comment on the historical legends of the Polynesians, finally, is of particular interest in view of the latter's ultimate place of origin:

Probably no race has ever held its history in higher esteem than the Polynesians. In their devotion to their early records they are comparable to the Chinese. The proportion of attention to events of centuries long past, and personalities long dead, is the more remarkable since these records have always been carried on without the aid of writing. Such a task could only have been accomplished by generations of specialists, saga-tellers highly trained in the art of memorising as well as in their critical faculty. And such a class of men could only exist where their art was held in high esteem and supported on generous lines. We have seen that the very absence of written records has afforded one of the main incentives of Polynesian chiefs towards the support of their oral record keepers. The result of this happy circumstance has been the production in Polynesia of one of the two finest oral historical literatures in the world.★

Even so, the presentation of an overall selection from this literary hoard has not been attempted until now. In J. C. Andersen's *Myths and Legends of the Polynesians* (1), published in 1928, the stories were given in summary and blended with commentary, in a way that tended to obstruct the reader's imaginative entry into the Polynesians' world of the marvellous; and Andersen had, of course, no access to the mass of important material that was subsequently published by the Bishop Museum. An undated book of about the same period by D. A. Mackenzie, *Myths and Traditions*

★ Chadwick (9), pages 400, 234, 232–233 and 260.

of the South Sea Islands, was impaired in similar ways. Only in Hawaii and New Zealand, on a mainly local basis, can it be said that there is public acquaintance with the poetry and tales that filled the minds of the Polynesian people. Since their collections are available elsewhere, I have not been concerned to represent Hawaii and New Zealand by their best examples in this book.

Principles of this Collection

It remains to say something of the principles followed in selecting and adapting the material now assembled, before we discuss some final points that may perplex or interest the modern reader.

As can be seen from the list of contents, we begin with three sections, 'The Creation', 'The Heroes' and a group of poems, which are all thematic anthologies drawn from Polynesia as a whole. We then range over some of the different island groups, in a sequence which has no particular geographic or historical significance but which does include (in the Easter Island section) some examples of migration literature. We end with a strictly historical section of modern material from the period of contact and just before, for which I have used a title taken perhaps with irony (though I am not quite sure) from one of the books of W. Wyatt Gill which show so vividly what was involved for Polynesians in the transition to Christianity. Beginning with a Polynesian Creation and ending with a Polynesian Genesis, we thus set our view of the whole within the only sort of frame that is thinkable, for Polynesians. The fact is, they were unable to conceive of religion and life itself as separate things until they met us, and one of the matters that had to be explained to them early on—by missionaries!—was that religion is something one can speak of separately from the very fact of being. Religion, then, is the frame. Next, I have tried to ensure that we have a balanced representation of (a) all the island groups; (b) all the principal myths that come from a long way back; (c) most types and styles of literary composition, in the Chadwicks' sense; and (d) the range of Polynesian life in terms of subject matter: peace and war; men and women; old and young; loyalty and fickleness; violence and tenderness; occupations, sports, fog and sunshine, volcanoes and surf, etc. I admit having indulged a whim to represent as many as possible of the fourteen islands I have been lucky enough to know or visit, while particular passages undoubtedly owe something to my having witnessed the equivalent 'classic Polynesian situation' in modern times: a grown man's humiliation at being berated for his bad conduct *by his mother*, in the hearing of the entire village; a deacon's family, lined up one behind the other on the verandah, picking and eating the lice from each other's hair before going to church on a Sunday morning; the faery sight of atoll-dwellers netting flying-fish at night by the light of palm-frond torches, from little canoes outside the reef; an exciting departure from Atiu on a vessel teeming with people; and even, on Manihiki, a play by children re-enacting the legend of Maui's fishing up their land from under the sea.

Negatively, I have tried to avoid all the instances I could detect of the 'feed-back' of European motifs, which inevitably occurs where material is collected late. One instance is referred to in the notes on the story of Tahaki; some traces of Greek myth are noticeable in printed Samoan sources,⋆ but not elsewhere; one Wesleyan collector has injected certain observations about the temperate use of the kava drink into a Tongan tale, and so on. But in general the reputable sources are remarkably free from these signs of contact.

It will be obvious that I must have had to make different adjustments for different kinds of collector and translator. With the best missionary material it is often simply a matter of translating the 'thees' and 'thous', and 'hithers' and 'yons' into current English. But Richard Taylor of New Zealand, Shand of the Chatham Islands and Handy of the Marquesas (one missionary, one amateur and one ethnographer!) are setters of standards I have tried to match.

The missionaries, incidentally, seem to have been outright

⋆ A god comes down to a maiden in a shower of rain, in one Samoan tale collected in the Tokelaus.

romanticists with regard to Polynesian love, and if a study of the
introduction of romantic attitudes into Polynesia were ever made, I
believe the stock-figure of the top-hatted 'mikinare' would be
found to be the party responsible. 'He earnestly besought her to
become his wife,' writes Gill somewhere, when we know quite
well the matter is one of much greater urgency. 'He fell ardently
in love with her,' writes another collector, when we know from
what ethnographers wrote later that a more probable expression
was 'he desired her', or even 'the jerks in his ure★ were strong to
have that woman'. Conversely, I have tried in some cases where the
translator is an ethnographer to restore something of the religious
feeling which the missionaries conveyed so much
better.

I have sometimes used constructions which come
from Polynesian rather than English thinking. The
use of the passive mood at points where we would
expect a style 'packed with action', is a Polynesian
characteristic and will be found fairly often. The
Western storyteller's device of getting the hearer
ready for a surprise is not a Polynesian usage (any
more than it is, for example, in our own Holy Bible).
The hearer of a Polynesian legend had heard it all
before, a dozen times. The element of suspense
should not be looked for: causation and the passage
of time do not have the same roles to play in Polynesian story-telling as in ours.

Polynesian languages reflect the extent to which
the individual was fused with his society. Most Polynesians had no word equivalent to our 'please' and
'thank you'; they had pronouns for speaking of two

Marquesan flute

★ Translations of Polynesian words are given in the index.

people and of more than two; and the language and kinship system together made no provision for any distinction between brother and cousin, mother and aunt, father and uncle, son and nephew, etc. The human separation implied by our usage in all these respects was not characteristic of Polynesian life, any more than were our concepts of property. I have therefore not inserted 'please' where it might often be expected; in the story of Tahaki I have deliberately alternated the English terms 'brother' and 'cousin' for Karihi, who was both because of adoption; and I have made some use of 'we-two', 'they-two', etc., always seeing in my mind's eye what one sees so often in the islands: two young people (not necessarily lovers) unselfconsciously walking hand in hand, or talking with an arm around the shoulders.

The expression 'this word', as an introduction to a short speech of some importance, does not come, as might be supposed, from the television screen, but from Polynesian usage.

Feeling that the book should contain at least one specimen of Polynesian narrative in literal translation (or nearly so), I have been fortunate in being able to give a little tale from Tikopia, almost in Dr. Raymond Firth's word-by-word rendering.

Since poetry and prose have clearly separated roles in Polynesian oral literature, it may be as well to consider them briefly before we turn to the prose. We shall see that two things, especially, distinguish the poems from the tales. First, their authorship is often known—that of the stories, never. Second, there is reason to believe that in many chants we are hearing a form of words that has been preserved by rote through many generations. The myths and legends are much more plastic. Subsidiary characters often change their names, obviously on the whim (or failing memory) of the narrator. They even shift from one generation to another, and Maui's father Taranga, to cite a well-known case, becomes his *mother* in New Zealand. Moreover, ancient myths are often strongly localized, with abundant circumstantial detail being used to give them an air of great veracity. Of myth, indeed, it might be stated as a defining principle that authorship should be beyond determining, and in the fullest sense irrelevant. For as Claude Lévi-Strauss has observed in his *Structural Anthropology*, myth is 'that part of language where the formula *traduttore, traditore* reaches its lowest truth value'. Poetry, he says, 'is a kind of speech which cannot be translated except at the cost of serious distortions; whereas the mythical value of the myth is preserved even through the worst translation. Whatever our ignorance of the language and culture of the people where it originated, a myth is still felt as a myth by any reader anywhere in the world. . . . Myth is language, functioning on an especially high level where meaning succeeds practically in "taking off" from the linguistic ground on which it keeps rolling.'

The poems of the Polynesians, on the other hand, are almost a private property at the outset. Their diction is regarded as fixed, and to remember their authors is a courtesy respected at least for a generation or two. On Rakahanga, when Buck saw a play performed, he learned that it was usual to obtain the consent of 'the person who thought it out' before repeating it. The names of the authors of four out of the five pieces that end this book are all known. These instances are recent, and needless to say there are older chants and poems which have become anonymous with the passage of time. But there is strong internal evidence in some cases that the *texts* have been kept intact, even when certain meanings have been lost. A well-known instance, referred to in the Notes on page 371, is the mention of the eel and the coconut in a Creation chant of Easter Island, where the terms in question have long been meaningless (or rather have become mere names), since neither eel nor coconut is known on the island. In another instance, from New Zealand, a reference in a chant to breadfruit (unknown to the Maoris for some six hundred years) threw light on an obscurity in a tribal legend and proved antiquity for both. Our own nursery rhymes, of course, are full of illustrations of the same sort of thing. The prosody of Polynesian poetry must have played an important part in this retention, but as far as I am aware it has not been seriously studied.

The Function of Myth and Legend

And so to the stories and the mode of thought they represent, which will often perplex the Common Reader, who I think can be heard inquiring from time to time, 'Where is the *point*? There's not much *point*, is there?'—thus lightly raising in an instant the immense question of what we mean by 'point' in Western literature. The end of an introduction is hardly the place to settle it, but since it undoubtedly comes up, we might try to clear the ground by at any rate defining our present material. For if we are to talk of 'point', we must consider *purpose*.

A classification once found convenient for primitive spoken literature was that of Malinowski, who distinguished three types: Myth (regarded as sacred, believed to be true); Legend (believed to be true but not regarded as sacred); and Fairy-tale (not believed to be true, not regarded as sacred). But these three divisions, even if they fit the Trobriand Islands material which Malinowski studied, will not do for Polynesia. As Raymond Firth has well shown in his *History and Traditions of Tikopia* (143), the 'true or false' criterion is too gross—a myth being sometimes believed by one man and not by another in the same village; or believed at one time and not believed a few years later, and so on.

The prose pieces in this book might be thought to fall approximately into four classes, on the meaning of whose names we may roughly agree: Myth, of very ancient origin, and wholly or essentially marvellous; Legend, of regional origin and partly marvellous but in no way political; Tradition, of local origin, partly marvellous but essentially political; and Folk-tale, of local origin (?), not necessarily marvellous and not political. But in Polynesia, where both the secular and the sacred material were fully surrendered to collectors,★ the class called Myth must be regarded as two. Starting again,

★ Which is not always the case; see page 30, and Chadwick (9), page xiv.

then, we have *five* classes, subject still to what has just been said:

RELIGIOUS MYTH, which is the learned work of priests and may be altered by them to suit immediate circumstances,* but generally in accordance with very ancient laws, no doubt unconsciously observed.

SECULAR MYTH, which is evolved rather than composed, and probably changes much more slowly. Its origins may be even more ancient than those of religious myth.

REGIONAL LEGEND, which again is the preserve of learned experts who are to some extent bound by facts, or at any rate traditions as to facts. This class of legend, being often concerned with personages claimed as ancestors, may sometimes serve 'dynastic' purposes.

TRADITIONS OF THE TRIBE, which also are the work of experts, and are concerned with who owns what, and why. They are usually associated with migration and settlement.

FOLK-TALE, which is the popular preserve, and of great variety. The experts probably take a hand in it, but the true arbiter is the common experience of the people.†

Examples of religious myths in this book are the opening pieces, both prose and chant, that deal with the origins of the universe and with the gods. Examples of secular myth are the tales of Maui the trickster hero—'ovenside tales', as Maori priests in New Zealand

---

* See note on Tangaroa, page 369.

† Finding a satisfactory compendious term for all these classes is an unsolved problem. 'Mythology' and 'myths and legends' are both in use. 'Oral literature' is inevitable, but is an absurd contradiction in terms. 'Stories' and 'tales' can be resorted to when the main thing is to get on with what one has to say. The original meanings in Greek of 'myth'—a word, something said, a tale, fiction, plot or even legend—and in Latin of 'legend'—a selection of the lives of the saints, something to be recited—give little help. Both words have become so diversified that the use of 'legends' in the title of this book is merest compromise.

have slightingly described them. Examples of legend (or are they myth?) are the long tales of Tahaki and Rata, and the shorter tales of Tinirau and Hina, and of Kae—all widely known, however localized by the narrator. Traditions of the tribe are represented here by the Easter Island migration and settlement stories. As examples of folk-tale we might choose 'Te Kanawa and the Visitors by Firelight' or almost any of the Tongan tales. The reader may care to try the endless game of classifying all the rest: of deciding, for example, whether 'Hine and Tu' is a true story of ancestors, as claimed, or just another tale of the ubiquitous Hina getting into someone's private pools.

To return, then, to our point. That the Polynesian concept of the 'point' of a story could be radically unlike ours may be seen when a single motif turns up in several different areas—for example, the 'misdirected dart and importunate woman' motif, which is discussed in the note on 'Tu'i Tofua', a Tongan tale with parallels in three other areas. It is obvious from the stories concerned in this case that *something* was transmitted—over the long periods of time that separate Tonga, the Marquesas, Hawaii and New Zealand—which had some 'point' for Polynesians. But what that something was is extraordinarily difficult to describe in English. To us, in short, it 'has no point'.

The point of a folk-tale like 'Te Kanawa' seems clear enough to us. The point of such tribal traditions as those we have from Easter Island becomes clear as soon as we acquaint ourselves with a few external matters. It is mainly when, working backward through the classes, we reach the regional legends and the myths themselves, that we experience strangeness and confusion. For this there are three outstanding reasons, which is not to exclude any possible others.

The first is the absence of our concept of 'justice', which is founded on notions of good and evil that the Polynesian did not entertain. This reason is so obvious that it need not be dwelt on.

The second is an apparently widespread characteristic of primitive literatures, that *persons* are not described,* and so do not quickly become 'characters' to us—who live in a world which discovered the Individual during the course of the Renaissance. The fact is, Maui, Rata, Tahaki and others did have clearly distinguishable personalities, even in our terms, and Miss Luomala has shown what they were in her book, *Voices on the Wind*. To help the reader a little I have somewhat emphasized them here, but this is licence. The Polynesian story-teller assumed that his hearer already knew those persons well. The *only* description of Maui's appearance that I know of is in a late, perhaps suspect source—a Stimson version, collected after 1920.

The third reason, possibly the chief one of the three, is the primitive concept of time. Many of the stories in this book will strike the reader as being 'open-ended' in regard to time. They begin, clearly enough, and they continue, and then the narrator stops. But has the story an 'ending', in our sense? Often it seems to have ended (perhaps with the death of a principal character), only so that it can be continued at exactly the same level of tension with another character, who may be the son of the last.

A Marquesan story may tail off with the words, 'It is concluded'. A fable from Kapingamarangi always ends with the words 'Waranga tangata hua'—'just a tale that people tell'. The stories of Rata and Tahaki, it is true, are sealed off in the version given here, but how justly I am not quite sure. The Maui cycle lacks the rounded ending which it uniquely has in the famous New Zealand version. Stories of Tinirau and Hina go on for ever.

Somehow the typical Polynesian story seems to stand outside of time as we believe we understand it.† In Western fiction (to use a

---

* Mrs. Chadwick (9, p. 832) says that descriptions of persons 'seem to be brief and rare almost everywhere'. Where they occur, as in Ireland, 'they tend to be conventional, varying only according to the age and standing of the person described'. Norse sagas, she says, are an exception. There, the descriptions 'frequently show marked individuality'.

† For a succinct discussion of the factors involved, see C. M. Bowra's *Primitive Song*, page 235.

term deliberately not introduced till now) we ask for an 'ending'—
or have done so in the past—and Professor Frank Kermode has
lately published a book-length study on this very subject, called
The Sense of an Ending: Studies in the Theory of Fiction. We like the
clock to go *tick-tock*, we do not like *tick-tick*; and we seem to need
our years and decades, centuries and eras—and apocalypses—for
the reassuring sense of order they provide.

If this be 'false' (and 'fiction' is our word for the literary art that
is based on the desire), then what are we to say of the Polynesian
literary mode, which is its contrary? In Polynesian story-telling,
solstices and seasons play no part and 'life goes on', as do the
months. The Polynesians had never heard *tick-tock* until Captain
Cook arrived with his two chronometers, and the whole sad ending
was begun. They had no word for 'years'. The Polynesian tale,
correspondingly, is open at both ends, like life, and not like fiction
—nor like this book, which the author now realises he has rounded off in a European manner. The desire equivalent to ours, for
something fictive, was evidently satisfied for the Polynesian by the
marvellous—which the native hearer perhaps no more believed
in than we may be said to 'believe in' the neat completions of our
fiction. 'Romantic' attitudes he never had, nor prudish ones. What
we call history, he would have looked upon as myth. With all his
credulity and his love of the marvellous he retained a capacity for
truth, in certain directions, that we seem willing to have given up
for something else.

PRONUNCIATION
AND SPELLING

THE Polynesians had no writing. The various dialects of their language that are used in print are spelled according to clear, consistent principles which were worked out, with a surprising measure of agreement, in the different areas during the missionary period. The simplest way to enable readers of this book mentally to pronounce the native words and names is therefore to suggest that all the consonants, including 'ng' and 'wh' when they occur, should be sounded as they are in English, and all the vowels as in Italian. No syllable ever ends with a consonant. In words of two or three syllables, let the stress fall on the first. In longer words, let it fall on the first and third.

Given these rules, a written Polynesian word is already a set of instructions for pronouncing it, and further 'helpful' spellings can only confuse. However, the following guides from Standard English may be used for the vowels: 'a' as in 'art' (or shorter): 'e' as in 'epic' (or longer); 'i' as in 'machine' (or shorter); 'o' as in 'orb' (or shorter); 'u' as in 'ruby' (or shorter). It is wrong to pronounce 'a' as in 'man' or 'i' as in 'it', and 'e' is never mute. Names like Hine and Pele therefore have two syllables. So much will hold, more or less, for the vowels, in all the dialects.

When we come to the consonants, some readers may be bothered by 'Ng', if it begins a word. It is really no problem. Anyone who can say 'a tongue' can say 'ngata' (the same sounds in reverse), or a name like Ngae. The sound of 'ng' is always as in 'singer'—never as in 'anger'. There is, however, the difficulty that several dialects use the glottal stop (represented in print by the hamzah)—sometimes for 'ng' or 'k', sometimes for 'h', and sometimes for 'r'. Moreover, some authors do not *show* this glottal stop, and it is beyond the scope of this book to amend every case. Since our object here is to experience the stories and poetry and not to take lessons in the intricacies of Polynesian orthography, I have followed one or two *ad hoc* principles which ignore linguistic requirements but should make things simpler for the reader: 1. For certain common words and proper names I have adopted a standard spelling regardless of local inconsistencies thus caused. 2. When use of the hamzah would merely leave the ordinary reader not knowing what to 'say', I have sometimes inserted the missing consonant. (For example, *Kui kura* for *'ui 'ura* on pages 140 ff; or *Tangaroa* for *Ta'aroa*, in many places.) 3. In Mangarevan texts I have used *'ng'* rather than *'g'*, as is done in the name of the island itself, but the *'g'* remains in some Tuamotu and Samoan stories, and should be thought of as *'ng'*. 4. In general, I have taken frequent liberties with names, omitting hundreds, shortening dozens, and making no fetish of 'consistency', which is beyond all reach when fourteen dialects and twenty-six collectors are involved. 5. I had hoped not to use our pluralizing *'s'* on Polynesian nouns, which have no plural form, but have surrendered for the reader's sake. Some other oddities, including inadvertent ones, may cause a lifted eyebrow for those who know; but if they know, then they appreciate the problem.

Some of the common words that have been standardized are: ariki (high chief, sometimes almost 'king'); atua (god or deity); kava (the plant and the drink); kura (red or redness); kumara (the sweet potato); tapu (taboo); tapa (bark cloth); umu (earth-oven); and the names of Rangi, Rongo, Tiki and Tahaki. 'Tattoo' (tatau) is a special case—the only word I have knowingly mis-spelled in European fashion.

Many other points that may leave questions in the reader's mind are dealt with in the Notes, which should be frequently consulted.

THE CREATION

Maori fish-hook

THE OFFSPRING OF
THE SKY AND EARTH

IN the beginning were Rangi and Papa, Sky and Earth. Darkness existed. Rangi adhered over Papa his wife. Man was not.

A person arose, a spirit who had no origin; his name was Rangitokona, the Heaven-propper. He went to Rangi and Papa, bid them go apart, but they would not.

Therefore Rangitokona separated Rangi and Papa, he thrust the Sky above. He thrust him with his pillars ten in number end to end; they reached up to the Fixed-place-of-the-Heavens.

After this separating Rangi lamented for his wife: and his tears are the dew and the rain which ever fall on her. This was the chant that did that work:

> Rangitokona, prop up the heaven!
> Rangitokona, prop up the morning!
> The pillar stands in the empty space,
> It stands in the baldness of the sky.
> The thought stands in the earth-world—
> Thought stands also in the sky.
> The kahi stands in the earth-world—
> Kahi stands also in the sky.
> The pillar stands, the pillar—
> It ever stands, the pillar of the sky.

Then for the first time was there light between the Sky and the Earth; the world existed.

When he had finished this work Rangitokona heaped up earth and of it he made man, he created Tu. This was his chant:

Stem heaped up, heaped, heaped up.
Stem gathered together, gathered, gathered
　together.
Heap it in the stem of the tree,
Heap it in the butt of the tree,
Heap it in the foundation of the tree.
Heap it in the fibrous roots,
Heap it in the thick root of the tree,
Heap it together, it grows;
Heap it together, it lives.
The heaven-stem lives, it is living, E!

Stem heaped up, body heaped up—
Let the heaven stand which lives.

Heap it in the flower of the tree,
Heap it in the leaf of the tree,
Heap it in the swaying of the tree!
Heap it in the spreading branches of the tree,
Heap it in the pattern of the tree,
Heap it in the finishing of the tree!
Heap it, it grows!
Heap it, it lives!
The heaven lives—E!

Stem heaped up, stem heaped up.
Let the heaven stand which lives,
Let Tu remain.

This was the forming of the body of Tu. Then the spirit was gathered in. And this was the chant for that work:

Let the spirit of the man be gathered to the world of being, the
　world of light.
Then see. Placed in the body is the flying bird, the spirit-breath.
Then breathe!

Sneeze, living spirit, to the world of being, the world of light.
Then see. Placed in the body is the flying bird, the breath.
Be breathing then, great Tu. Now live!

Tree-carving from the Chatham Islands

Then man existed, and the progeny of Tu increased: Rongo,
Tane, Tangaroa, Rongomai, Kahukura, Tiki, Uru, Ngangana, Io,
Iorangi, Waiorangi, Tahu, Moko, Maroro, Wakehau, Tiki, Toi,
Rauru, Whatonga—these were the sons.

Ruanuku, Motu ariki, Te Ao marama, Tu mare, Ranganuku,
Matariki, Wari, and Ro Tauira the pattern-maid—these were the
females. These were Rangitokona's descendants born of heaven
and the earth.

The last, Ro Tauira, being made, the children of Rangi and Papa
went forth their ways, they went out to the world of being.

Then Te Ao marama had her son, his name was Rongomai
whenua. He was the first man of this land; he was the land.

From this time grew the tribe of men, until the time of Maru-
puku and Rongopapa, whose tribe was called Te Hamata.

These people dwelt in this land here, before the coming of the
canoe Rangimata, and the rest.

Those ancient ones were hiti, they were giants. The long bones
of their thighs lay formerly at Te Awa patiki, showing that giants

lived formerly in this land; but the flood of that lagoon swept all away.

Ro Tauira the pattern-maid brought forth her son Tahiri mangate, who took for his wife Rangi maomao, 'Mackerel Sky'. As children of these two were born the winds.

The East wind was the first-born child, he came from where the dawn is seen. The West wind was the last.

The other sons were Wairehu, the warm month, and Tuhe a Takarore, the month before. These two kept counting and disputing when their season should begin.

It was Wairehu, that is January, who prevented Rehua, heat-of-February, from turning and devouring men by drying all things up.

Mihi torekao and Rongo, they are March and July. They were incited by Tahiri the father of winds to fight against man, and thus they do, with cold rain and the southerly, with sleet.

Tu matauenga, Tu-of-twisted-face, was a son of the rough West wind. It was he who placed strength in fishes and birds and trees to injure man.

TANGAROA MAKER OF ALL THINGS

*Here in Tahiti we state that Tangaroa was the
ancestor of all the gods. He alone made everything.
From the time without knowing there was Tangaroa
tahitumu, Tangaroa the origin.*

FOR a long time Tangaroa lived within his shell. It was round
like an egg and in the lasting darkness it revolved in the void.

There was no sun, there was no moon, there was no land nor
mountain, all was moving in the void. There was no man, no fowl
nor dog, no living thing; there was no water, salt or fresh.

At the end of a great time Tangaroa flicked his shell, and it
cracked and fell apart. Then Tangaroa stepped forth and stood
upon that shell and called:

'Who is above there? Who is below there?'

No voice replied. He called again:

'Who is in front there? Who is behind there?'

Still no voice answered. Only Tangaroa's voice was heard, there
was no other.

Then Tangaroa said, 'O rock, crawl here!'

But no rock was, to crawl to him.

He therefore said, 'O sand, crawl here!'

There was no sand to crawl to him. And Tangaroa became angry
because he was not obeyed. He therefore overturned his shell and
raised it up to form a dome for the sky, and he named it Rumia,
that is, Overturned.

After a time great Tangaroa, wearied from confinement,
stepped out from another shell that covered him; and he took this
shell for rock and sand.

Tangaroa creating other gods

But his anger was not finished, and so he took his backbone for a mountain range and his ribs for the ridges that ascend. He took his innards for the broad floating clouds and his flesh for fatness of the earth, and his arms and legs for strength of the earth. He took his fingernails and toenails for the scales and shells of fishes in the sea.

Breadfruit

Of his feathers he made trees and shrubs and plants to clothe the land. Of his guts he made lobsters, shrimps, and eels, for the streams and for the sea.

And the blood of Tangaroa became hot, and it floated away to make the redness of the sky, and also rainbows. All that is red is made from Tangaroa's blood.

But the head of Tangaroa remained sacred to himself, and he still lived, the same head upon a body that remained.

Tangaroa was master of everything that is. There was expansion and there was growth.

Tangaroa called forth gods. It was only later that he called forth man, when Tu was with him.

As Tangaroa had shells, so has everything a shell. The sky is a shell, which is endless space, where the gods placed the sun, the moon, the constellations, and the other stars.

The land is a shell to the stones and to water, and to the plants that spring from it. The shell of a man is woman, since it is from her that he comes forth. And a woman's shell is woman, since it is from her that she comes forth.

No one can name the shells of all the things that are in this world.

CREATION

The first period: of Thought

    From the conception the increase,
    From the increase the thought,
    From the thought the remembrance,
    From the remembrance the consciousness,
    From the consciousness the desire.

The second period: of Darkness

    The knowledge became fruitful;
    It dwelt with the feeble glimmering;
    It brought forth night:
    The great night, the long night,
    The lowest night, the loftiest night,
    The thick night, the night to be felt;
    The night to be touched,
    The night not to be seen,
    The night of death.

The third period: of Light★

    From the nothing the begetting,
    From the nothing the increase,
    From the nothing the abundance,
    The power of increasing,
    The living breath;
    It dwelt with the empty space, and produced the
       atmosphere which is above us,
    The atmosphere which floats above the earth.

★ 'During this period all was dark—no eyes.' (Richard Taylor's note.)

The great firmament above us dwelt with the early dawn,
And the moon sprung forth;
The atmosphere above us dwelt with the heat,
And thence proceeded the sun;
They were thrown up above, as the chief eyes of Heaven:
Then the Heavens became light,
The early dawn, the early day,
The mid-day. The blaze of day from the sky.

The fourth period: of Land
The sky above dwelt with Havaiki,
And produced lands:
Taporapora,
Tauwarenikau,
Kukuparu,
Wawau atea,
Whiwhi te Rangiora . . .

The fifth period: of Gods
Ru; and from Ru, Ouhoko;
From Ouhoko, Ruatupu;
From Ruatupu, Rua tawhito;
From Rua tawhito, Rua kaipo;
From Rua kaipo . . . &c.

The sixth period: of Men
Ngae, and from Ngae, Ngae nui;
From Ngae nui, Ngae roa;
From Ngae roa, Ngae pea;
From Ngae pea, Ngae tuturi;
From Ngae tuturi, Ngae pepeke,
Ko Tatiti, ko Ruatapu,
Ko Toe, ko Rauru,
Ko Tama rakeiora . . . &c.

HAVAIKI THE LAND

Tangaroa made the rocks and all the land. He made
the roots and all that grows. He made the seawater;
he made the fresh water. He called forth Tu to be his
artisan. He fixed the dome of sky upon its pillars.
Then Havaiki existed—the birthplace of man.

CLOSED in, the earth was enclosed, firmness held it. Atmosphere, the earth was atmosphere. Searching, there was searching for land. Nothing, there was no land.

Inland was not yet formed, seaward was not yet formed. Above was not yet formed, below was not yet formed.

The time for night passed by. There was quick growth, there was slow growth. There was thinness, there was thickness.

The first generation of growth was born, it was affinity-rocks.

Rock of the cliffs and ocean rock may meet and unite, there is affinity between them.

Slate rock and clay rock may meet and unite, there is affinity between them.

Pebbles and crumbling rock may meet and unite, there is affinity between them.

Sandy rock and earthy rock may meet and unite, there is affinity between them.

Rock of the point and rock of the bay may meet and unite, there is affinity between them.

Yet in affinity there is otherness which will not let all things unite.

Rock that is sharp and rock to sit upon, these may meet but not unite: there is no affinity between them. A man would grow impatient trying to unite these things.

Behold great Tangaroa! In himself were the devices that made uneven the surface of Havaiki. The first unevenness took place, and there was applause: the earth looked well.

Te tupo o 'ai 'ai dwelt with Tumu iti, and there was born Taune'e. Land was creeping in. Taune'e dwelt with Pau tere fenua: land came rushing in. Pau tere fenua dwelt with Ara 'arahu in the foundation: charcoal came in on the land.

Then Tangaroa cried: 'Let the stratum-rock stand out that sand may come, that Te Pori may be born for Ta'ere in the murmurings!'

Sand—there came sand to kneel on, also flying sand, fine sand, and muddy sand. Havaiki became full of sand: sand in the space for armies, sand in the plains; sand in the stream-beds, sand for the mountains, sand for the forest.

As the land came rushing on there was a narrow course around the base of Tumu nui Great Foundation. Fresh water flowed from the right of Tumu nui and seawater flowed from the left.

Tangaroa's standing place was above the churned-up waters of the passage in the reef. Upon the reef on one side he placed one foot, upon the reef on the opposite side he placed the other foot, and he looked on all and said:

'Let the hard rocks stand to support the mountains! Let the sandstone lie as a bed for the earth and the sea!'

This chant of Tangaroa made the substance of the land. Havaiki became land by the chant of Tangaroa.

Then Tangaroa shaped the substance of the land: he shook it, and it did not break. And he said, 'What good property I have in this land of mine!'

He therefore said this chant: 'O Tu, come forth to be an artisan for me!'

And there came Tu, the sacred one, the great artisan of Tangaroa. And Tangaroa ordered him: 'Lay out the sand for my small
canoe! Lay out the sand for my great canoe! Run and do, run and
do, run and do till all is done!' And Tu spread out the sand, he ran
and did as Tangaroa commanded him.

Roots were born for growth in the world. When the Chief of the
first generation of roots was born, he lived for the second generation. When the Chief of the second generation of roots was born,
he lived for the third generation. When the Chief of the third
generation of roots was born he lived for the fourth generation.
When the Chief of the fourth generation of roots was born he lived
for the fifth generation. When the Chief of the fifth generation of
roots was born he lived for the sixth generation . . .

> There were tens of roots.
> There were hundreds of roots.
> There were thousands of roots.
> There were myriads of roots.

Roots that spread upwards and roots that spread downwards.
Roots that spread inland and roots that spread seaward.
As the roots spread out they held the sand: the land became
firm.

Tangaroa fixed the dome of the sky, Rumia. He fixed it upon
pillars. He said: 'O Tumu nui and Paparaharaha, bring forth
pillars! Let there be a front pillar and a back pillar! There shall be
pillars upon our land. There shall be pillars, many pillars!'
When this was accomplished, there was applause, there was
extension.

There stood Hotu i te ra'i, for a front pillar, and Ana feo for a back
pillar, and Ti'ama tangaroa for the inner pillar. And there also
were the pillar to stand by and the pillar to sit by; the pillar to

*'There were tens of roots,
There were hundreds of roots . . .' Banyan tree*

blacken by, the pillar to debate by; the pillar of oratory and the pillar of going out.

There was extension of Tumu nui, there was extension of Paparaharaha, there was extension of the horizon. The sky was extended, it was widened, with the pillars of the land of Havaiki.

> The world beneath grew larger, darkness
>   extended.
> Mountains grew larger, mountains multiplied.
> Water increased, it rushed on.
> The ocean increased, it rolled forth.
> Rocks grew and increased.
> The skies increased, till they were ten in number.

Rain increased, it fell everywhere.
Moss and slime grew and increased.
Forests grew and increased.
Food grew and increased.
The tree that gives tapa cloth grew and increased.
Creeping plants grew and increased.

Living things grew in the sea and the rivers, and on the land. And they increased in the sea and the rivers and on the land.

Then Tangaroa looked below and he looked above, and he laughed with his pleasure at what he saw.

The face of clearness above looked down upon clearness below. The face of clearness below looked upward to clearness above.

*   *   *

Then Tangaroa cried, 'Who is behind, there?' and these now answered him:

'It is I, Tu moua, Standing-mountain'—'I, Tu fenua, Standing-land'—'I, Puna heuheu, Rushing-spring'—'I, Vai ariki, Chief-of-rivers. Tangaroa produced us all!'

Then Tangaroa cried, 'Who is in front, there?' and these now answered him:

'I, the twin-bodied Tino rua, lord of Ocean'—'I, Tahuri mai to'a, Rock-that-overturns'—'I, Tupu o te moana. We myriads of ocean rocks were made by Tangaroa.'

And Tangaroa cried, 'Who is above, there?' and answer came:

'I, Atea, the moving space, the sky space, the moving fatness, the fatness of the sky thrown off the earth.'

And he cried, 'Who is below, there?' and he was answered by Pit-of-great-foundation, Pit-of-ripeness, and Pit-of-noise. All these answered him.

He asked, 'Who dwells upon the land? Who lives in the ocean?' and the answer came to him: 'We living creatures, that are running to and fro, that crawl and swim. Tangaroa made us, he is master of us all!'

*   *   *

A great spirit pervades the sea for all time and his name is 'Oro pa'a, and he has a roaring voice, it roars eternally.

When Tangaroa saw all that was, he applauded. The earth had become land and it was filled with living things. Fresh water flowed through all the land, salt water filled the ocean; and they were filled with living things.

But silence was in the thick darkness of the closed-in sky of Rumia; in Havaiki, the birthplace of land; in Havaiki, the birthplace of gods; in Havaiki, the birthplace of chiefs; in Havaiki, the birthplace of men.

WHEN THE SKY LAY ON THE EARTH

Earth's covering then was creeping plants;
Her covering was the tutu,
Her covering was the wehewehe,
Her covering was the bramble,
Her covering was the nettle.
Do not grieve that the earth is overflowed with
    water,
Do not lament for the length of time.

The ocean's reign shall be broken,
The ocean's surface shall be rough—
With lands that spring up in it,
With mountains standing forth,
Girdling round the sea—
Yes, round the sea.
Broken up shall you be, O earth!
Do not grieve—yes you, even you,
Lest you should grieve through love,
Lest you should grieve for your water-covered
    surface;
Lest you should lament for the time.

THE CONFLICT OF
THE GODS

*We people of the Tuamotu tell of Atea, that is Space,
and of Tane also, that is Husband. These were gods,
their separate realms were in the layers of the sky.
Their peoples fought, and Tane came for safety to
the earth, he lived for a time with men. Afterwards
he obtained lightning, and throwing it upon Atea he
killed him. Yet Atea's mana lives.*

WHEN Atea first existed he was formless. It was the enchant-ress-woman Vahine nautahu who uttered chants and moulded him into comely shape. Then he became the god of the expanse above the third layer of the world.

Atea's wife was Fakahotu. They had handsome sons and daughters, and birds, butterflies, and all kinds of creeping things also were born to them.

Tane was the son of Te Hau and Metua. He dwelt with his parents and ancestors in the heaven called Vavau, and at length they all came down to fight with Atea, but Atea's warriors defeated them. Some were killed, some escaped, and Tane the youth fell behind in the realm of Atea. When he saw his danger Tane stepped down to the third layer of earth and dwelt with human beings. They received him kindly, and from them he learned to eat food, which was not known above.

When Atea saw the young god on the earth below he set a guard at each corner of the earth and sent gods to capture him. But Tane dodged back and forth and evaded his pursuers, until at last he found a doorkeeper crouching with his arms around his knees.

Thus he slipped through and escaped to his own heaven, where his parents had mourned him for dead.

Up in the heavens, Tane who had eaten food on earth grew hungry. 'There is no food here,' his father said to him. 'All you can do is open your mouth and swallow wind.'

'That cannot satisfy,' said Tane. 'How many men have you here?'

His father answered: 'Most of our men were killed by Atea. Only your two grandfathers and their parties escaped alive. And there are your ancestors, who did not leave this place.'

So therefore Tane killed one of his ancestors and ate him, and this was the beginning of the eating of men.

When Tane grew to manhood he vowed revenge against Atea

*A bone figure
from the Marquesas*

for the former defeat of his parents. His father warned against folly, but Tane went to his ancestor Fatu tiri, that is, Thunder, and he obtained lightning from him. Then Te Hau said to his son:

'Do not go yet, Tane, lest you fail. Wait until my hair is grey with age. This will tell you that Atea also has grown old. Then try your skill against him.'

So Tane waited until his father's head was grey. Then he made spears, and he gathered his warriors. They were led by Tall Ru, Short Ru, Tottering Ru, Ru the humpback, and Ru the turtle. All these came with chants of great potency to make war upon Atea.

'Now go to your grandfather Mata'i,' said Tane's father, 'and ask him for seeds of the pia bush.' And Tane did this.

'Now, my son, go down to the earth,' said Te Hau, 'and if you see ants gathered at the stump of a toa tree to feed upon its flowers, it will be the right time to plant your seeds, and you will know what to do.'

So Tane and his warriors went down to the earth, and ants were gathered round the toa tree to feed upon its flowers. So they planted their pia seeds, and they grew. And on the spreading top of a pia bush Tane chanted:

> Prop, now props the warrior
> With the pillar of the friend of the skies.
> Cast up by enchantment will be the heavens!
>
> Tall Ru, the man, propped up the sky,
> Which is held now by the warrior.
>
> Remain raised up, O sky,
> Remain raised up,
> Upon the pia tree, the teve, and the au.

Then the pia rose up with Tane upon it, and so he extended the heavens and fixed them in their proper places. And the pia remained as a post for the centre of the first sky; and Foundation Rock remained on the lowest layer of earth to hold up the world.

When Atea saw what had been done, and that Tane had come into his realm and fixed the heavens in their places, he said:

'Am I to remain and kneel in the presence of the friend of Havaiki who will seek Atea's blood?' So he made spears, and gathered all his warriors to meet the warriors of Tane.

But Tane wished to kill Atea alone. He therefore went to him one day and asked him to make some fire. Tane held the piece of grooved wood while Atea used the rubbing stick. But when it began to burn, Tane blew upon it and put it out, and this he did a second time, so therefore Atea changed places with Tane, and requested him to make the fire. So Tane worked the rubbing stick, and he used enchantments, and when Atea blew upon the fire, it only blazed more fiercely.

Now one of Tane's men when he saw this fire became jealous of Tane, and he stole some flame and set fire to the heavens above them. But Tane saw the flames and put them out, and when he came back he threw lightning on Atea, so that he died. And Tane took Atea's body on his great canoe, the name of which was A toa e ruru ai hau.

Atea's mana did not die. It remained great in these islands and it descended to men, and it came down to the Pomare family, as is shown in the genealogy of these chiefs.

TIKI THE FIRST MAN

TIKI was the first man.

It was said among our people that when Tiki was born Atea himself set Tiki apart to bring forth all the children of men in this world below.

When Tiki was young his parents said to him, 'You, Tiki, go outside and play,' and they remained together inside the house.

One day when he was playing by himself Tiki grew tired of the games he knew. He returned to the house and saw his parents at their own enjoyment. Tiki desired this. He therefore went away from the house and he heaped up earth in the form of a woman. He gave it a body and a head, with arms and legs, and breasts and ears and all that was required to make a woman. Having done this he acted in the manner of his father, and he there became a man.

Tiki took that woman for his wife, and her name was Hina one, that is Earth Maid.

The child that was born to Hina one was a human being, and they named her Tiaki te keukeu. She grew handsome. One day Hina one asked her husband to go to the world below to fetch some fire for them, for all the fires in that village had gone out. But Tiki was lazy and he refused, and so his wife said, 'Then indeed I shall go myself to get us fire.'

'No, no,' said Tiki, 'let us stay here quietly,' and they argued thus; but Hina was strong in her will. She said to her husband, 'You stay here. You have your daughter. I will go to the world beneath, as the moon goes.'

And Hina went below. And she was swollen with child, like the moon. In the world below she gave birth to her twin sons Kuri and Kuro, who knew not their father.

⋆ ⋆ ⋆

Tiki remained in Havaiki with his daughter; yet it was not seemly that he should have her openly. He therefore built an inland house in a valley of that land, and he said to his daughter: 'You live up there, and I shall live down here by the sea. Up there you will find the house that I have built and a man there who resembles me in every way. You will think it is Tiki, but you will be mistaken.' So Tiaki te keukeu did as her father had told her; she went up the valley to that other house.

Now Tiki ran swiftly by another path, and he reached the house before her. When Tiaki arrived he greeted her saying, 'Welcome, respected one! Enter this house of mine! Be seated on this mat!' That girl did so, she went into the house, and Tiki desired her. He took her with his hands. She cried out, 'No, I do not wish to. You are my father.' And Tiki pressed her, saying, 'It is true that your father and I are as like as two drops of water, but he is down there by the sea. I am of the upland.'

Soon that girl consented to live with Tiki in that house, and children were born to them. But after a time she became disgusted with her father, and she left him to seek her mother in the world below.

Her mother was disgusted also when her daughter told her, and they two made a plot to kill Tiki. They lit an oven in which to cook him, and sent the god Tuako up to fetch him. But Kuri and Kuro, the twin sons of Tiki, who knew not their father, made objection, and they prevented it. When Tuako went to the world-above he brought back a man named Katinga. It was Katinga whom they cooked and ate instead of Tiki.

⋆ ⋆ ⋆

While Tiki and his daughter were living together he told her one day that he was going out to catch fish. He asked her to follow him later with a basket for the fish. 'You will come to the beach,' he said, 'and go to a place where you will see a flock of birds hovering about something which is sticking out of the sand. That will be the place.'

And so Tiaki did as he had told her, she went to the beach with her fish basket. She saw the flock of birds and also something standing up above the sand. Thinking that it was their pointed stick for stringing fish, she took hold of it and pulled. And Tiki, who had covered his body with sand, jumped up crying, 'Who's this, pulling on my ure?' And he laughed at her shame.

When she saw that it was her father and that what she had in her hand was his, Tiaki reproached him: 'O Tiki, this is a dreadful thing that you have done, a most horrible act of yours!' And he laughed at her again; and she called him 'Tiki the slimy', and 'Tiki the rigid', and 'Tiki the trickster'. That is how Tiki earned those names of his.

After these events were known, the women of that land did not like Tiki. They called him 'Tiki the god of kaikaia', meaning a person who eats human flesh or who sleeps with his relations.

*   *   *

It was said of Tiki that he was two men, a handsome Tiki and an ugly Tiki; and the people saw his ugly and his handsome side at different times.

One day Tiki asked his womenfolk to make him a maro to wear around his waist. To tease him they gave him a maro full of slits and holes. He therefore made one for himself, and he wore it back-to-front so that the tail hung down before him. Then with his

Vaaroa, the 'long-mouthed' sea eel

eyes and nose all streaming with the mess that comes from there, and uttering noises from his bottom, he made his way up the valley, taunting them.

'Kill him! Kill him!' cried the people when they saw this. But when they tried to catch him Tiki disappeared, and suddenly he returned to them in his handsome form. It was said that Tiki kept all his ugly features in the hole in his bottom and took them out when he wished to wear them.

One day when Tiki appeared in that valley in his evil form the people caught him. They tried to pull his eyes out but they could not. They pulled out his tongue and tied it in a knot, but he untied it. They tried to knock his teeth out but they would not loosen. They cut his ears off, but he picked them up and stuck them on again. They cut off his ure, but he picked that up and put it back. They cut off his feet, but he put them on again, and the same when they cut off his arms. At length those people cut open Tiki's belly and they unravelled everything in there. At that he burst into tears and he ran away from all those people to the beach, and he remained there for a long time, sleeping in the sand.

They caught him again. They tried to rub off his skin with pieces of coral, but it would not leave his body. They lit an oven to roast him, but they could not drag him into it. Suddenly while the people were doing all these things the ugliness of Tiki left him, and he was handsome again before their eyes. Immediately all the women desired Tiki, and there was a great commotion. The women cried out to the men, 'Now leave him alone! Leave him alone!' So the men gave Tiki to the women, and at once he was ugly again; therefore they seized him and tore him to pieces. Yet every time they did this, Tiki was restored.

When they had torn him apart three times Tiki escaped from those women, and he slept once more in the sand by the sea, all covered up except his eyes. As he lay there a great sea-eel came, and it seized him by the foot.

Tiki cried out to his wife, Hina one, 'Bring me my knife, my cutting-shell!' Hina one was wearied of Tiki's tricks, and she answered, 'I am tired of sleeping with a demon.' But she took his head and pulled, and the eel pulled also, and there was a tugging match between them. Suddenly while the eel and the woman were pulling, Tiki disappeared.

This story of Tiki is concluded.

HINA AND THE EEL

We speak of Hina and her love with Tuna, first of
eels. From Tuna's death we have the coconut, which
bears his face.

HINA-MOE-AITU who was daughter to Kui-the-blind
lived in the shadow of the inland cliff of the makatea, her
house was near where the cave Tautua has its opening.* Now the
water from Kui's taro swamps disappeared beneath that cave into
the makatea, it ran out to the sea beneath the land; and Hina's
pool where she washed herself was there below that cliff.

In Hina's pool lived many eels, those tuna liked the darkness of
that pool. One day when she was bathing an eel of great size came
from its place beneath the rocks, and startled Hina by its pleasing
touch: that eel went sliding under Hina in the place where pleasure
is. And the tuna was wicked, and the same thing happened many
times, and Hina permitted it. That eel gave Hina pleasure with its
tail.

One day while Hina-sleeping-with-a-god was gazing at the eel
it changed its shape, it became a handsome young Mangaian. The
young man said, 'I am Tuna, god of all the eels. It is because of your
beauty that I have left my home and come to you, O Hina-moe-
aitu, and I desire you to have me.'

So they did, they two; they went into Hina's house together, and
afterwards he always turned into an eel once more, so that no
person should know about them. Their love grew strong.

One day Tuna said to Hina, 'I must go, I must leave you now for

---

* Mangaia is a 'raised coral' island, at one time an atoll. It therefore has a high
encircling rim, the ancient reef, called 'makatea', which has cliffs both inland and
seaward.

ever. Tomorrow there will be long-pouring rain, there will be flooding rain, there will be rain from the rivers of the sky. The rain will fill this place, the water will rise until it covers all the taro beds; it will reach up to the door of this house; but do not be afraid, for then I will be able to swim here to your very threshold. I will lay my head on that paepae and you will know that it is I. Then quickly take the adze of your ancestor and cut off my head on the threshold, bury it here upon the high ground. After that, be sure to visit the place each day, to see what will appear.'

Therefore Hina did as Tuna said. In the night she heard the heavy rain, the thick rain, the long-pouring rain; and she waited until morning for the light to come. Then Hina saw that all the waters streaming down from Rangimotia had filled the taro swamps and covered all the taro-tops. And water lay beside her door.

On that moment, a great eel came to the house and laid its head across the paepae. Therefore Hina took her adze, she took the sacred adze of her ancestor and she sliced off the head of that eel. She took it behind her house, and buried it.

Then the rains ceased and the floodwaters moved away, they passed out through the makatea to the sea; and each day Hina-moe-aitu visited the place where she had buried Tuna's head. For many days she saw no thing that grew, but then at last she saw a firm green shoot, it sprang up through the soil and it was not like any thing that grew upon this land. Therefore Hina guarded that shoot, and on the next day she saw that it was two.

Those two green shoots sprang forth and Hina guarded them, and soon she had two fine strong trees that grew. Those trees grew tall, they climbed toward the sky until the wind was rustling in their tops, her children climbed them for the nuts they bore.

There one tree was which had a red stem and a reddish fruit; it was sacred to Tangaroa. The other of her trees possessed a green stem and a green-hued fruit; it was sacred to Rongo.

After that time there were coconuts in this land. There was niu to drink, from the green nuts; there was niu mata, the soft white flesh that comes later; and motomoto from the ripened nut; and creamy roro that is squeezed from it; and there was uto, that forms inside the nut that sprouts; and from motomoto that is dried out in the sun the people of this land got oil to put on their hair and skin; and from the leaves they made kikau for baskets and for walls; and from the husks old men make twisted cord; and from the shells, round bowls; and from the dead tree past the time of bearing they had strong hard wood for houseposts, and for paddles.

All of these things were given to the land by Tuna the lover of Hina-moe-aitu. Therefore we call the white flesh of the coconut te roro o te Tuna, 'Tuna's brains'.

When all the husk is taken from a ripened nut the face of Hina's lover may be seen, the face of Tuna-god-of-eels, with his two small eyes and mouth.

A CHANT OF CREATION

God-of-angry-look by lying with Roundness made the poporo
  berry,
Himahima marao by lying with Lichen-in-the-soil made the lichen,
Parent-mother by lying with Pipiri hai tau made wood,
Ti by lying with Tattooing made the ti plant,
Elevation by doing it with Height made the inland grass.
Sharpness by lying with Adze produced obsidian,
Twining by lying with Beautiful-face-with-penetrating-tongue
  produced the morning-glory,
Parent-god by lying with Angry Eel produced the coconut,
Grove by doing it with Trunk produced the ashwood.
Veke by lying with Water-beetle made the dragonfly,
Stinging-fly by doing it with Swarm-of-flies produced the fly,
Branch by lying with Fork-of-tree made Beetle-that-lives-in-rotten-
  wood,
Lizard-woman by lying with Whiteness made the gannet.
Hard-soil by lying with Covering-below made the sugar cane,
Bitterness by doing it with Bad-taste produced the kape,
Tail by lying with Hina oio produced the crayfish,
Killing by doing it with Stingray made the shark.
Tiki-the-chief by lying with Heap-of-earth made Hina kauhara;
Kuhikia by lying with Wetness made the bulrush;
Kuhikia by lying with Pigeon made the seagull;
Small-thing by doing it with Imperceptible-thing made the fine-
  dust-in-the-air.

> It runs red, the blood of the kovare.
> Abundant the kovare, rough the eels.
> The rain falls in long drops.

A tapa-covered headdress from Easter Island

TURTLE, FOWL AND PIG

IN Havaiki were the beginnings made of many things that concern this world above. It was persons of that land who brought forth turtles, fowls and pigs, all from one family. These people were Tu moana urife and his wife named Rifarifa, and their son whom they called Metua puaka, that is Pig-parent.

While Tu and his wife were on a visit to the island of Pupua, turtles were born to them. These turtles crawled down to the sea and swam away, and produced their young throughout all the low sandy islands of the Tuamotu.

When Tu and his wife returned to Havaiki they had a family of chickens. They let them go in the bushy valleys of that land, and all the fowls in the world are descended from those progeny of Tu and Rifarifa. These things happened when the world was new.

Fowl and Turtle met one day, and at once they began to argue. 'You!' said Turtle, 'you are common! *You* will be eaten by women and children, but I shall be sacred to the gods! I shall leap into the gods' house!'

Fowl replied, 'How can *you* leap into the gods' house! It is you that is common. You yourself will be eaten by the women and children, but I shall live in the depths of the sea and escape their hands!'

Just then Turtle was picked up by a strong man who took him to the chief of all that land. The chief was so pleased, he sent Turtle straightway to the marae to be offered to the gods. Thus it is that the turtle is tapu and may be eaten by none but chiefs and priests.

On seeing Turtle's fate, Fowl made off to hide in the sea, but she had only got her head under the water when a party of women and children who were gathering shellfish seized her legs and took her

'It was persons of that land who brought forth turtles, fowls and pigs . . .'

home. Thus the fowl became common, the food of women and children. Only white birds are offered up at the marae of the gods. White birds are tapu, like the turtle.

Tu and Rifarifa had one child like a man, Metua puaka. When Metua grew up his parents took him to Porapora to marry a young woman whom they had chosen.

These two dwelt together, but one day that wife teased Metua for having no land in Porapora. This hurt his feelings and he went to his mother. She said, 'Is that all your trouble? Well then, tomorrow morning go into the bush and open your mouth wide, like this. There will rush out a great number of small animals making a noise. They will be puaka maohi. Tie them together by their legs with sinnet, and gather many stones to make a wall. By night they will be fully grown. Put them in the pen and bring your wife and present them to her.'

All this Pig-parent did next day. It happened as his mother had said, and Metua's wife was pleased. All the pigs in the land are descended from those pigs of Metua's.

THE WOMAN IN THE MOON

The Woman in the Moon is there because of her annoying noise, her noise of beating tapa-cloth at night.

THERE was noise at night at Marioro, it was Hina beating tapa in the dark for the god Tangaroa, and the noise of her mallet was annoying that god, he could endure it no longer.

He said to Pani, 'Oh Pani, is that noise the beating of tapa?' and Pani answered, 'It is Hina tutu po beating fine tapa.'

Then Tangaroa said, 'You go to her and tell her to stop, the harbour of the god is noisy.'

Pani therefore went to Hina's place and said to her, 'Stop it, or the harbour of the god will be noisy.'

But Hina replied, 'I will not stop, I will beat out white tapa here as a wrapping for the gods Tangaroa, 'Oro, Moe, Ruanu'u, Tu, Tongahiti, Tau utu, Te Meharo, and Punua the burst of thunder.'

So Pani returned and told the god that Hina would not stop.

'Then go to her again,' said Tangaroa, 'and make her stop. The harbour of the god is noisy!'

So Pani went again, and he went a third time also, but with no result. Then Pani too became furious with Hina, and he seized her mallet and beat her on the head.

She died, but her spirit flew up into the sky, and she remained forever in the moon, beating white tapa. All may see her there.

From that time on she was known as Hina nui aiai i te marama, Great-Hina-beating-in-the-Moon.

Tapa beater

THE HEROES

Handle of a Tahitian fly-whisk

ATARAGA AT THE POOL

*Attend now to the stories of the demigod Maui, the
maker of mischief. We speak first of Maui's parents
and how they made him.*

THIS is a story of Ataraga who fathered Maui and all those
brothers of his. A tale of Ataraga when he was young and
handsome.

One day Ataraga was in the bush looking for timber to make
the barge-boards of his house. He was near a certain shady bathing
pool when two young women met him, Hina uru and Hina hava.

'Hallo, Ataraga,' said those two, 'where are you going?'

'To the pool to bathe,' he replied.

'Let us all go together,' said those girls.

'Well, your legs are your own,' said Ataraga. 'Come on.' But he
strode ahead and would not wait for those girls, they had to gather
up their dry clothes first.

Before he reached the pool Ataraga hid himself in the undergrowth and soon he heard the voices of those two young women.
They were saying 'Where can Ataraga be?' 'He cannot have gone
back', and they were looking all around them. Then Ataraga
heard them talking about him, and there was much giggling
and laughter. 'If only Ataraga wanted us, we could enjoy it with
him over there in the trees,' said one of them. And the other one
said, 'There are just the two of us. One could have him first, and
then the other one!' And they laughed and giggled, and danced
along the path.

Just as they were passing Ataraga's hiding place one of them
stopped, and she put her hand on the other one's arm. 'What do
you think would happen if he saw our lovely Huahega at the pool?'

she said. 'I should think he would sweep her off, don't you?' And they two screamed with laughter.

Now Ataraga heard all this. In a while they stopped their giggling, and one of them said to the other, 'Well, if he isn't coming, let us go in anyway.' And they ran down to the pool and dived in, and swam about, and ran their fingers through their long black hair, and splashed each other with their hands, and shouted silly things.

Beside that pool there was a coconut tree that leaned out over the water, and the tree was worn smooth in the curve where people used it for a diving place. Dark Hina climbed on to that diving place, and she shouted:

> *Ataraga is the lover!*
> *Hina uru is his mistress!*

Then she dived in with a splash; and Hina-the-smeared climbed out and took her place, and she shouted across the pool:

> *Hina hava's the mistress!*
> *Ataraga's her lover!*

And she dived in, and those two young women splashed about and laughed and called out silly things, until it was time for them to wring their hair dry and depart. Then Ataraga came dry from his hiding place.

'Where have you been?' they said. 'We have had our bathe without you. Why didn't you come?'

'Never mind,' said Ataraga as he slipped his maro off. 'I will bathe by myself. You two go home.' And so he dived in with a manly dive.

Those girls remained, however, and they watched that man. With their arms around each other's shoulders they stood and admired Ataraga, while he dived many times from the diving place.

'That's a good one you've got there,' cried Hina uru while the man stood on the tree.

'Yes, it's a lovely one,' cried Hina hava; and they-two laughed and giggled till they nearly died.

Ataraga came to the surface, he shook the water from his head, and he said to them:

'It would be no good if you two had Ataraga first. It is Huahega that I am wanting.'

Utu flower

So then they knew that he had heard them—he had heard what they were saying along the path. Those two young women looked at one another and then they said:

'If you'll take us two first, you shall have Huahega afterwards.'

Those words astonished that man. He did not know until that moment that these girls were servants of the chiefly Huahega. He therefore came out of the pool and stood before them so that they could admire him.

'Very well,' he said, 'but you must arrange for me to have Huahega as well.'

'That is agreed,' those two girls said. And Ataraga dried himself, and they all three went away into the trees. And Ataraga first had Hina uru; then he called out to Hina hava, and when he had also finished with her he said, 'You are the first satisfying woman Ataraga has ever had.' Then they walked back to the village together, all those three.

Near Huahega's house those women said to Ataraga, 'You stay here. We two will go and see what Huahega is doing.' And they went on to the house of their mistress.

Huahega saw them coming, she commanded them to sit, and they two went in and sat respectfully beside her. She asked them, 'Where have you two been hiding since this morning?'

'We were bathing in the pool,' they said, 'but just when we were enjoying ourselves an enormous eel-with-a-slit-skin rushed at us, and Oh, we were so frightened. We had to come away.'

'That is amazing,' said their mistress, 'I have not once seen an eel-with-a-slit-skin in that pool, and I have bathed in it since I was a child. I should very much like to see that creature too. We shall all go there tomorrow morning, then.'

When they had finished their talking to their mistress those two pretended to be going to their home, but they ran instead to Ataraga and they told him what they had arranged.

In the morning when Ataraga went to the pool he saw Huahega in all her chiefly beauty, dancing with those young women. With swaying of hips and twining of fingers those three were performing the item which is called the Dance of Havaiki, they were singing this song beside the pool, it is a song of man-love for the woman:

Te kiri vi! Te kiri vi!
Te momotu, te momotu!
Tu i mimi takeo.
He vahine, ki raro te hakonokono
He tiriga pa na a Tu-kohe-roa.
Mahora i te maikuku,
He kupenga e vaha aua, ko taria!
Hutia, hutia, e te manu kore ra e!
E te tangata hekeheke nui e!
Ka pu te i vaho ra!
Ka horo ra, ka horo ra!
Kake, kake, kake!
Toropi, Toropa!
Oni ake—
   Kokokokina!

Ataraga said a chant under his breath to cause them to make an end of what they were doing. He then climbed into the leafy pua tree that shaded that pool, and waited there for his spell to have effect.

It did so. Huahega said to the others, 'Let us stop our dancing now. I'm hot. Let us have our bathe.' Then Huahega walked toward the pool and Ataraga's hiding place, and that man spoke another spell:

That woman who comes this way:
May she take her flower-wreath off her head!
May she undo her girdle-strap!
May she let her skirt slip down!
May she run this way quite naked!
This indeed will be the first time that a girl
   comes running naked here
For Ataraga to possess!

And this spell also did its work: Huahega stopped at the edge of the pool and she removed the wreath of perfumed flowers from her head, she undid her belt and let her skirt fall down, and she removed her tapa loin cloth which she wore for modesty and cleanliness. In Huahega's thoughts as she undressed, no thought of men! Then in she plunged, that girl, and swam about that pool and dived below, and rose up dripping, and she ran her fingers through her hair.

Tiare, the fragrant flower that Polynesian women wear above the ear

Then Ataraga picked a flower from his pua tree and threw it down, it fell on Huahega's shoulder, and she took it in her fingers, saying:

This is the first charming flower of mine
   that ever fell like this!
Never yet, at one time or another time,
   till now,
Has a flower thus fallen down to me!

And she tossed her pretty flower on the pool, and dived again in her delight. And when she rose she floated on her back, and trailed her fingers in the water. Then indeed Ataraga picked another flower and threw it down, it fell upon her breast. And Huahega picked it off and softly sang:

This is but the second charming flower of
   mine that ever fell like this!
Never yet, at one time or another time
   till now,
Has a flower thus fallen down to me!

And Ataraga did not wait for Huahega to dive again, he picked another flower while she sang, and softly nipped its petals with his teeth, and threw it down. It fell upon that part of her where pleasure is. And Huahega took that flower between her fingers, singing softly:

This truly is but the third charming flower
   of mine that ever fell like this!
Never yet, at one time or another time, till now,
Has a flower thus fallen down to me!
Oh!—A pigeon has nipped it!
It has been pecked by a pigeon!

Then truly Ataraga laughed out loud, and cried out from the pua tree: 'Pecked by a pigeon! It has been nipped by a man!'

Then Huahega was confused. She quickly turned her back toward that man and sank down in the pool, and her long hair floated forth.

So Ataraga came down from the tree and stood there wanting Huahega to come to him.

'Oh no,' said Huahega from the water, 'that would be shameless!'

Therefore Ataraga picked up Huahega's under-cloth of soft tapa, and held it out for her. And she came out from the water and took that garment, and wrapped it round her. Then Huahega also felt desire, for Ataraga rampant stood before her. She therefore gathered up her other clothes and they two walked away together, they went into Huahega's land. And her companions, seeing their work concluded, went to their houses.

Ataraga and Huahega walked away until they reached a thick part of the bush where no one should see them. And Ataraga, tingling with his wishes, said, 'This is the place.'

'Not yet, O Ataraga,' said that chiefly woman, 'we must go further on.'

So they walked on further, to a place more hidden yet, and Ataraga said to Huahega, 'Surely this will do.'

Then Huahega turned to Ataraga and admired his splendid ornament, but she said to him:

'In the sea is for sharks and remoras. In the bush is for land crabs and hermit crabs. But in a house is best for us two, O my sister's husband!'

'Oh, but that is far too far away,' said that man. 'This is a good place here.'

Then Huahega had no more to say, for she too felt desire. She therefore lay upon the ground and Ataraga took one of her legs and bent it back; and next he took the other leg, and bent it back. And the whole leg came away, it broke off like a lizard's tail.

Now this astonished Ataraga. He exclaimed, 'This girl's bewitched! Her knee's come off! There's witchery at work! Her leg's come off!'

'Not so,' said Huahega. 'There is no witchery in this. My knee has come off simply because of this most improper place that we have chosen for our pleasure. Long ago the same thing happened to my witch-mother because the place was wrong. Her leg was cut off by edges of sharp coral. There will be wars of vengeance over this knee.'

Then they two forgot about the matter and enjoyed what was to be enjoyed. And when that was concluded Ataraga said to Huahega:

'This living thing that we have made, if it should be like you, a girl, then name it with a girl's name from these leaping thighs of yours. And if it should be born like me, a boy, then name him Maui tikitiki a Ataraga.'

Then Ataraga let Huahega go. As for him, he went on looking for the right timber for his barge-boards, and when he had found it he took it back with him to his homeland.

MAUI-OF-A-THOUSAND-TRICKS

In Manihiki we tell of Maui's mischief-work: of how
he went below to find his father and in that nether
place restored the sight of Hina-the-blind, then stole
the fire-god's gift of flame for cooking in the world.
Returning above, he slowed the sun; with Ru he
raised the sky. He also fished up land.

MAUI MURI lived in that land from which our people
came, in Rarotonga.* Manu ahi whare was his father, Tongo
i whare was the mother. They were offspring of the god Great
Tangaroa-of-the-tattooed-face.

These were all the children of those two: Maui mua the first-
born son; Maui roto the second-born son; Hina ika the daughter;
and Maui muri the last-born son, the potiki, his sister's pet.

Those children played at hiding. One day Hina hid small Maui
underneath some leaves and rotten wood, and she said to her
elder brothers, 'Find your brother.'

They-two searched and searched, nowhere could they find their
little Maui. Therefore Hina pointed to the heap of sticks and
leaves. That heap had vanished! All the leaves and sticks were
scattered on the ground. No Maui muri!

This was the first time that those three knew what their brother
was, what he could do.

Maui muri was his father's favourite: each night he slept by Manu
ahi whare on his sleeping-mat. But every day at dawn his father
disappeared, he stayed away from their house all day and he only

---

* The story of Maui is now continued on another island, where his parents have
different names, and he is known as Maui muri.

returned at night. No one knew how he went, or how he returned. Therefore Maui wished to find this out.

One night he lay awake until his father came to the mat and undid his maro to sleep. Then Maui, secretly, took one end of his father's maro and put it beneath him, so that he would wake up when his father pulled it out. In the morning when his father arose and drew out the maro to put it on, young Maui lay quite still, he breathed like sleep. Through one eye then he saw his father go to the housepost, and he heard him say this chant:

> O you housepost, open, open up!
> Open so that Manu ahi whare may enter,
> May descend to the world below.

That pillar lifted, left a hole, and Maui's father descended to the world below. Then Maui muri closed his eyes again, he slept, he waited for the light.

That day those children played their hiding games once more. Said Maui-the-youngest to his brothers and his sister, 'You-three go outside. I will hide here in the house.' They went outside, they wondered where inside the house young Maui could find a hiding-place.

Umi, a Tahitian fish

Then Maui went to the housepost and he chanted:

> O you housepost, open, open up!
> Open so that Maui muri may enter,
> May descend to the world below.

That post obeyed, it lifted, left a hole. Small Maui went down there, he went below. He entered the body of a bird and flew to where his father was, became himself again.

Manu was greatly surprised to see his son in the world below. They pressed their noses, made the hongi. Then Manu went on quietly with his work.

Maui muri went to find, he went journeying in the world below. Came he to the house of an old blind woman, she was stooped over a cooking-fire with her fresh green tongs, her piece of kikau midrib split and bent. Fingered she apart the tongs, went to pick up food—picked up burning wood instead!

Maui muri stood there, watched that old blind woman try to pick up food. What she picked was embers with the tongs! She left good food to be burned.

Then Maui spoke to her, he learned her name. She was Hina porari, his ancestor Hina-the-blind.

Old Hina asked the boy his name, but he would not tell it. He stood there watching, sorry for her, sorry for the blindness.

Near that place there grew four nono trees. Maui took a stick, he struck it against the nearest of those trees. Said angry Hina porari: 'Who is this, meddling with the nono tree of Maui-the-first?'

Maui muri did not answer; he went back to the next tree, tapped it with his stick. Old Hina shouted angrily, 'Who is this that meddles with the nono tree of Maui roto?'

Then Maui struck the third tree, and found that it was the tree of his sister Hina ika. Very angry now, the Old one.

Then did Maui strike the fourth tree, nono tree of Maui muri,

'Near that place there grew four nono trees'

last-born child. Cried the Old one, 'Who is this maggot who meddles with the sacred tree of Maui muri, here in this world beneath?' Then said the visitor, 'I here am Maui muri.'

Was then surprised the Old one. 'Oh, then,' she said, 'you are my grandson! And this, here, is your own tree!'

Now when Maui muri first looked at that nono tree it was bare, it had no leaves nor fruit. After Hina-the-blind had spoken to him he looked again, and the tree had leaves, with fruit as well, not ripe.

Therefore Maui climbed up the nono tree and he brought down one of its fruit. He bit off a piece, and threw it into one blind grey eye of Hina. That Old one smarted with the pain, her sight returned. She saw! Then Maui picked another fruit, he bit off a piece and threw it in the Old one's other eye. Her sight was given back, she saw him plain! Delighted then was Hina porari, to see her grandson Maui muri. She said to him:

> All that is above here,
> All that is below
> Now is subject to your sacred mana,
> Grandson of Hina porari!

Then Hina-the-Old, once called Hina porari, gave to her grandson Maui muri sacred knowledge of all things that are found in her land in the world below, and power in the world above.

She taught him these things: in Havaiki there are four kinds of nono tree, one for each child of her son Manu ahi whare. In Havaiki also there are four kinds of coconut tree, one for each of those children. There are, besides, four kinds of taro, one kind for each of the children of Manu.

Maui asked this question of his ancestor Hina: 'Who is the god from whom fire comes?' She answered, 'Your ancestor, Tangaroa tui mata.'

'Where does he live?'

'He lives over there, my grandson,' Hina answered. 'But do not go to him. Anger is in that god. You would die, being near to him.'

'I wish to see him.'

'You would die, my grandson. Do not go to him!'

But Maui insisted in his asking, therefore Hina yielded to his wish, yielded to this grandson who restored her sight. She spoke thus:

'There are two roads to the house of Tangaroa-of-the-tattooed-face. One road, my child, is the road of dying: men who go by that path die. The other is the common road. You, Maui—take that common road.'

Now Maui did not do as that Old one had told him. He spurned the common road. He chose the path of dying.

Tangaroa tui mata saw this small man coming on the road, he raised his right hand up to kill him. No man had ever lived, struck by that hand of the god of fire. But Maui lifted *his* right hand, he raised it up. Therefore Tangaroa pulled a face of fearful looks and lifted up his right foot, he would kick to death this Maui. But Maui muri lifted his foot also, he showed the god no awe.

Was astounded the god. He asked the visitor to give his name.

'I here am Maui muri, son of Manu ahi whare and Tongo i whare. I have come.'

Then Tangaroa tui mata knew his grandson, and they made the hongi, said their greetings, wept.

The god asked Maui: 'For what purpose have you come to this place?'

'To get some fire,' that young man said.

Then Tangaroa tui mata gave him a burning stick and sent him away. Maui walked a certain distance, he came to water, put the stick in water. Out the fire!

Maui returned to Tangaroa tui mata. 'Oh sir, my fire went out. The water killed its flame.' Therefore Tangaroa gave him another burning stick, but Maui did the thing again, put out the fire, returned to the god for more.

When Maui returned to his ancestor a third time, all the burning sticks were gone. Therefore Tangaroa had to fetch two dry sticks to rub for fire. This, young Maui had wanted, wished to see it done.

'Hold this for me.'

So Maui held the grooved piece, kau ati, while Tangaroa with his two hands worked the kau rima: he ground it in the groove until there was smoke. When the dust in the groove was smoking, Maui blew it—*Pu*! He blew the tinder all away.

Was then enraged the god, he drove young Maui off! And he called to his pet tern, his white kakaia, to come and hold the kau ati. The kakaia came; and with her pretty foot she held the grooved piece firm for Tangaroa while he worked the fire-plough with his aged hands. The fire began, the dust was smoking. Tangaroa put it with some dry stuff in an open basket, waved it in the air. It flamed. Fire was.

Then did jealousy of that tern drive Maui to his mischief. He took up the charred fire-stick of the god, and he put two black marks on the beautiful face of that pure white bird. The kakaia flew away, she left that place for ever. That is why the kakaia has a black brow above its eye, and another below. Maui muri put them there.

Then Tangaroa wept because his tern was gone, his favourite bird. And Maui lied to him: 'Your bird will come back.' But the tern did not; it left Havaiki, the world below, it flew up through a cave to the world of light, this world. It lives above here, in the world of light.

One day Maui said to Tangaroa tui mata, 'Let us go up there to where your tern is living.' The god asked, 'How can we-two go up there?' Said Maui, 'I will show you the way.' Then he changed himself into a bird and flew high up, toward the entrance which leads to this world from the world below.

Then Tangaroa laughed and was pleased, and Maui flew down and said to him, 'Now you will try.' The god asked how he should, and Maui made him put on his most glorious girdle, his girdle of sacred kura which the people of this world call anuanua, that is rainbow.

Therefore Tangaroa girded on his rainbow; and by its sacred mana rose he above the highest coconut tree in all that land.

They flew, they-two flew high; but Maui flew below the god, he did not fly beside him. They passed beyond the clouds, to open sky, this world of light. Then Maui snatched the loose cord of the girdle of the god, he pulled it sharply; Tangaroa fell, he fell from cloud-height to the ground of world-below. And falling thus, great Tangaroa-of-the-tattooed-face was killed.

Then Maui was pleased and he returned to his parents, he showed them the secret of making fire with wood, which no one in that land had known. He did not tell his parents that he had killed Tangaroa his ancestor.

Maui's parents were filled with happiness because he had brought them the gift of fire, and they-two wished to visit Tangaroa. 'But do not go at once,' said Maui, 'wait until the third day. I myself wish to visit him tomorrow.' Those parents agreed. 'Very well, we will wait until the third day.'

On the next morning Maui went alone to Tangaroa's place, he found that his body was rotten. Only bones. Therefore Maui gathered up the bones and put them inside a coconut shell, he closed up the hole which is known as 'Tuna's mouth', and he vigorously shook that shell, he rattled the bones of the god.

When he opened the shell again his grandfather was alive and whole. Then Maui let him out from that degrading place, he washed his body, gave him food; he rubbed scented oil on Tangaroa's skin, and left him in his house to recover from the trouble. Then Maui returned to his parents. They said to him, 'Now we must visit your ancestor Tangaroa tui mata. We shall go tomorrow.'

But Maui urged them not to go, he asked them: 'Wait until the third day, as I said.' For Maui feared his parents' anger, knew what they would learn. He wished to reach this world before they-two could speak to Tangaroa.

On the third day Manu and Tongo made their journey, went to Tangaroa's house. When they saw him they-two wept, his mana and his pride were gone from him, his face showed feebleness, its tattoo marks were rotted off.

Then Manu, softly weeping, asked the god what was the cause. 'It is that son of yours, he has been ill-treating me. First he scorched the face of my bird, my tern. Then he made me fly, and he pulled my girdle to make me fall, and the great fall killed me. I was dead. Then he gathered up my bones and degraded them—he rattled them around inside a nut! Then he made me come alive again, as you see me now, all scarred and feeble. Aue! Aue! That son of yours!'

Then Maui's parents wept, and they returned to their home in Havaiki to scold their son. But Maui had left that place; he had returned to this world of light, where his brothers and his sister all were weeping for him, mourning for his loss. For they thought their brother dead.

Delighted were those brothers and Hina, filled with joy, when Maui appeared at their house. Their brother then did boast to them: 'I have found a new land! I have found how fire is made!'

'Tell us where! Tell us where!'

'The place is down there.'

'Down where?'

'Down there—down there below.'

Those brothers and Hina did not know of the cave beneath the housepost. Therefore Maui said that if they would promise to follow him he would show them the world below. He went to the post of the house and said this word:

> O you housepost, open up,
> That we all may enter, go below;
> That we may go to Havaiki, the world
>   beneath.

Upon this word of Maui's the housepost lifted up, and all those four went down, they visited Havaiki. When Maui had shown his brothers and his sister the world beneath, they returned to their house and all lived quietly together there.

After Maui had brought back fire from Tangaroa the people of this world ate cooked food. Before that time all food was raw. It was Maui who brought the gift of fire and of cooking to this world above.

One day Maui said to his family, 'These days are too short. There is not enough time in the days for men to do their work. There is not enough time in the days for women to cook the food. The sun-god goes too quickly across the sky. Before our food is cooked, Ra has gone to the world beneath.'

Therefore Maui considered how Ra might be caught and made to move more slowly across the sky. With his brothers he made a great cord of coconut fibre. He took this cord to the far horizon, to that pit from which the sun rises, and he laid the noose around the pit to catch the god. This trick of Maui's did not work. The cord was too weak, it was soon broken.

Maui made himself stronger ropes, he gathered all the coconut husks of this land and rolled the fibre, and he plaited it into ropes of very great strength. But these ropes also were of no use, for the sun-god made them frizzle up.

Therefore Maui took the sacred tresses of his sister Hina, he cut off lengths of Hina's hair and plaited it, to make a rope whose mana could not be destroyed by Ra. He took that noose of Hina's hair, he travelled eastward to the border of the sea; he placed his ropes around the pit from which the sun rises, waited there, he waited for the dawn. Then Ra came up, he came up from the spirit-world which lies in the east.

Maui pulled the cord, he caught the sun-god by the throat! Ra struggled, kicked, he screamed against the sky.

'Then will you go more slowly if I turn you loose?'

The sun then promised Maui, 'Let me go, and I will move more slowly, I will make longer days for your fishing.' Since that time, men have had longer days in which to go about their work.

When he had done this task Maui left some ropes of Hina's hair hanging from the sun, and they are still there. We see them when the sun is going down through clouds, outstretching to the sea, the Ropes of Maui.

The first man to find this land of Manihiki was Huku. He found it before Maui did, when it was still beneath the sea.

Huku was a man of Rarotonga. He was fishing for bonito, far

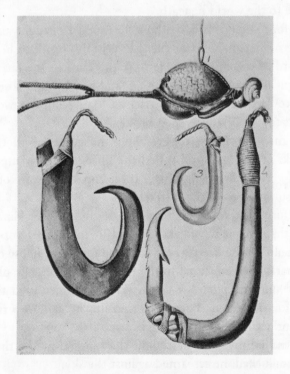

Polynesian octopus lure and fish-hooks

out from that land. Looking down, he saw a great coral-head that was growing up in the sea. Then Huku said this word:

> Huku looked down and saw
> Foundation-of-the-rock.

After that Huku returned to his land, to Rarotonga.

Huku went fishing for atu again; he returned to this place and looked down, his rock had grown, it had moved upwards. Therefore when he returned to Rarotonga he gave his canoe a new name, he called it Tapuaua—'coral-coral'.

Afterwards came Maui and his brothers: they came because they knew of what Huku had seen in this place. They came together in their canoe Pipi mahakohako, and they found the rock, that growing reef.

Then Maui the youngest dived into the sea, he went below to the house of Hina i te papa. And after he had spoken to Hina-in-the-rock he returned to his brothers in the canoe. They started their fishing in this place, threw out their lines.

Maui mua baited his hook and let his line down, chanting:

> Maui roto, Maui muri,
> Guess the name of my fish—
> What is it?

Maui roto could not guess, but Maui muri said:

> Your filthy fish is a haha shark—
> Then haul it up!

And when that fish was hauled to their canoe they found indeed it was a shark, the haha kind.

Then Maui roto let down his hook, and chanting asked his brothers to name the fish that he had caught. Maui mua could not guess, but Maui-the-youngest said, 'Your filthy fish is an urua. Haul it up.' And so it was.

Then said Maui muri, 'You-two have had your chances, now let me try.' And he baited his hook with puroro, that is spathe of coconut, and with aoa, that is sprouting kernel of the nut; these two were wrapped up in a puke leaf by Maui muri.

Maui let down his line so that it would be seen by Hina-in-the-rock. That woman fixed the hook for him, she hooked it on the coral growth. Then Maui asked his brothers:

> Maui mua, Maui roto,
> Guess the name of my fish,
> What is its name?

They-two both said, 'Your filthy fish is a haha kakahi.' But Maui hauled his line, the weight of his fish was very great. When it came near, the whole sea broke in angry waves, they saw that Maui's fish was land, and were afraid.

Sprang then Maui muri out of the canoe, he leapt on to the rocks. But his brothers Maui mua and Maui roto were dashed on the reef; their canoe broke up, they were hurt in the breakers, and they drowned.

Then Maui named his land Manihiki, and he stayed here looking at it, looking at this land. His only food was fish, the rain from the skies was his drink, no coconuts were growing here in Maui's time. Then Maui said his chant:

> The sea was churned, churned up,
> It became an angry sea—
> Then upward came the land.
> I, Maui, severed Manihiki,
> Severed it from Rakahanga.
> The sea was churned, churned up,
> It became an angry sea.

Maui walked about on his land. He came to a house built of earth, and he asked them, 'Who are you?' They answered, 'We are a house of tupuas.'

There were eighty of those spirit-people in the house of earth. Maui also heard the voices of men inside the house, for there were ten-score people living there. Then Maui sang a dancing-song before those tupuas, with gestures of contempt, and he claimed the land for his. Just when he had finished, Huku came back to his reef that he had found. Great was his anger at seeing Maui there! They two fought together! Did come combat, did come combat!

Then Huku chased Maui across the land to Tumukau. Fled Maui from Tumukau to Paahi, chased by Huku's anger. But at Paahi, Maui found that Huku had trodden on the land and spoilt it all. Therefore Maui with a great spring leapt up to the heavens, never was he seen on Manihiki more.

The force of Maui's leaping broke off Rakahanga from Manihiki. These two lands afterwards were separate for ever.

After this Huku returned to Rarotonga, for the land here was barren, no coconuts were growing in this place. It was only later that Huku returned and found that Wheatu, having heard him speak of this land, had come to take it. This led to the great disputes between those two.

A 'fisherman's god' from Rarotonga.

MAUI AND TUNA

*Here in the Tuamotu we tell of the rivalry of Maui
and the eel-god known as Tuna. These two compared their force for Hina's sake, and Maui won.
Afterwards, seeing grey hairs on his mother's head,
Maui wished to conquer death; but men cannot do
this.*

HINA was living with Tuna in his land beneath the sea; but
she became tired of her eel-husband, also of the coldness
there. One day she said to eel Tuna that she was going out to
fetch food for them. Then she travelled far away, to find a new
man for herself.

She came to the land of the Tane tribe. When she saw those
husband-people Hina sang her chant about what she wanted:

> Inland eel here—manly thing!
> Eel of the sea there—watery thing!
> I here am a woman for the eel-shaped one,
> I have come to find him at Raronuku,
> I have come to find him at Raro vaio.
> Your fame, O Tane tribe, is known to me!

But the men of the Ngati Tane, Husband-tribe, all shouted to
that woman who invited them, 'There is the road! Keep going on!
We will never take Tuna's woman—he would kill us in a day!'

Therefore Hina went on to the land of the Ngati Peka, and she
sang her chant to them. But the men of that tribe answered in the
same words as the Tane men.

Therefore Hina went on until she reached the Tu tribe's land.
They would not have her there; no man-erect of Tu would take
her, Tuna's woman.

Then Hina passed the house of Huahega, sang her chant. And Huahega said to her last-born son, to Maui tikitiki a Ataraga: 'Take that woman for your wife.' Therefore Maui did so, and they all lived quietly together there.

After a time the people of Tuna's land told Tuna: 'Your woman has been carried off by Maui.' Tuna replied, 'Oh!—let him have that woman to lie on!' But they kept on going to him, always telling him, 'Your woman is taken by Maui.' Therefore Tuna grew angry, and he said, 'What sort of man is this Maui tikitiki?'

'He is a small man, and the end of his ure is bent.'

Said Tuna, 'Then just let him see this dirty cloth between my legs, and he'll be showing us his heels.' Then Tuna said, 'Go and tell this Maui that I am coming to have it out with him.' Then Tuna sang his song of lamenting for Hina:

First voice:

Kua riro! Stolen from me!

Second voice:

Grieving for the wife is the heart.

Chorus:

Kua riro! Stolen from him!
The winds have brought the word
That she is taken. Now we go—

First voice:

We leave for Vavau, land of speeding wave
To see the loved one—

Second voice:

—Kua riro!
The wailing winds lament it!
Grieving love!

Then the people told Maui that Tuna was coming to have it out with him.

'Just let him come!' said Maui.

But they continually told him of Tuna's threats; therefore he asked them, 'What sort of ure is this Tuna?'

'*Aue*! He is huge! He's as big as a whale's!'

'Like a standing palm-tree?'

They lying answered, 'Like a *leaning* one!'

'He is weak and bending?'

'Always drooping.'

'Then just let him see the crooked end of mine and he'll go flying for his life!' said Maui.

Maui waited with his family, he dwelt there quietly in that place. One day the sky grew dark and thunder rolled, the lightning flashed. All the people, knowing this was Tuna, were afraid, their skin was trembling, and they cried out blaming Maui: 'This is the first time that one man has stolen the woman of another man! We will all die!' But Maui said to them, 'Just keep together. We will not be killed.'

On came the monsters, came Pupa vae noa, and Poroporo tu a huanga, Toke a kura, and Tuna nui himself—they all came rushing on the land. And Tuna stripped off his loincloth, and he held *it* up; at once a mighty wave reared up and swept toward that land. Then Huahega shouted to her son, to Maui tikitiki, 'Quick now! Show them yours! Pull it out!'

Did Maui then as Huahega told him, did as his mother said. That wave fell back, the great wave of the monsters soaked away. The bottom of the sea was bare, and all the monsters floundered on the reef, they flapped in pools. And Maui went out, he went with his weapon and he beat them dead, each one. He killed them all, excepting Tuna.

Then Tuna went to Maui's house with him and they two lived together quietly. One day Tuna said: 'We two are to fight this out. When one of us is dead, the other can have the woman.'

Said Maui, 'What kind of combat do you wish?'

Said Tuna, 'One of us enters into the body of the other, goes completely in. When it is over I will kill you, and take the woman

back to my land.' So Maui agreed, and Tuna said, 'I will try it first.'
He began his chanting:

> Hiki tautau orea,
> Tautau orea,
> He tangata nui i whano mai
> I tena motu ra
>
> . . . . .
>
> It is I, Tuna,
> That now enters your body, O Maui!

With this word Tuna went completely into Maui's body, he
went through the place for entering and disappeared. After a
while he came out again. Said Maui, 'Now it is my turn,' and he
spoke a chant like that which Tuna said:

> . . . .
>
> Ko vau, ko Maui, e tomo ki roto
> I ia a u, e Te Tuna!

With this word Maui entered into Tuna's body, and all of Tuna's
sinews came apart, he died.

Maui came out again; he cut off Tuna's head to take it to his
ancestor. But Huahega his mother took it from him and she said:
'You must bury this head of Tuna beside the post in the corner of
our house.'

Maui did so, and that head grew up, it sprouted, it became a
coconut tree. On the nut which is its fruit we see the face of Tuna,
eyes and mouth. All coconuts have this.

Maui and Hina lived quietly together with Huahega. One day
when his mother was sleeping, Maui saw grey hairs on her head.
He said to Hina his wife, 'Your hair and my hair are the same—
quite black. But Huahega has both black hairs and grey hairs.'

He woke his mother up and asked her why this was. Said
Huahega, 'Grey hairs in my head say that I am growing older.

When all my hair is white you will know that I am an old woman, soon I shall die, and you will bury me; you will never see me more.'

Then Maui grieved, and he asked his mother, 'By what means can people go on living in the world?'

'If you can get possession of the stomach of Sea-slug-of-the-deep-set-eyes,' that mother said, 'then you will never die.'

Therefore Maui went to the shallows of the white lagoon and he searched for Rori. He found him living in the clusters of the coral. Said Rori:

'You must have some reason, Maui-of-the-many-tricks, for coming all this way to the coral-beds of Whangape.'

Said Maui: 'That is so.'

'What is your purpose?' Rori asked him.

'I have come to get your stomach for myself, O Rori. In return, I shall give you mine.'

Said Rori, 'If my stomach were taken by you, this would cause my death.'

'I will not kill you if you give it to me,' Maui said, 'but if you will not, then I must kill you.'

'Never, never will I give it up! It is my stomach.'

Therefore Maui in his anger snatched up Sea-slug, squeezed his guts; it came. Then up he sicked his own. Began he swallowing the stomach of Rori-of-the-deep-set-eyes.

Just then, his brothers who had followed him cried out, 'Here is Maui swallowing that demon's guts!' They ran at him, those brothers, ran to stop him doing it.

So Maui had to bring up Rori's stomach when he had almost swallowed it. He took his own and put it back. Was furious with his brothers Maui then. He cried at them, 'Why did you stop me at my work? I sought the means by which we all might live, we need not die. Now, because of you, it will never again be mine to try this deed.' Then Maui sang his solemn chant concerning quest for everlasting life.

Afterwards Maui returned to his house. Huahega asked him,

'Have you taken Rori's stomach?'

He answered her, 'I had it indeed, O my mother. But suddenly my stupid brothers rushed at me; I had to bring it up again.'

Then grey-haired Huahega said to her last-born son, 'Evermore, O Maui, must you follow me upon this path which I do travel, until you yourself grow old and die.'

Not speaking then was Maui, he was silent.

One day Huahega said to Maui, 'Do not ever go again to seek adventures, O my son. Remain here in our land.' And Maui consented. They all lived quietly together.

After a certain time had passed, Hina bore Maui's first-born child, a girl. Her name was Rori i tau. Afterwards Hina conceived again, she gave birth to another girl. Her name was Te Vahine hui rori. No sons were born to them. Maui named both of his daughters for Rori so that they might never die; for Rori can live beneath the waters of the sea.

The fame of Maui's thousand tricks was known to all men of the land, all lands. Therefore people spoke of him and handed down the word; and afterwards he was called Maui peu tini, 'Maui of a thousand tricks.'

I have not been told of Maui's death. There are many other tales of him—forgotten, cannot be remembered; I have ended this telling with those things that I know.

HINE AND TINIRAU

*Here on chilly Rekohu we tell of Tinirau the handsome
chief, and Hine's love for him. Because of Tinirau's
unkindness Hine's pigeon-brother carried her away
toward the skies, her child as well.*

ALL the tribes were gathered at Rakau whatiwhati for the
baptizing of the child Rangi hiki wao. They were gathered
for the feast tuaporo, to eat the tapu-ending food.

One people and another came. Those guests assembled, each
chief with his pute, his ornament-basket; and when they had put
on their chaplets of red feathers and their other finery, they hung
those baskets on the branches of a certain tree. Alas! A squall blew
up, it broke that tree. *Pa-a!*—the tree that held the baskets of the
visitors was smashed!

The chiefs rushed forth to catch their pute, but those pute were
not caught by them, so great was wildness of the wind.

Young Tu moana sprang for his pute, he darted after, caught it—
Pe!

Spoke Kahukura then of that young chief, 'Ea! One valiant
person only shall arise over Rakau whatiwhati: you only, youngest
born!'

But Horopapa said (for he had not caught his pute): 'Those
valiant ones are those valiant ones. These valiant ones are these
valiant ones.'

This was the first occasion of that saying.

And Kahukura said: 'Ea! A real kura—a true chief!'

Then Horopapa was provoked and said, 'An inferior kura! My
heart is clear to Tu. Tu, the god of war, knows me.'

These were the words spoken by those chiefs at the tuaporo of

Rangi hiki wao, after the wind had scattered all their pute from the tree.

Tinirau was one of the chiefs who attended the baptizing of that child. It was then for the first time that Hine te iwaiwa saw that handsome chief, desire went into her for him.

Seagull pendant, Chatham Islands

Hine's complexion was light, her skin was fair. Tinirau was ehu also, he had auburn hair. Those two were handsome persons both, and there for the first time Hine saw Tinirau, and she desired him much.

Afterwards the guests departed, each people returned to their land. They placed their kura ornaments in their pute and departed. Tinirau returned to his land, Tongi hiti ate. Other tribes returned to their lands. Not Hine.

When Tinirau reached his home he had a dream, he dreamed that his sacred house of Tapeirihou had been entered. Therefore he made his children go and look, he sent them to that sacred house.

Hine was wearing her rauira, her scarlet ornament upon the head. Those children also, children of the chief, were wearing their rauira. Hine's rauira flashed; the children's rauira flashed. Then said they-two, 'Who is the stranger?'

'It is I—Hine. Who is the indweller?'

'We-two children—we of Tinirau.'

'Where is your father?'

'Over there.'

'Then you-two go to him and tell him to come here.' And Hine patted her hand upon the mat where she was sitting.

They-two returned. When they were nearly at their home they called from the canoe: 'Invaded is the land of Tapeirihou! Invaded is the land of Tapeirihou!'

Called Tinirau: 'Invaded by whom?'

'Invaded by Hine—Hine te iwaiwa hingara wharara. She says you are to go to her. She pats her mat—like this.'

Therefore Tinirau put on his warm cloak of sealskin and he went to his sacred house. Time passed, and home he did not come. His wives were waiting there, Mongomongo tu a uri and Mongomongo tu a tea. They-two waited, then they sent the children forth to look for him: 'Find Tinirau.'

Those children went again in their canoe. When they reached the sacred house of Tapeirihou they raised the outer door, lifted the inside door, lifted the inmost door. A sealskin cloak upon the mat.

'U-u! There are only two feet. Our father is dead.'

Three legs showed. 'U-u! Our father is alive.'

A fourth leg showed. 'Oho indeed, he is alive!'

Then Hine said to them, 'You-two go to your mothers and tell them to come here.'

They paddled home, they said to their mothers: 'You-two are told to go there to the sacred house.'

'Yes yes, we will do so.'

Those women went, they stayed outside the house, the children entered. They came out with this word: '*Ooi*! You-two are told to go and get stones.'

'Yes yes, we will do so.'

The children came out from the house again. 'You-two are told to get firewood, make an oven.'

'Yes, we will do so.' This was done.

'You-two go for coverings for the oven.' They brought these things. For Tinirau, they thought.

Then did Hine come out of the sacred house, resplendent in beauty to the soles of her feet.

Then Mongomongo tu a uri and Mongomongo tu a tea rushed at Hine in their rage. Hine seized hold of them, she seized them both. Into the oven! Those wives were killed there by Hine resplendent in beauty.

After this, Tinirau lamented for his wives. This was his chant:

> You are dead, Mongomongo tu a uri,
> Truly, indeed truly.
> And you are dead, Mongomongo tu a tea,
> Truly, indeed truly.
> As truly my voice said to you, Mongomongo
>   tu a uri,
> It is come about.
> Truly, indeed truly.

Then Hine and Tinirau lived quietly together. After a certain time Hine said to Tinirau, 'Do not send me outside to have my child, do not build the birth-house there. In here is shelter from the wind.'

Tinirau did not listen, did not do as Hine asked. She said to him, 'Wait, and you will suffer.' Then she cried to her brother Rupe in the heavens: 'Rupe, help me! Tinirau is cruel to your sister.'

The birth-house was made outside and Hine's time arrived. When the child was to be born the fog came down, thick mist came all around: and in the mist came Rupe's people to deliver Hine's child.

Those people were pigeons from heaven; they were rupe which had flown to Hine's house. It was from Hine's blood, when helping at the birth, that the rupe got its red beak. Rupe's people took Hine with her child, the mat as well. They lifted all toward the skies.

Cried Tinirau, 'Think of our child!' But Hine answered him this word: 'Later on you will go to the tuaporo, to the baptizing of our child. Then you will see him.' And thus it was. It was not until the tuaporo that followed the baptizing of this child that Tinirau saw him, and Hine also. That story is another tale, we do not have it here.

That woman Hine was a person from the Wai ora a Tane. It was from the Living-Waters-of-Tane that she came. There in that bright land are the mantis and the butterfly, the large and the small dragonfly, the shining cuckoo and the long-tailed cuckoo and the pretty black-capped tern of summer. These are all the things of that land bright as day.

TAHAKI OF THE GOLDEN SKIN

Great Tahaki son of Hema here is spoken of. This
auburn chief was noble—all a chief. His cousin Karihi
was a common person. Yet they-two journeyed to the
world below to avenge the shame of Hema, who was
degraded there.

OUR ancestor Tahaki of the Golden Skin was descended from
that female maneater known as Rona nihoniho roroa, therefore when we tell the story of Tahaki we begin with that woman,
Rona long-teeth. She had good looks and was of high rank in the
land, but because of her teeth and what she used them for her
husband did not remain with her, he went away from that woman.
She remained in their house, and after the man was gone she gave
birth to her daughter, and named her Hina.

Hina was brought up properly by that mother. Rona washed her
well when she was born, she rubbed her body every day with oil
of sandalwood, and pressed her head to make it of handsome shape;
she bit Hina's eye-lashes to make them grow long, and she rolled
the tips of her fingers with her thumb to make them tapering and
slender. She saw that she was fed with all good things; she fished
the reef herself to catch the tenderest of crabs for Hina. That girl
grew well, she became a beautiful young woman with chiefly
manners, and she did not know what food it was her mother ate.

Rona's hiding place was in that hole through the cliff at Taharaa,
the path which people use at low tide, to avoid the climb. She
waited there and caught men as they passed, and ate them. Therefore people became scarce in that district; there were houses without people, and there were bones in Rona's Cave.

Fishing in the lagoon at Tahiti

One young man escaped that woman's teeth. Monoihere was his name, and he desired her daughter. He was handsome, and Hina desired him also, therefore they used to meet at Orofara, in a shady place near where the spring flows into Hina's Pool. That cave in the rock-face there was only known to them. For others it was quite closed up in former times, but it opened and closed as they-two wished, and hid Monoi.

The time for their being together was when Rona had gone out on the reef for crabs. She was expert at this and was often to be seen far out off Matavai, bending over the reef to collect food for her daughter. Then it was safe for Hina and Monoi. Then Hina took a basket of food and went up to Orofara, and she said these words:

> Monoihere is the man,
> Hina is the woman.
> Come out from there!

and from inside the rock the man replied:

> Where is your mother with the long teeth?
> Where is Rona?

and Hina answered him:

> She is on the long reef,
> She is on the short reef,
> She is catching food for us,
> O my lover!

Then Hina said:

> O rock-foundation—
> Break you open!

These words split the rock and let Monoi out, and they-two had their custom in that shady place. Then Hina returned to her home and left Monoi closed up in the rock.

After a certain time Rona noticed that the food she caught was quickly gone. 'This daughter of mine eats much,' that mother said. One day therefore, when she had cooked the usual quantity for keeping, she said that she felt unwell, and lay down on her sleeping-mat, and snored. And Hina, believing that her mother was asleep, took out some food and crept away; and Rona followed her. When she saw where Hina was going that woman took a short cut by enchantments, and she concealed herself at Orofara in a pua tree. And Rona saw what happened in that place. She heard the words that Hina spoke, and she watched her daughter with the man: and she desired his flesh, that vahine kaitangata. Therefore she returned to her house, and snored on her mat when Hina came.

On the next day that eater of men said to Hina, 'Tonight I go fishing by torchlight, so I will go now to collect dry leaves. Stay here, for I shall not be long.' But Rona went inland to Orofara; by enchantment she made the distance short and soon she stood before the rock, and she pretended to be Hina, saying:

> Monoihere te tane,
> O Hina te vahine.
> A puta mai i vaho.

But Monoi knew the voice of that vahine kaitangata and he answered, 'You are not Hina, you are Rona. You are Rona of the Long Teeth.'

She therefore knew that he was in that place and she said the words that are for splitting rock:

> Te tumu o te papa e, vahia!

And the rock split open. Rona rushed in, she caught Monoi in the cave, and made a meal of him. She ate the best parts first, she ate his fingertips and toes; she scooped his brains and ate them, she swallowed his liver, and she found out his kidneys and ate them also. She also ate his ure and the two that hang; but Monoi's heart that woman could not find. His heart concealed itself, it remained still beating in the mess of guts, and therefore Rona did not eat Monoi's heart. When she had finished her meal she closed the cave behind her. Then she gathered up dry fronds to make her torches, and went home to Hina.

So soon as the moon came up that woman got her crab spear, and taking a young person to carry her torches, she went out wading on the reef. Then Hina filled a basket, and went inland to have enjoyment with Monoi. She stood before that rock and softly called:

> Monoihere te tane,
> O Hina te vahine.
> A puta mai i vaho.

But the rock was silent. Therefore Hina said the rest; she said:

Te tumu o te papa e, vahia!

and the rock split open, and she saw her lover's bones and guts.

She spoke no word, that girl who loved, but straightway took her lover's heart, it was beating yet, and placed it by her own. Then she returned to her home to act.

Sad Hina cut the man-long stem of one banana tree, and laid it on her sleeping-mat, and she covered it with her sheet of soft white tapa. Then at the head she placed a drinking-nut; and she hurried from that place. Well guided by her lover's heart, she ran to Uporu, to the house of that hairy chief whose name was No'a huruhuru. No'a received her with kindness, and she remained at his house.

Now in the middle of that night when all her torches had been burnt, that woman Rona came home with her catch, and she called to her daughter in the house, 'Here's food!' But the house remained silent.

And Rona cried, 'E Hina! If you don't answer, you will be eaten by me!' But there came no answer from the house.

Therefore Rona rushed to where her daughter was sleeping, she seized her body in the sheet and sliced it with a single bite. And when she saw how she was tricked she was enraged, and cried out, 'Aue! My food has escaped!' All through that night she was enraged.

So soon as the cocks were crowing in the valley and the first men were astir, Rona rushed out to look for Hina. She asked for her at every house and they told her which way that girl had gone. That woman therefore hurried to the house of No'a huruhuru, and when she saw her daughter there she became all teeth.

There were teeth on Rona's chin, teeth on her elbows, teeth on her belly. But No'a huruhuru raised his spear, he cried out in a loud strong voice:

'This spear, Tane te rau aitu, has dealt with Te Ahua and Hine te aku tama!'

Then he thrust that spear down Rona's throat, right down through all her teeth. She writhed and died.

Thus perished Rona nihoniho roroa, the vahine kaitangata of Taharaa, the ancestor of Tahaki kirikura. Her daughter Hina was the grandmother of that golden chief.

*   *   *

Hina remained with No'a in his house. When a certain time had arrived she bore a son, and they-two named their first child Punga. After that Hina had another son whose name was Hema, and no more children were born to them.

Those sons of Hina grew well, they became expert surf-riders. One day when the surf was good and they-two were leaving for the reef, Hina asked her first-born son to pick her head-lice for her. But Punga grumbled, and refused. Then said Hina: 'Your wife will not be anyone of note.'

She therefore asked Hema to delouse her hair, and Hema put his surfboard down and did that service for her. And his mother said: 'Your wife, O Hema, will be a woman of quality.'

Afterwards Punga took a wife, who was no one in particular, and she bore him five sons. The first-born son was Karihi nui apua, and he and his brothers were common persons. But Hema, helped by Hina, found a wife who was connected with the gods. It happened in this manner:

*   *   *

One day Hema's mother told him: 'Go, my son, in the coolness of early morning, to the east bank of the Vai po'o po'o. You must dig a hole beside that stream and hide yourself, and then a beautiful young woman will come there from the world below to bathe. You will find her very strong, but she has long hair, so you must catch her from behind by that. You will need to carry her past four houses on the road before you put her down: then she will come.'

Hema therefore did this in the way his mother said. He dug his hiding-place beside the stream, and as soon as it was light a young woman of great beauty came up from an opening in the earth, her name was Huauri. Before she entered the pool to bathe she squatted to relieve herself, and Hema watched her from his pit; and the jerks in his ure were strong to have that woman.

Then she dived into the pool and swam about, and rinsed her long black hair, and Hema waited for his chance. Then Huauri came out on the bank and wrung her hair, and Hema sprang. He took a twist of Huauri's hair around his hand, he grabbed her in his arms and carried her away, she kicked her legs.

When they had passed two houses on the road, Huauri stopped her kicking. She said to Hema, 'Put me down, then I will walk.' He therefore did so, and she rushed away—she darted to her opening in the earth, it opened for her, she was gone.

When Hema told his mother this she frowned and said, 'But I told you: you must carry her past four houses on the road, my son. Then she will come.'

Therefore Hema went next morning to the same place, and Huauri came to bathe. He seized her by the hair once more, and he carried her past four houses, and all the way to his house.

It was because people of this world had seen her in Hema's arms and therefore looked upon her as his wife that that spirit-woman consented to remain.

Huauri bore a son to Hema, and when this son was born she found that he was ehu, auburn-haired, and that his skin was the colour of kura. Therefore she named him Tahaki kirikura.

*　　*　　*

Tahaki played in childhood with Karihi his elder cousin, and with those other sons of Punga. They played at flying kites and spinning tops, at sailing toy canoes and riding surfboards on the reef; they also played at offering a person to the gods, they used the man-long stem of a banana tree, and fire. After a time Tahaki and Karihi lived as brothers, for Hema and Huauri became Karihi's feeding-parents.

One day Tahaki's cousins made round balls of sun-dried clay and bowled them fast on level ground. The ball that lasts the longest is the one that wins this game, the first that cracks is out. Huauri showed Tahaki how to mix fine sand with his clay to make it even, in the manner of her people of the world below, and when Tahaki had made his ball he ran to join his cousins. They had begun their game but when they saw his ball they cried, 'Come on, Tahaki, have a throw!' He replied, 'Not so, I will wait my turn. The first must be first, and the last must come in last.' So they played by the rules, and young Tahaki won the game. His well-made ball outlasted all the rest, and there was jealousy of him.

At the season of the south-east winds those cousins played totoie; they made toy canoes of sharpened sticks, with sails of plaited leaf and leaflet rudders at the stern. Then they ran down to the cool lagoon to make them race. They swam them to the starting place, then they let them go and shouted all the chants they knew, to make them race more quickly to the beach.

Tahaki's mother showed him how to make totoie from a pithy stem. Its lightness made it fly before the wind and so Tahaki won— he played correctly, and he won. One day therefore his cousins grabbed Tahaki and they beat him up. He lay quite still, so they left him buried in the sand, they thought him dead. But Huauri knew; by her magic powers she knew what had been done to him. She therefore dug him out and brought him back to life— and this occurred again. At other times those cousins did the same.

Because of the unkindness of those cousins toward Tahaki, Hema his father became deeply aggrieved and he left this world. From deepest shame he went below to live; he descended to the Po, and was degraded by the gods. They put him in the dunny where they went to squat, and he lived in that place. But Huauri remained, she continued dwelling in this world of light.

Tahaki excelled in all he did because his mother imparted to him her knowledge from the world below. In a secret place where none could see she made Tahaki open his mouth above the crown of her head, and breathe. Then her iho entered into him, and he felt great workings in his heart. Then lightning flashed from Tahaki's armpits, and those who saw this knew that he was of the gods.

Tahaki the son of Hema grew to chiefly greatness in his mother's care. All about him was sacred, wherefore his name is told to all who are of rank and would excel.

A giant chief he was, his shoulders were above the heads of other men, and when he walked the earth his tread left footprints in the rock.

Kura, the sacred colour—that is the colour of Tahaki of the Golden Skin. All those birds and flowers and fish that have red parts have them from him.

*   *   *

Tahaki's first great deed for this land was the cutting of the sinews of the fish.

Tahiti the fish was moving no more, it was turned to land. But men to cut the sinews were required, so that Tahiti nui might remain for ever stable in the world.

No mortal men came forward who could do this work. No gods there were who would assist! But then Tahaki took the adze, he took up the immense adze called Te pa hurunui.

> *Haapapura'a whenua was the ceremony!*
> *Te pa hurunui was the adze!*
> *Tahaki was the chief!*

Immense Tahaki took the adze in his hands and said:
'This is the adze Te pa hurunui, for the ceremony of Tinorua

Lord of Ocean, to cut the sinews of this great fish Tahiti. The sinews must be cut, well cut! That the growth of the land might find room, that the lowering blackness might pass through, that the wind-with-clouds might pass through, that the wind might sweep around the mountains, that the mountains might be walked upon by man—all for heralds of the awe-inspiring sky!'

Then the adze became possessed, it became light in Tahaki's hands and he chopped the land, he chopped the sinews of the fish.

Then all the warriors who were with Tahaki did not cease their chopping until the sinews of the throat were severed. Then the head of the fish was drawn far back and there remained still land, unmoving plain, between the two great mountain-ranges of Tahiti nui mare'are'a—yes, of Great Tahiti of the Golden Haze.

So was formed Tara vao, that narrow part of land which joins Tahiti and Taiarapu. So was completed the cutting of the sinews of the fish, that Great Tahiti of the Golden Haze might be forever firm, that it might have fixedness in the world.

Afterwards Tahaki crossed the sea and rendered stable other lands. He took his shoulder-spear, the spear no other man could lift; he took his paddle which no other man could wield, and many wooden fish-hooks also which were magic at his touch; and in the great canoe named Rainbow he sailed with warriors north-west to Mo'orea, and he cut the sinews of that land also, that it might remain forever firm.

And they did the same at Maia'o iti, and at Tetiaroa. Then eastward they sailed toward the Shaven Sea, and there from beneath the foaming breakers of Reef-that-extends they hauled up all the islands of the Tuamotu. These have ever since remained.

Tahaki also drew up Mangareva, and Hiti au rereva, and other islands in the eastern sea.

*   *   *

After these acts were complete Tahaki determined to go in search of his father Hema, to restore him to this world of light. He therefore asked his mother, 'Which is the way to the world below?' and she promised to tell him as soon as he was ready to depart.

Then Karihi asked that he might go as well, and Tahaki gave consent. And Huauri, when the time was propitious, caused the earth to open for them. They went down through that hole, those cousins, and they travelled many days through the long damp caves that lead toward the Po.

At last they reached an open space and there they saw a house, it was the house of their ancestor, an old blind woman named Kuhi.

Kuhi was sitting on the ground counting yams, she was talking to herself.

Then Karihi as a mortal felt great hunger for that food, for his journey had been long. When Kuhi had counted ten yams he took one away, and Kuhi, finding there were only nine, exclaimed, 'Who is this little maggot who has come here to the Po?'

Then Tahaki feared for his brother, and he answered in his chiefly voice, 'It is I, Tahaki,' and the old ancestor said, 'Oh then, be seated properly.'

Then Kuhi drew out a splendid fish-hook, it was dressed with finest kura and its line had magic strength. Tahaki warned Karihi by a sign that he should never touch that hook, but Karihi did so, he could not resist its golden sheen.

Then Kuhi had that common person on her hook!

'Aha, my food!' old Kuhi cried, and Karihi tried in vain to run from her, he feared her open mouth and her distending belly. But he only ran in circles while she pulled on the line with all her strength.

Cried great Tahaki then: 'O Kuhi, set aside your fish, lest the Great Shark come for you!' But Kuhi answered, 'He shall not escape. This is the fish-hook Puru i te maumau! He is my food!'

Therefore Tahaki seized the line, and saved his cousin from that old blind woman. And finding that her hook was loose, she cried, 'Aha! There is a personage of note beside me here! Can you restore my sight?'

Tahaki replied, 'E ora ho'i ia ia'u.'—'I can restore it.' And he took a piece of coconut and cast it in her eyes, and that old woman saw.

Then Kuhi looked admiringly upon her grandsons, and she asked what service she might do for them.

'Please tell us where my father is,' Tahaki said.

'He lives further on along your road,' that woman said. 'You will find him in a certain forest where the gods throw all their filth and where they squat. They have torn out his eyes and given them as lights to the girls who weave mats for the orators. The sockets they have filled with shit of birds.'

Then Kuhi called two children to direct those brothers to their father's place, and when they reached the gods' dunny Tahaki snatched up filthy Hema in his arms. Before the gods found out, Tahaki and Karihi had restored their father to this world of light. They also snatched his eyes as they departed from that place.

Then Hema was scraped, the hard-caked filth was picked out from the sockets of his eyes and he was washed, and they restored his eyes. Hema was happy to be with his wife and sons again, and they all dwelt quietly together in that place.

HOW TAHAKI LOST HIS GOLDEN SKIN

In Mangareva more is told of great Tahaki, the grandfather of Rata. His journey to below is made again. There are women who desire him, when he shines; but Tahaki resplendent leaves Nua weeping on the shore, and ascends to the heavens. There he remains.

TAHAKI was of this land Mangareva. His father Hema lived at Ngaheata. Punga the father of Karihi lived at Rikitea, on the far side of the land. Tahaki and Karihi were of natures unalike because of something which their fathers did when young. It was this:

One day the mother of Punga and Hema asked them to pick her head for lice. They did so, and Punga caught a black louse of the common sort, but Hema caught a red louse. When their mother said, 'Now eat your lice', Hema obeyed his mother, but Punga would not. Because of his obedience Hema's son was born with a ruddy skin, which gave him beauty in the land; but Karihi his elder cousin had only a common, dark-hued skin.

Nua naheo was Punga's daughter, and Tahaki desired her. It was his custom to go to her in secret in the night, and go home before the sun came up.

Now all the land had heard about Tahaki's ruddy skin, and when word got out that he went to Nua naheo at night, those Rikitea people made a plot to catch him in her house; for they very much desired to see that kirikura.

They said to Nua, 'We would like to see your lover's golden skin.' And Nua, greatly pleased, agreed to do what they suggested. They therefore stopped up all the chinks and crevices in Nua's house so that Tahaki should not know when daylight came.

Tahaki came that night, and was with Nua. Toward the day he heard the first cry of the karako, the bird that wakes us in the mornings in this land. 'Hear that,' he said. 'The herald of the dawn. Night's candles are burned out.' He roused himself; but Nua said, 'Must you be gone? It is not yet near day. Believe me, love, here at Rikitea those birds call out in the middle of the night.' Tahaki therefore stayed; he rested yet in Nua's arms.

The karako cried again, and great Tahaki stirred, but Nua said, 'It cannot be dawn, for see how dark the house remains.'

But the birds cried more. Tahaki rose; and when that chief slid back the door he found the sun was shining on the sea, and all the Rikitea people lined up by the path from Nua's house. Thus Tahaki naked left that house before their eyes. With pride but not with boasting did Tahaki walk between them. He had indeed a skin of gorgeous hue, with auburn hair as well; and great was the stature, great the glory, of that golden chief.

After this there was jealousy in Punga's village, that a man of Ngaheata should so surpass them all in handsomeness. They therefore resolved to get Tahaki's skin, they made a plot to take it from that chief and make him common. And low Karihi, out of envy of his cousin, joined that plot, he schemed with Punga and the Rikitea people.

At the edge of the lagoon-shelf, where the water becomes blue, they built a diving-platform, high and strong, and they sent out word to all the land that there would be a diving festival.

'I would like to be in that,' said great Tahaki to his mother Huauri when he heard this news, and Huauri did her best to put him off.

'It is a plot against you because of your beauty, O my son,' that mother said. 'They will steal your handsome skin, those Rikitea people.'

But Tahaki disregarded her advice, he crossed the land to join the diving festival.

Then all the haters saw him coming and they shouted, 'Who will be the first to dive?'

'I will,' Tahaki cried, but the people said, 'Who is this person? Did he help to build this platform here? He will be lucky if we let him dive at all. Let him go last!'

Then the Rikitea people dived, but none of them came up again, they remained below. By the magic power of Punga they were turned to fishes or to coral rocks, and they waited for Tahaki to arrive.

Then came Tahaki's turn; he sprang up from that platform and he dived, all golden in the sunlight, to the dim green fathoms of below. His waiting enemies were there, they darted in and tore off pieces of his skin. Tahaki twisted and he turned, and as he turned a thousand enemies took nibbles of his skin. Then the living rocks leapt up, and they too scraped off pieces of the glory of that chief, until they had it all.

Tahaki rose to breathe, he shook the water from his head and swam to shore before the crowd, his kura gone. Those people jeered. And great Tahaki, stripped of redness, strode the island to his home.

' Well, you were right,' he said to Huauri when he reached their house. 'They took my skin.' He sat in silence then; nor did Huauri speak her thoughts.

After that occasion Nua naheo was no longer flattered to be Tahaki's lover, and she deserted him, she took another man. His other woman Tumehoehoe also turned her back upon that chief, because his golden skin was gone.

*   *   *

Now Punga's and Karihi's plot was foiled; it was foiled by that ancestress of Tahaki whom we know, old Kuhi of the blinded eyes. From gratitude for sight she saved Tahaki's kirikura.

Those Rikitea people stole it indeed, they nibbled it off in pieces when he dived; but Kuhi as well was beneath the water on that day, she came from the Po, and sat among those people who were fishes and rocks. She brought her sacred basket, kete katorangi, and when the fishes bit off pieces of Tahaki's skin deft Kuhi snatched them back. Each little piece she took from nibbling lips, and put it in her kete katorangi, saying to herself, 'My young grandson gave me back my sight for this.' She also took those pieces which the rocks scraped off; and when she had the skin complete she returned with her basket to her house in the Po te Moamua. And Huauri knew what Kuhi had performed.

As soon as Huauri considered that her son had learned the lesson of his stubbornness, she said: 'If you have courage, you will go to your ancestor in the Po.' Tahaki answered, 'Indeed then I shall go to Kuhi, if that is your advice. And I shall take Karihi with me. We know the way, we two.'

Then Huauri was dismayed, for she knew of Karihi's jealousy. She did her best to make Tahaki go alone, but he was obstinate.

Those two set off, they took Tahaki's drum to keep in step, and after journeying they came to Kuhi's house. But seeing Karihi there, old Kuhi went within—she made herself not seen.

Those cousins stood outside. Then Kuhi called:

'Tahaki dear, as a man, remain outside.'

Tahaki did not move. And Kuhi called again:

'Tahaki dear, as a god, come in. Your skin is here in the katorangi basket.'

Tahaki therefore put down his drum and entered that old woman's house, and his cousin remained outside. And Kuhi took the basket from the ridgepole, she picked out all the thousand pieces of Tahaki's skin, and put them back in their proper places. She put them on, tapiripiri, and they stuck.

Then did Tahaki stand forth in his golden skin once more. It was complete save only where he trod—for Kuhi could not find the pieces for the soles of Tahaki's feet.

Those pieces had been stolen from her basket by the stick-insects, the 'e, who live on the fronds of the coconut tree. Kuhi guessed this and she went outside, she stood beneath the tree that leaned above her house, and she called to them, 'Ho, you red-faced 'e! Give back the grandchild's skin!'

Those thieving insects lied; they answered her, 'We have not seen it.'

'Of course you have,' she cried, 'you have it in your armpits, every one of you!' But the insects would not give the kura back, they had used it on themselves.

'Oh, let them keep it,' Kuhi muttered as she went inside. 'No one will notice that you have no kura on your soles, O man erect.'

This is how the 'e obtained the kura that is in their armpits still.

Then Tahaki came forth from Kuhi's house, and Karihi was amazed to see him restored to his former handsomeness; and there was confusion in Karihi's heart.

Then they-two started on their homeward journey to this world of light. To lead the way—that was Karihi's task. To beat the drum to make their striding firm—that was Tahaki's. But Kuhi worked upon their thoughts with magic power. With power of her divinity she made Karihi feel so greatly confused that he fell behind, instead of leading. And she caused Tahaki's drumming to become faint and full of doubting, wherefore our people have this song:

> Let us leave on the rising tide—
> Though doubt arises with the waves.
> The sounding drum is the younger son's,
> The elder goes in doubt.
>> Drum softly sounding,
>> Cause of doubting,
>> Drum that sounds so secretly!
> I have adorned myself with fragrant flowers—
> But yet one wonders.

> Karihi here, move over now

Toward the first Night-World,
To the first Night-World
Where doubt exists.
   Drum softly sounding,
   Cause of doubting,
   Drum that sounds so secretly!
I have adorned myself with fragrant flowers—
But yet one wonders.

Toward the first Night-World
Move over now,
To where the woman planned
To pluck the eyes out of Karihi,
Whom she held in doubt.
   Drum softly sounding,
   Cause of doubting,
   Drum that sounds so secretly!
I have adorned myself with fragrant flowers—
But yet one wonders.

By the power of Kuhi from the gods Karihi fell so far behind that
he heard Tahaki's drum no more, he fell from sight. Then Kuhi
seized him with her scaly hands, she took him to her house and
tied him up with cord. And she plucked Karihi's eyes out and put
them in her katorangi basket, and she lit an oven in order to cook
him. But Huauri as Karihi's feeding-mother came from the world
above. She asked, 'Why have you done this to Karihi, O my
mother?' and Kuhi answered, 'It was this pig who took the word to
Punga.' Then Huauri made her mother untie Karihi, and she gave
him back his eyes, and he returned to this world above.

*   *   *

After this journey Karihi went to the land of the fishes, where he
lived quietly for some time. But this was his trouble in that place:
the fishes did not like Karihi, he felt alone among them, and

ashamed. Since they would not make friends with him he sought for some way to please, and it was this: he peeled off his own black skin and gave it to the fish called Hamikere, the black hami. Then he told that fish to say to all the others, 'It was Karihi nui who gave me this handsome skin'.

When Hamikere went home all his relations were delighted and amazed by his appearance, they crowded round and questioned him.

'Well,' said Hamikere, 'it was like this: I simply went to the land of Sea-moss and I was nibbling the moss on the coral when I saw this black thing. I was frightened, and I was going to leave when I heard someone calling me, and I looked at this person, and he was coming toward me shouting, "Don't run away, lest I kill you." Then what did he do—he took off his skin and gave it to me, saying, "Here is your handsome skin." And he told me to say I got it from Karihi nui.'

'Where is he now?' the rest all cried. 'We'll have to find him and ask him for skins like yours!' So they all swam off to that place where Karihi was staying; but not Hamikere: he remained.

Karihi in the meantime built himself a fish-trap. He gathered many coral rocks, and in a shallow part of the lagoon he built a

Tatihi, a Tahitian fish

walled-in place with inward-curving entrances, one entrance leading to another one. And when those fishes arrived he asked them, 'What is the purpose of your journey here?'

They answered, 'Is the skin of Hamikere really yours?'

'It is,' Karihi said, 'I gave it to him.'

'The purpose of our journey here,' the fishes said, 'is that you should give us new skins also, like Hamikere's.'

'I will gladly do that for you,' Karihi said. 'What you must do is this: all come in here to this place which I have made for you, and when I call you you must come to me one at a time—not all at once.' So the fishes agreed, and they swam inside, to live in that place.

'Aha!' cried Karihi-the-man, 'no shortage now! I shall have what I want every day!' And he closed the entrance and returned to his own place.

Soon Karihi felt hungry, so he called a fish, and it came to receive its skin. Karihi bit its neck and ate it up. In time he did the same to all the rest, they came to him singly and Karihi ate them, until there was none left but the sand-borer, Hamohamo ngaere.

Hamohamo knew quite well what had happened to the other fishes, but the opening of the trap was shut, there was no way out. It was then that he thought of boring into the sand to hide.

One day Karihi called Hamohamo to come to him, but no fish came. He searched and called, and searched again, but no fish came: no trace could he find of Sand-borer. At length he went home tired out, and he neglected to close the entrance to the fish-trap. Then Sand-borer came out of the sand and darted through the opening, he sped away.

Karihi saw that fish escape, and chased it, but he could not catch Hamohamo ngaere.

It was Hamohamo who warned all other fishes not to believe Karihi, and that is why no fish ever obtained a gleaming black skin like Hamikere's.

This explains why we say that the black hami got its skin from

Karihi and the red hami got its skin from Tahaki. How the hami-kura got Tahaki's skin has not been told.

*   *   *

Tahaki kirikura returned to this world of light and showed abroad his golden skin, but those lovers who left that chief had gone to other men. Tumehoehoe was sharing Tangaroa's mat and Nua naheo was beating tapa for Tuku, a good-looking fellow who lived beside the coast and fished with nets.

Therefore Tahaki resolved to carry his pillow to Tuku's place, to win back Nua whom he loved. By incantations he turned himself into an ugly old man, and in that form he trudged to Tuku's house.

'O Tuku,' said Tahaki in the thin voice of an old one, 'may I live with you and help about the house?'

'What can an old man like you do for me?' said handsome Tuku.

'E 'iro'iro a'o, e tata manongi,' Tahaki answered: 'Twist good lines and make you hand-nets.' So Tuku let the old man stay, and told his wife to give him food.

When Tuku went out fishing, Tahaki made approaches to his wife. But Nua pushed him aside and said, 'You have the bad breath of an old man. Go away!'

Tahaki therefore spoke a certain chant which gave that woman pregnant cravings for the fish called ta, and when her man came home she said to him, 'Oh Tuku, I am longing for some ta.'

So Tuku took a hand-net which his visitor had made, and he returned to the reef to fish for ta.

Then great Tahaki made himself not seen, and he followed Tuku to the reef. He stirred the water with his hands, and Tuku, seeing red fish among the coral, let down his net. He caught no ta, and tried again, and scooping deeper caught his hand-net in the coral. Then Tuku had to strip his maro off and dive to free the net. And Tahaki watched him, he observed that man.

While Tuku was mending his net that old man of stinking breath returned to Nua naheo. 'I saw your husband on the reef,' he said. 'He has a poor kind of ure, that man. It is short and crooked.'

At last Tuku gave up trying to catch the fish that Nua wanted, and he returned to his house. 'Has that old man been saying anything to you?' he asked; and Nua told him what their visitor had said. 'I thought as much,' said Tuku, 'it is that pig of an old man who has brought me this bad luck.' And Tuku went off to collect his friends to kill Tahaki.

But great Tahaki sent forth potent force, and not a man of Tuku's party could approach his sacred person.

Then lightning flashed from the armpits of that chief, he threw off his disguise and stinking breath, and he stood before Nua naheo in all his shining divinity, his youthful handsomeness and golden skin. And Nua instantly desired him, and made this known to him. But pride and bitterness were in Tahaki's heart, he spurned that woman.

Tahaki left Nua naheo weeping on the coast and crossed the sea, he trod the ocean till he reached the green tree of Havaiki, the sacred tree whose roots are in the Po, whose topmost branches touch the sacred sky of Tane. And while sad Nua sang laments beside the sea that golden chief climbed upward, he ascended to the topmost heaven.

THE LEGEND OF RATA

We tell of Rata and his parents' fate; of his impetu-
ous acts; the building of his magical canoe, and how
he journeyed to avenge his father's death and mother's
degradation, far in Puna's land, Hiti marama.

ATTEND now to the story of Tahaki's grandson known as
Rata, the son of Vahieroa and his wife called Matamata taua,
a chiefess of the Scarlet Girdle, who held the title in her own right
of Tahiti tokerau, for she was ariki nui of North Tahiti.

Rata was born to these parents at the season of maroro tu—that
time when all the flying-fish come leaping near the reef and many
are caught for food. On the night after he was born there was a
fishing expedition which his parents wished to join. All their
relatives and friends were at the beach with nets and torches,
singing this chant to Splashing-gladness the fishing god:

> Now tie the torches, tie!
> Their length is for the length of night.
>   There are torches here,
>   There are torches to light—
>   Let my torch have its flame!
> With our prayer to Splashing-gladness
> Let us please the god and go!

Tahiti tokerau wanted to eat fish so that her baby would find milk
in her, therefore she asked her mother Kui kura to look after the
child, and they-two joined the fishing party. Young Vahieroa, with
lighted torch, took the bow of one canoe; his wife was there behind
him to enjoy the sport, and those canoes passed through the reef

Kotuku, the Tahitian reef heron

and felt the ocean swell. Then all the maroro flew toward those torches to be caught, they made a flittering as they flicked the waves. The people all caught many fish that night.

Now while they were about this work, an intense darkness swallowed up the stars that hung above the heads of Vahieroa and his wife. It was Matuku tangotango the demon-bird, the chief of all the demon-birds of Puna's land called Hiti marama.

No person felt the coming of that bird. And Heron-of-Darkness, swallower of stars and sons of chiefs, swept down and seized young Rata's parents, he snatched them up and flew away: with slow and silent wings he flew to Puna's land, Horizon-of-the-Moon. That land lay where the moon comes up; but it now is sunk beneath the sea. After he had flown for many days across the trackless ocean Matuku tangotango came down on the shores of Puna's land, and there divided up his catch.

Rata's mother he gave to the wife of Puna, and that woman used her for a food-stand. She had her planted in the ground head downwards with her feet in the air to be used as hooks for the baskets in which her food was brought. This was the fate of Lady North Tahiti—to be a *food-stand* for the wife of rotten Puna whom we hate!

As for Vahieroa, son of great Tahaki—Matuku bit his head off and he swallowed it; he *swallowed* that chief's most sacred head! Then he threw his body in the sea to be a meal for Puna's filthy fish-gods—for Pahua nui the monster clam, who waits in the middle of ocean to capture men; for Shoal-of-Monsters, who smashes and swallows their canoes; for Totoviri, Giant Billfish, who eats the hands of paddlers; for Beast-of-Heated-Flesh as well, and for that awful creature called Consuming-Ghost-of-Ocean-

Reefs. These monsters all dwelt in a sea-cave beneath an ocean reef near Puna's land.

The priests of North Tahiti learned these matters from their gods, extensive was the wailing in the land. But Rata's grandmother Kui kura resolved to keep the knowledge from the child, lest she lose him. It was she who dried the cord off, she who saw to it that Rata grew in fatness. With her hands she squeezed his head to make it shapely, with her palms she rubbed him all with oil of sandalwood. And when the cord fell off, it was Kui who took white core of young banana stem and rolled it on the child, and said the chant that is used on such occasions. Kui saw to it that Rata's fattening-parents brought him nothing but the richest food; three women gave their breasts, he grew immense, and he knew Kui kura as his mother, kindly caring for him as he grew.

The Chiefs of the Scarlet Girdle chose Kui kura to be the regent chief of North Tahiti, until the qualities of Rata should be known.

One day Rata and some of his cousins made toy canoes to race in the lagoon. The rest used purau wood, as their fathers had shown them, but Rata made a canoe of clay and dried it in the sun, as Kui had shown him. Rata's heart was strong to win, he wished to beat those other boys; but their totoie raced away, while Rata's turned its side toward the wind. He shouted its name to make it go, the rest all jeered.

'How can that thing of yours win, Rata?' they cried, 'when your father's head is in Matuku's beastly stomach and your mother is a food-stand upside down for Puna's wife?'

Then Rata wept, he ran with tears to Kui to ask her what was meant and where his parents were. She answered him, 'I here am your parent, Rata.'

But Rata asked her, 'Where is my father?' and she replied in the words we use when truth is hard: 'Look in the housepost there.' Therefore Rata fetched a digging tool and dug beneath the post to find his father; and Kui had to stop him, lest the house fall down.

Tahitian canoes

'Then let me see you call my father forth!' cried Rata, and Kui said that she was both his mother and his father. Rata wept.

One day he played totoie with those other boys again. The rest made their canoes of purau, but Rata used bamboo for his. Its hull was light, and Rata launched it with this powerful chant:

> Beat all the others, my totoie!
> Speed faster than the others,
> Than the tens and thousands
> That may follow you!

His canoe raced off, it left the rest behind, and Rata's heart was filled with joy.

'All right,' those cousins said, 'your canoe has beaten ours. But what sort of house has your father's soul got when his head is rotting in Matuku's guts and your mother does a dirty job for Puna's wife?' They made a dancing-song of these insulting words.

All Rata's joy fell down. He went with tears and hanging lips to Kui, she was grieved to see his face. 'What is it, Rata?' said that mother, 'tell me what it is.' And Rata burst out saying, 'When are you going to tell me about my parents?'

Good Kui then was sorely anxious, thought within her: 'If I tell this child the truth he will no more remain with me.'

Then Rata told her what those boys had said, he begged her to tell him where his parents were, and she did so. And Rata's face went dark when Kui told him of Matuku, and of his mother's beastly fate.

When the tale was ended Rata asked, 'How can I go to that land, Horizon-of-the-Moon?'

'You would surely die if you went there, my son,' said Kui kura. 'Matuku tangotango is of Puna's land. There is no one who can conquer that foul bird. He took your parents there and they are lost—let that suffice. Remain here with me in my old age.'

'But I *must* go, Kui,' Rata said. 'You know that I must go.'

And Kui in her silence knew.

'You would have to be a warrior, my son,' she said. 'You would need a great canoe, and many friends.'

*　　*　　*

In Kui's house young Rata grew in manly strength. There were good things there of every kind. The floor of Kui's house was thickly strewn with clean white shingle from the beach, and Rata slept on softest mats; he wore none but chiefly clothes, he ate rich food. In due time was his youthful character approved on every side—though some there were who said, 'The boy's impetuous'. It was said of him, that when he was of age and knew his proper duty, Rata would inherit the sacred title which his mother held.

There was prosperity then throughout the land. In every space were seen banana trees that bore good fruit, the coconuts were plentiful, cocks were crowing in the bush, and fowls increased. Kava plants matured, pigs' tusks grew upward, sugar-cane leaned forwards, taro ripened. The gods kept famine from the land and numerous children were born, there was no need to throttle them at birth. In years of fatness therefore Rata grew to the stature of a powerful chief, his body strong, his mana seen by all.

At length there came the time for Rata to assume the title, then was held a great assembly of the chiefs. The whole hui ariki were present—the Chiefs of the Scarlet Girdle, old and young. And beneath them in rank the hui rangatira—persons all of worthy dignity. These took their places in the presence of the regent Kui kura. Then, as they had already agreed in their secret councils, they gave their assent when Kui announced her wish—let Rata succeed to the sacred title of his mother who was lost.

Forthwith the people began preparing for the ceremony of installing their ariki nui. The chiefs fixed the time at four moons afterwards—so that the people could accumulate the food, weave mats, beat tapa cloth for gifts, so that builders could complete the ceremonial canoe. And when this time was past and all was ready, then the whole of the three-day ceremonial was held, with human sacrifices made, and all the ritual of pa'i atua. And Kui kura made this following address:

'O tribes that are here assembled—tribes of Pe'eai and Papahonu, tribes of Hiti uta and Hiti tai! I have words to say to you!

'I am surveying you here, yet my eyes cannot include you all because you are so many! You have heeded what I said on a former occasion—when one of us here present was a child I said to you then: "Dwell on the land, cultivate food. Let the people grow in fatness and take care of the offspring, that they may replace those who are lost on the trackless ocean."

'These things you have done, and you are numerous; there now is fatness in the land. It is therefore right that we should think of what was done to us when our ariki nui and her husband were taken by that evil bird Matuku tangotango. You all know what that creature did with them, and where they are.

'Since that day you have had a woman for your ariki nui. You soon will have a man. There must be chiefs among us who are willing now to cross the ocean and avenge those hateful deeds. Chiefs who are willing, chiefs who are strong! They will cross the ocean in canoes, these men; they will defeat the monster-enemies who await them there. I speak of Pahua nui, the slimy sea-brute who would clamp his shell on human bones; of Totoviri, who bites off paddlers' hands; of Shoal-of-Monsters; of Consuming-Ghost-of-Ocean-Reefs. There must be men—are they among you here? —who will destroy these creatures and assail the land of Puna whom we hate: men who will find the bones of those whom we intend should be restored to us.

'Now this is what I have to say to you, my people of North Tahiti—of Pe'eai and Papahonu in the uplands, of Hiti uta near the hills, and Hiti tai: Because our land is filled with people and with fatness, let us have a boar-chase as a test of strength and courage. Let us have on the one side Pe'eai and Papahonu; and on the other side, Hiti uta and Hiti tai. You all know what the rules are: "Catch by the hind leg, tie by the rope." Then let the men run down the slashing boar, the tribes all show what they can do against an angry beast. In this way shall we learn which men of ours are fit to meet Pahua nui, Shoal-of-Monsters, Giant Billfish, Consuming-Ghost, and all their kind. And we shall know whether one among us here is fit to slit the guts of him who swallowed Vahieroa's sacred head.

'Shall such as Puna and Matuku tangotango seize our sacred chiefs?' cried Kui to the crowd. 'Shall these keep Tahiti tokerau as a food-stand for a queen of Hiti marama?

'But if there be no men among us who are fit to do this work, then let us all remain and merely loiter on the land. Let us abandon our revenge, be known for feeble weaklings. What is your opinion, clans here present, of what I have proposed?'

Then Kui kura sat. She cooled her face with waving of her chiefly fan.

There was murmuring then among the chiefs; and after there

had been some private talk there stood up one who spoke for all:

'We agree to it, Kui, since what you say is good. You have spoken with the voice of the authority that was placed in you. You have spoken for the hundreds. You have spoken for the thousands! Let the new generation, who have grown up in the midst of strength and fatness, show us what they can undertake. Let the fatherless become like men! We have dwelt in the land, we have cultivated food; much offspring has been given to us. Let the young show their courage and their strength. Let the chosen be their leaders!'

So it was agreed, and hefty Rata joined in all the work. There was captured in the mountains a great wild boar with savage tusks, he was commended to the god of bravery and tied up to await the chase. Then Kui kura made it known that she would judge the conduct of the chase, and all agreed with this; for she was known for wisdom in the land.

It was therefore time for Kui to speak to Rata of certain matters that were in her mind. She had heard an old man say, 'The boy's impetuous', and she resolved to tell young Rata what was said; for she feared lest he might do some clumsy thing in front of all the commoners and lose respect.

In the private silence of her well-kept house she therefore said to him, 'O Rata, you must take no part whatever in this chase. You must join me as its judge and keeper of the rules. On no account, my son, take one side or the other. Sometimes you do not know your strength. On this occasion, be strong within: be calm and patient while the chase is on. Let all the people plainly see that you are fit to be their ariki nui, the chief of all.'

Young Rata promised Kui that it would be so.

Upon the day, therefore, in the cool air of early morning, the young men of the two opposing sides arranged themselves on both sides of the tahua, with their drummers and their priests. That grassy flat had been cleaned by the children, cleared of sticks and fronds, and while the visitors arrived the teams lined up. Those of

Hiti uta and Hiti tai had their backs to the stream which runs down to the beach beside the tahua; those of Pe'eai and Papahonu lined up facing them.

Then Rata and his parent took their seats upon the platform that was built. Huge Rata wore the splendid headgear of his rank. Its towering height made great the movements of his head, its wealth of kura feathers glistened richly in the sun.

When the priests had made their prayers for bravery before the teams, and the pig-priest, too, had spurred that beast toward the fight, all the assembled people waited for the word.

At a sign from Kui kura the boar was jabbed with pointed sticks, it squealed, it dashed out on the open ground, while drummers beat the tokere—those fearful drums that sound for human sacrifice—and all the people screamed with joy.

That boar stood still, it stood bewildered. It remained for a time not moving; but then the gods put anger in its blood and savagely it turned, it made an inland dash toward the bush.

The rival parties kept their ranks, and led by chiefs they both closed up the path the boar would take. It glared at some of the Pe'eai, they thought that it would charge them, some drew back; but then it swung about and with its head down it rushed toward the Hiti uta lot, they almost had it. A man made a dive to catch the boar's hind leg and turn it on its back, there were others ready with the rope. But in the muddle and the clamour soon that boar was off again and heading back the other way, both sides were caught off guard.

'O *come on*, Hiti uta,' shouted Rata crossly from his judging seat; and when the Hiti uta people heard his voice it fired their hearts to win. But fearful Kui snatched at Rata's cloak.

'Be calm, be silent, be a chief,' she said, and pulled him down. But Rata in the frenzy could not hold himself. He leapt up from the judging-seat, and all the chasers saw his golden helmet dancing in the sun.

Then the boar got down to the beach, where the stream flows

out. With frothing jaws and muddy flanks it slipped through a hundred chasers, and it saw the open sea. There was a man who dived upon its back, pulled out its forelegs by the feet, and held them flat. It could not tusk his hands! But the boar was slippery with mud, and those who had the rope were far behind. The boar got loose, the man let go, the boar dashed to the sea.

At this young Rata clean forgot himself, and who he was. He removed his helmet, tossed aside his kingly cloak, he left his mother's side. Big Rata dashed out on the ground among the Hiti uta and the Hiti tai, shouting 'Come this way! *This* way!' Then Kui stood, and cried out in her anger, 'Rata! Come back! You are their chief! Come back and sit!'

But hefty Rata, all forgetful amidst the yelling and the drumming of the priests, ran swiftly to the beach, where some of both sides had turned the boar back from the sea; and there he joined the Hiti tai. That pig was wet and slippery, no man could hold his grip, and though the Hiti tai had it surrounded, not a man could hold it down; therefore men of the upland tribes were scrambling in to seize their prize. Then Rata quite forgot himself. He did not know his strength, that lad, he lashed out with his mighty fists at some of the Pe'eai and Papahonu people. With single blows he peeled the skin from foreheads of those men. Some died at once, the rest lay stunned upon the ground.

Thus suddenly the sport was at an end. The people stepped back in horror from this most unseemly act; the boar made off, pursued by none. The only thought, then, was for those who had been killed or hurt. Young Rata, ariki nui of all the tribes, stood silent with his head hung down. There were some there who had teased him once; those men despised him now.

Then Kui kura came to stand with the silent crowd. To her the Pe'eai and Papahonu people turned, and said with bitter hearts: 'Well, Kui—here are people of your tribes of Pe'eai and Papahonu, fattened for their journey to the land whence none returns!'

Good Kui had no word to say to them, but only tears of grief.

Then, taking Rata with her, she returned to her house, and wept.

For two whole days and two whole nights the people heard their chief upbraided by his parent in her house. So great was his shame, his akama, that Rata would not show his face outside. He remained within, he ate no food, and Kui kura lashed him with her tongue.

'Why did you murder the people, most unworthy son?' she cried. 'Was that your way of keeping the promise that you gave? You behaved like a lout. Is that the conduct of a chief of North Tahiti? Recall your father Vahieroa—a good man loved by all. Did he beat up his friends? Recall his father Tahaki, a perfect chief. Do you count yourself their son? You have murdered harmless people of the land, not hated enemies—not those whose deaths we wish. Such bravery, such strength!

'Can friendship be recovered now? Can you regain respect? Were you a man worth anything at all you might eat pork and turtle like your forebears in this place. But you are worthless now. Go and eat globe-fish then, and die. And if globe-fish doesn't kill you, Rata, go and eat shit! Do not pick up the food of decent men, lest you blight the goodness of this land.'

These words were overheard by persons who hung about the walls of Kui's house; and Rata knew that all were told of them. He wept and wailed, till people pitied him. Then he answered Kui kura:

'O my mother,' Rata cried, 'you have hurt my heart enough with cruel words. Give over now! I only wish that you would beat me as you did when I was small—it would warm my heart again! Or get the people of the tribes to come and beat me till I bleed. A shark's-tooth knife would hurt me less than does your scolding tongue! Then must you still go on? My ears retain your hurtful words. Do you think they can forget?'

And Rata wept, and beat his head, and Kui kura left him to his pain.

Then Rata called to her, he spoke again: 'I wish to ask you this, my parent—this that I have asked before: How can I go to that land of Hiti marama, to avenge my father's death?'

'To go there you would have to build a great canoe,' that old one said. 'Can a great canoe be built without the help of friends?'

Then Kui left her son to weep. In a while she gave him food to eat; they spoke no more of what was in their thoughts.

*   *   *

After a certain time had passed the people ceased to speak of all that happened at the boar chase. They went about their daily tasks forgetful of that day; nor did the chiefs discuss those matters Kui once had mentioned in her speech. On that subject there was silence in the land.

One day Rata went to Kui, he asked her again that question he had asked before. For her answer Kui did not speak; she handed him the adze Te pa hurunui—the sacred adze, passed down from the ancestors, which his father Vahieroa had preserved. And Rata knew her meaning.

The edge of that adze was blunt. 'You will have to sharpen it, my son,' said Kui kura. 'You must sharpen it on Kui's back.' Then she bared her back and stooped before him. And Rata ground the adze upon her whetstone back, while she intoned a chant to give it power. She chanted this: 'E oro hia ho'i te tua tapu no Kui kura e'; which is to say, 'The sacred back of Kui kura must indeed be rubbed.' Thus that adze was sharpened, and endowed with godly power.

Then Rata asked his parent, 'Where shall I go, O Kui, to find a tree for my canoe?'

'In the sacred place of Tongahiti-of-the-Cheerful-Face,' Kui answered. 'There you will find your tree. No man of this world has ever ventured in that place—but Rata must. Long-lasting is the love for one's parents! Sorrow for them does not soon die!'

So Rata knew that he must journey to the green depths of that inland place called Sacred Valley, to the house of Tongahiti, god of forest.

Early in the morning, before the first grey light of dawn, he ate fish and taro, he strapped on a working maro of tough material, and he set out with his father's adze. He took that adze to the marae and awakened it with prayer and water. And carrying as well some drinking-nuts and mid-day food, he went far inland to that place of leaves and moss and mountain rain where Tongahiti lives.

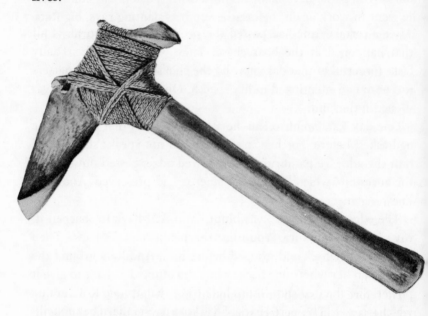

'She handed him the adze Te pa hurunui, the sacred adze'

As the sun was rising Rata came upon a fine tall aha tea tree, and he would have chosen that. But he was sure that higher, in the cloudy realm where no man ever ventured, he would find a tree more perfect still. He therefore climbed again. Before the sun was glinting from the sea, strong Rata found a very tall maomea with a clean straight trunk. Its head stood far above the heads of all its neighbours, breathing mist.

Then he spoke to the gods called Lord-of-hosts and Keel-of-all-skill, he called on them to possess his adze. They did so, and that adze began its work. All morning sweaty Rata toiled without the help of friends. He made a falling-cut, then worked from the other side; and at last that tree fell over, with a crash so loud, it echoed far down Sacred Valley and alarmed a thousand birds and insects. Then Rata rested, he ate and drank. Afterwards, he gathered leaves and wove a garland, to shade his head from the noonday sun. Then he went to work again; before the sun had slanting rays, big Rata trimmed the branches from that tree and made it ready to be hollowed out.

He then went home, and rested in his house. While food was being fetched good Kui asked him if his work had been propitious. He said it had; but Kui, being informed of certain matters by the gods, replied, 'The foliage of your tree is standing up.' Tired Rata ate, then slept.

Next day at sunrise Rata returned to his log, but he could by no means find it. For Kui's words were true; that tree was standing up alive once more, with every twig and leaf in place and all its bark restored. No trace at all could Rata find of all his work—no chips, no marks of where the tree had lain, nor broken undergrowth. No fallen tree was in that place; all things were Tongahiti's still.

Therefore Rata stood dumbfounded; but at last he saw his living tree, he saw it in its perfect state. Then he knew that in the night those thousands who inhabit Tongahiti's realm had come there and undone his work. He therefore felled the tree again, he toiled all day. But he did not cut its branches off, he left them on. And in the thickest of their greenery he hid himself, he waited until evening for the forest people to return.

As the sun sank into the sea the moths and flies came out, and shortly Rata heard a soft murmuring of many voices in the forest. There were buzzing sounds, and clicks and whistles, pretty chirrupings, and many sounds of scratching and tapping in the trees. And as he waited in his hiding-place big Rata saw through leaves the forest god himself, he saw great Tongahiti-of-the-Cheerful-Face; and with him his tough little artisan Tavaka, Hewer-of-canoes. And behind and all around them, alighting on the branches of the forest, all their company; of whom some spoke in harsh complaining terms of persons who improperly invade the sacred realm; but others sat good-naturedly among the branches. They sang this cheerful chant:

> Fly hither, fly hither
> Green leaves of my tree!
> Come gently, come angry,
> Fly hither, fly hither!
> Green sap and strong gum
> Make upstanding my tree!

This is a chant for making a tree stand up again which has been felled. Never before had Tongahiti's people used it without result. But hefty Rata hidden from their eyes held down his tree. It would not lift, and Tongahiti's leaf-green thousands were perplexed, they sang and chattered noisily.

Then was it for Tavaka to exert his power. That god leapt on the fallen trunk, and brandishing his adze of his divinity he cried, 'Let us drive out the anger of Kui! The anger of Kui must indeed be driven away!'

Then he ran along the tree from end to end, skittering among its branches as he went; yet he did not feel big Rata there. Then all the company of beaky persons sang their chant again:

> Rere mai, rere mai!
> Te vai toto o ta'u ra'au,
> Homai heti, homai heta!
> Piripiri tapau tu—
> Tu te ra'au, tu e!

On this the tree rose up with all the little gods remaining on its branches. The chips of Rata's adzing rushed back to their places, they were solid wood again; leaves sprang back on their twigs, and sheets of living bark returned, and stuck themselves in place. And hefty Rata remained, unnoticed by the throng.

When those forest persons had nearly finished their work, Rata shouted suddenly in a great voice, 'P-a-a-a-a!'—and he shook that whole tree back and forth. This terrified them all, they had not known a man was there. They flew out every side like dragon-flies, and fluttered in the air with anxious sound.

Soon order was restored, for the tree stood still; they all resumed their perches. Then artisan Tavaka shouted to the person who was hidden in the leaves:

'What is your purpose, O man, that brings you to this forbidden place, the valley sacred to Tongahiti?'

'I need a tree for my canoe,' said Rata in a gentle voice. And he came out of his hiding place, and took his garland from his head.

'Good gracious, Rata, it is you!' exclaimed Tavaka. 'We did not know that this was done to us by one who is entitled to be here—who is our grandson! Your person is sacred to us, O Rata, because of our friendship with your parents whom we adopted. Long lasts the love for one's parents! Sorrow for them does not soon die! The ship you want is for a journey of avenging—am I right? Then you shall have your great canoe! Just give us the necessary things, good tools, and plenty of cordage. Leave all the rest to us!'

So Rata was amazed. He returned to his home, he went to Kui kura to tell her this good news. But Kui already knew it all. She had the tools all ready for her son: adzes for hollowing, adzes for planks, adzes for fine work; sharp drilling-points to make the lashing-holes; well-hafted mallets, harsh lumps of coral for the work of smoothing off; and mats for sails, and many rolls of sinnet cordage made by old men, for the gods to use.

She also had ready for him baskets of red feathers, fine girdles and cloaks for the master craftsmen, and other wealth as payment for their work. Rata gathered up these things and took them inland, he put them all beside the tree. Then he returned to his home to eat.

Said Kui kura while her grandson ate: 'Your pahi will soon be finished!' After he had eaten, Rata lay on his mat and slept.

Toward the densest part of night big Rata dreamed, and as he dreamed he rolled about and sang this chant:

> O then my eyes did close
> And I did dream!
> My dream is to stand up tall
> Above the rest.
> My dream is to defeat—
> To destroy by Tane,
> Lord in scarlet cloak!
>
> This is Tane's darkness, Tane's night!
> My sleep is in the midst of boards
>   and adzing planks,
> Of singing by the bird of night
> That utters day,
> That utters night—
> That twitters and extends its wings.
>
> The springs now flow in dream of night—
> It is the gods!
> O it is gods that stir me so in sleep!

His shouting woke up Kui on her mat. Said Rata, 'I have been dreaming about my ship. I thought it was here beside the house.' He tried then to explain that dream, but fell asleep.

As day was nearly breaking Rata dreamt again; and he awoke, and said to Kui: 'My dream! I have had it again! I feel sure that my pahi is there, outside the door!'

'Throw pebbles, then,' said Kui. 'There is no mistaking pebbles on something hollow.'

And Rata picked up pebbles from their floor, threw hard.

With joy then did he hear the sound that told him of his great canoe! He went outside, and groping felt its greatness with his hands.

That chief could barely wait for daylight then. He sat beside good Kui's mat and talked—he talked of voyaging, and all that he must do.

At last full daylight came. Then Rata and his parent saw the ship, her two fine hulls of handsome length, her well-sewn seams, the master-carving on her sterns and prows. She was equipped with paddlers' seats, with bailing scoops, and paddles all with sacred names. A well-lashed platform joined her hulls, with a deck-house for her chief. There was also furnished for her chief a mighty spear of magic power, the spear Te Va'oroa ia Rata. On the ground beside her lay her masts, and woven mats to make her sails. Then Kui named that ship Te Ao pikopiko i Hiti—'The cloud that hangs over Hiti marama.'

Straightway then Rata with enormous strength drew his pahi to the water's edge, to launch her. Yet in his haste he forgot the proper prayers. Te Ao began to leak.

'This pahi is a bad ship!' he cried.

'She must be made to drink!' good Kui said. 'You cannot launch her without the fakainu!'

Therefore Kui showed impatient Rata what to do. When she had taught him the proper chant, he pulled the vessel out. And having dedicated her in gratitude to Tongahiti-of-the-Cheerful-Face, he launched her once more, she rode the water well. Therefore he pulled her to the shore again, and in the coolness of the dawn he stepped her masts, and put aboard her sails.

Then Kui showed Rata how to make a cooking-place of sand in that canoe, he laid in stores of food and drinking nuts. She wove for him a basket of pandanus lined with tapa fit for chiefs. 'This is the basket,' said that old one, 'for your father's head.' He put it safely in the sacred place which he had made, wherein he also kept his god.

Tahitian war canoe

Then Rata said a chant of hating to his filthy enemies; and weeping full, he took his leave of Kui kura, sailed away.

*   *   *

Rata took with him his captain, Tavaka, and a nimble crew as well of tiny persons who accompanied that god. They made their quarters in the lashing-holes. And when Te Ao had passed out through the reef and was lifting to the swell they all came forth and rigged the sails, and raised them to the wind.

Then Rata watched this land grow small. With heavy heart he sang this chant:

> O my land standing forth!
> Now hide your face—
> Be lost to view!

Let me be lost as well—
My face not seen,
My feelings known to none.

O hide my feelings, distance!
Make my face not seen
As I say farewell—

Aroha to the forests of my land,
Aroha till a later time.

Then Rata turned his tears toward the trackless ocean and the deeds he was to do.

For many nights they sailed, they kept their course toward that land of Hiti marama. Each day there came a frigate-bird, it soared above them; and Rata knew that bird was Kui kura's spirit, watching over him.

One morning early, roused by voices from the rigging, young Rata saw a shoal of anae threshing on the ocean's rim. 'Land ahead,' he cried, but Tavaka came to look and said, 'Those monsters are not land. We have foes ahead, my king!' So Rata drew his spear from beneath the flooring-slats, with chanting on his lips he braced himself to fight those beasts. They soon came rushing up to meet the ship, to weigh it down and swallow it. But Rata with a dazzling show dispatched those anae, every one of them, he killed them with his potent spear. They scattered and departed, all of them. And those he had caught, young Rata offered to the gods. Then he cooked their flesh, and the crew had food.

Their ship continued on its course. A small cry from the masthead told them that Totoviri, Giant Billfish, was ahead. Young Rata thought this beast was land, but Tavaka warned him, 'Totoviri is your foe, my king. He is sent here by Puna whom we hate.' So Rata stood prepared to fight, and Billfish came at speed, his jaws alert to seize this youthful chief. But Rata with his spear killed Totoviri, he sliced his body up and gave it to the crew.

They next met Beast-of-Heated-Flesh, whose breathing made the ocean boil. The spear dispatched that horrid whale, the sea went red. The monster met the same fate as the rest, the crew ate well. Their ship sailed on.

Next Rata, on his steering watch, saw seven great combers rearing up, they came to swallow his canoe. 'Come here and take the steering-oar,' he cried, and Tavaka came; then Rata got out his father's adze, Te pa hurunui; and standing on the bow he chopped the first of Seven-Combers into bits. The next great comber came and Rata leapt out on its crest, he chopped it also into ineffective parts; and so with all those mighty waves, he sliced them up. They were killed and cooked, the crew had ample food.

Then next they met the terrible Pahua, monster clam, who waited with his open shell to swallow all that company.

'What mountain is this?' cried Rata when at dawn he saw that cliff and heard sea-greedy caves which sucked and sighed.

'It is not land, sir,' said Tavaka. 'It is the monster clam, Pahua nui! Be ready, king!'

That clam sucked up all ocean, it was drinking in the waves on which the ship was borne. Horizon shrank, the world grew small, and Whirlpool swept Te Ao toward the monster's jaws. But Rata with his potent spear made severance of its vital part, he cut the sinews of Pahua's strength. Then he propped his spear between Pahua's shining jaws, they could by no means close; and with his adze he sliced Pahua's flesh, and had it cooked for all his spirit crew.

This was the last of those sea monsters whom Puna sent to fight off Rata's ship. He therefore made his offerings to the gods, and continued on his way.

After the sun had risen well next day there came a sudden darkness over that canoe. Obscurest night involved the sky, the sun was hidden, gloom filled all the sea and Rata, watching eastward, cried, 'There's rain ahead.'

'That is no rain cloud, Rata,' said Tavaka, 'it is the shadow of Matuku tangotango's wings. It is Matuku who has swallowed up the sun—your enemy, who comes to swallow you as well, and sink the ship. Be strong!'

'I am ready,' Rata said, and taking up his spear Te Va'oroa, he ran to the bow that cut the darkened sea. Not finding that place right he came back to the centre-deck; but there the masts and rigging blocked his view. He ran astern to where the steering oar, manned by Tavaka, was creaking in its slot; but the gods were against that place as well. Therefore Rata jumped over the side and landed on the steering-oar, and sliding down it on his heels he stood where the water swirled about his waist, and with his spear he swept the gloomy sky.

'This is the right place now, Tavaka!' Rata cried. 'Guide the ship! Steer well!'

Tavaka held in readiness that basket lined with tapa cloth that Kui kura wove. Then Rata, joyous in his good place in the foam, cried out aloud:

> Let the darkness descend
> While Rata stands
> Upon that sweeping oar!

> But he will be imbued,
> Far-soaring bird, with energy!
> With energy, far-soaring bird!

> *O bird of musical darkness,*
> *Bird of singing night—*
> *O bird far-soaring: be afraid!*

Then that evil bird of darkness hovered over Rata's ship, obscuring all the sky; and Rata shouted to Matuku-of-the-night, 'Come here, my friend!' The monster took its range, it closed its wings and made a gannet's-dive to snatch up hefty Rata. But he cried, 'Now down!', Tavaka raised the helm, the oar strove down, and Rata went beneath the waves. And foul Matuku checked his dive, he soared again, and hung above the wake with watchful eye.

From underneath the sea, then Rata threw his spear Te Va'oroa, it flew out dripping from the wake, and severed off Matuku's wing. And Rata caught the wing and handed it to Tongahiti-of-the-Cheerful-Face—who in that instant joined the ship. Then Tongahiti set the wing on end, he stood it up to be a sail.

When Matuku saw this done he gave a scream more terrible than any that men have heard. Then sliding down the rays of morning he assailed once more the son of him whose head was in his guts. But good Tavaka flung the helm up hard, he plunged his chief beneath the sea. Matuku on his one wing dived, and spinning fell. His blackness soaked the sea, and light returned throughout the sky.

'So you are mine!' cried Rata as he rose: and drove his spear into Matuku's other wing, and pitchforked all that monster's body to the deck.

Then Rata quickly sprang aboard again, and taking Kui's basket from Tavaka's hands, he placed it over Matuku's beak. Matuku retched—he gave up Vahieroa's sacred head. And Rata recognized his father. He wept, and softly chanted:

> Fall away, O fall away
> My father's head!
> Here is the safe receiver, O,
> Here is the safe receiver.

With reverence that weeping son then placed the basket in the ship's marae, he laid his father's head in safety in the presence of the gods.

Then Rata took his adze and sliced away Matuku's head, he killed that filthy bird, and ate its brains. And Heron-of-Darkness was no more, to be a danger on the sea.

Then Rata and Tavaka and their friends set to and plucked the bird, they pulled out all its sheeny feathers, they used them to dress the ship in handsome style. With artful hands they made the masts and sails and rigging all look well, with fluttering feathers of the bird of Hiti marama. Those feathers hid the ship entirely, no rope or mast of it was seen.

Then Rata took Matuku's other wing, and stood it up to be a sail. His ship, Te Ao, sailed on, toward Puna's land. And kindly night came down, true night; and gentle winds, that carried Rata's feathery canoe toward Horizon-of-the-Moon.

Next day at height-of-sun a distant cloud whose underside showed blueness-of-lagoon informed those travellers that reef and land were near. They steered toward that cloud; and the soaring frigate-bird, the spirit of Kui, showed them that it was the place they sought. At evening they saw many other birds returning to the land. So Rata hid, and all the crew as well; they crept back to their places in the lashing-holes. And good Tavaka made himself not seen. The black-winged ship sailed on toward the night, and with the dawn she lay off-shore, in Hiti's lee. Then boldly she glided into Puna's wide lagoon, the mirror of the setting moon.

In the middle of that land of Hiti marama there stood one mountain, all feathery with blossoms of the kakeho, the waving cane: therefore the name of that mountain was Maunga pua kakeho. Clear streams ran down its valleys, at its foot there fell into the ground a great dark cave. That cave was foul Matuku's place: in smelling darkness there his thousands lived.

Never before that day had Hiti seen so huge a seabird as Te Ao. A person who came early to the beach to squat ran back to rouse the rest, and all the people of the villages came out. Thin Puna was among them. All trembled when they saw the bird that entered their lagoon. And the priests came out, consulted with their gods.

Then Puna, chief of all that rotten tribe, cried out: 'E eitu no te moana mai!' 'It is a spirit-thing come out of the sea,' thin Puna told his crowd, 'it is an eitu made visible to us by Clearness-of-atmosphere.'

The ship drew near. As soon as shouting might be done Tavaka said to Rata, 'You had better come out now, O my chief. Be seen!'

Therefore Rata revealed himself: that hefty lad stood up and took the helm. Tavaka and the crew remained not seen; and all the people were astounded, for they saw that the bird was a great canoe, and only a youth was steering it.

Then a cry of 'E pahi!' ran along that beach: 'It's a ship! It's a ship!' those people shouted. Thin Puna's face went dark, and turning to his two chiefs Tupa uta and Tupa tai, he said:

'Something wrong has happened. Those feathers are Matuku's hair. That lout has murdered him. Go out and deal with him—guide him in! Just run him on the coral-heads! The next good storm will do the rest.'

So Land-crab and Shore-crab went to help young Rata pick his way among the coral-heads. But when those pilots shouted 'To the right', Tavaka said 'Steer left'. Those persons could not see Tavaka, he remained not seen. And when they said 'Steer left', Tavaka said 'Steer right'. And all the Hiti people were amazed, gaunt Puna fell silent, when the ship was safely beached on Hiti's sand.

Then Rata sprang ashore with his adze Te pa hurunui, and after obtaining permission he cut sufficient rollers for his ship, and spaced them on the beach to pull her up.

'He surely won't try that alone,' the people said. Then Rata swam out, and pushing from the stern he beached Te Ao. With a shove at the crossbeams of her deck he rolled her up beneath a breadfruit tree, and he covered her from the sun with fronds of coconut which children brought. After he had attended to all these matters Rata retired into his deck-house to rest.

Then the people crowded round their visitor, they gave him food, and drinking nuts. But Rata remained in his ship. No person dared to ask him to his face, 'Who are you?', for it was plain this person was of rank. Indeed they feared him, as a god.

Thin Puna, when he saw these signs, went apart with his two chiefs, Tupa uta and Tupa tai. They made their secret plan and Puna ordered that a house of finest quality be built beside Te Ao for Rata's use. He marked out the place himself, and it was done.

It was a house well worthy of a chief of noble rank; its thatched roof rose beside the breadfruit tree that gave its shade to Rata's ship. That house for floor had clean white shingle from the beach, and finest mats, and Puna furnished it with chiefly stools and everything for Rata's comfort.

When the house was finished, Puna sent his daughter Tie maofe, to invite Rata to use it. And good Tavaka, whom those people could not see, told Rata, 'Take the house. But do not go there without your spear Te Va'oroa.'

Therefore Rata went into the house with Te Va'oroa, and he found a great feast prepared. And Tie maofe and many other girls and young people were there to entertain him with their kindest services. Their king had told them, 'Tire him out. He has been sailing alone these many days, so keep the dancing up till dawn: and when he drops you must all pretend to be asleep. Then come away. Leave no one in the house but him. And bring away that stool of mine.'

They did all this, those young ones of Puna's land. They filled their visitor with food, they danced and sang till dawn was near;

'And bring away that stool of mine'.
A chief's stool from Atiu

then all lay down to sleep in Rata's house, and Rata snored. Some persons prodded him. He did not stir; they all crept out. Then Tie maofe took a lighted candlenut to Rata's side, she wished for a last look at that handsome visitor; and she desired him, touched him secretly and said these words: 'E tamaiti ra ho'i 'oe i te maitai, 'e 'a pohe e!'—'Oh, what a handsome youth you are to die!'

And Rata heard her word. Then with her light that daughter who obeyed crept out, she joined her relatives and friends, they all went to their sleeping-house.

Not sleeping, Rata waited for his foes to come. He heard men tie the doors with cord, and through the chinks he saw the light of torches that were brought. Then all those friends of filthy Puna fired the thatch.

'Now be my friend,' said Rata to Te Va'oroa. He stuck that spear beside the centre-post and swiftly climbed it to the rafters. Then through the roof, beneath the tree that shaded great Te Ao, big Rata tore a hole—with one grasp of his hand he pulled a man-sized hole, he swiftly darted through. He pulled Te Va'oroa behind him, and none of Puna's fools saw Rata as he sprang into that tree, and so came down, and went to bed aboard Te Ao.

All Puna's lot stood round and watched that house go up in flames. The thatch was soon ablaze, the rafters fell in sparky piles upon the place where Rata slept. No cry was heard from him!

There was a popping noise. Said Puna's chiefs, 'The Lizard-belly bursts. He's done for now.'

'That ship of his belongs to me,' said thin-faced Puna. 'In the morning let Matuku's sacred feathers be removed, and let the priests preserve them with respect. If anything is left of that lout when the fire cools down—put it down the crabholes! We all know what a crab will eat!'

Then the people returned to their houses, and they slept. When it was day they came to take possession of Te Ao. They were greatly abashed, those people, when they found that Rata was alive, his sacred person was unharmed. The ship continued to be his. And Puna was afraid, he had no word, his cloak was trembling. One by one, his people went away. Then fear came into Puna's heart. He spoke in anger to his daughter, to Tie maofe: 'You must have been asleep yourself. That lout has made us look like fools.'

★   ★   ★

After this Rata lived quietly for a time among those people, and he took his turn at playing tricks on Puna's chiefs. This was when he cheated Tupa uta and Tupa tai of all the crabs they gathered on the reef; and from their fishing canoe he hooked the sacred white rooster, the watcher for Puna that waked him from his sleep.

But at last young Rata said, 'The time is come,' and he laid his plans. To dispose of all Matuku's thousands, that was his first intention.

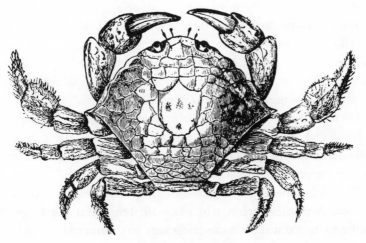

Tupa tai, a sea crab

They must avoid the sun, those people, or they died. They dwelt like woodlice in the mountain cave, they were never seen outside by day. Therefore Rata went in secret to the entrance of that place and hid himself until the sun was at the proper angle. Then with one kick he made the cave burst open, he split that cave along its length. Stinking monsters flew in Rata's face, they tried to bite his eyes and lips. But the sunlight did for all of them, they curled and died; and those that escaped went down below, they were never more seen by men. Then Rata closed the cave, went back to his ship.

Next Rata launched Te Ao once more and sailed her out to sea, he let all think that he was gone. For two days he was gone, not seen. Then Tongahiti came, he caused a hurricane to blow at Hiti marama. The sea piled up on Puna's reef, a thousand trees fell flat; but Rata sailed to safety on the other side, he landed there; and crossing over with Tavaka in the night, he came to Puna's house.

They found thin Puna on his sleeping-mat, shaking with the cold beneath his tapa sheet and muttering, 'This storm is goodness of the gods; now Rata will be drowned at sea, and that will finish him.'

With light of candlenuts they waited by his sickness bed, and shortly Puna, taking them for slaves of his, began to moan: 'O people here! O people here! I have got te mariri! It is the fever! Make an offering to the god!' But Puna's servants were stupefied by the enchantments of Tavaka; they slept on.

Then Rata and Tavaka took a rope and bound up Puna's feet; and the end of that rope they tied to a great stone pillar that stood outside Puna's marae. The name of that stone was Papa 'ari 'ari— 'Stone-with-tapered-waist'.

That pillar was the rock to which king Puna tied his victims for the sacrifice; therefore it was worn to thinness at the height of half a man, worn thin with strugglings of a thousand men.

At daylight Puna woke with groans. He saw the rope and where it went, he gave a great convulsion. Then Stone-with-tapered-waist was snapped by Puna's strength, the rope lashed back and tangled with his filthy limbs. With awful screams he strove to rise, but Rata speared him with his spear Te Va'oroa, and good Tavaka pierced his neck. Thus Puna died and rotted into filth. His wife and daughter, Tie maofe, slept on.

Then Rata went to Puna's cooking-place, he went to where his mother still remained, a food-stand upside down for Puna's wife. And with his spear he dug away the dirt and filth in which her head was set. Young Rata pulled his mother from that pit and started scraping her. And fair Tahiti tokerau, quite blind, supposed her hour was come. She gently said: 'You will have to wash the dirt off me before you eat me.'

Then Rata wept. 'It is I, your son,' he said. And Lady North-Tahiti could not see him, nor believe his word. 'That is not possible,' she said. 'Rata is across the sea. No man of North Tahiti could reach this land of filthy Puna. There are fiendish sea-gods who protect this place; there is also vile Matuku, the worst fiend of them all.'

And Rata in his sorrow wept aloud, and weeping sang these words:

> There was no pity shown, indeed!
> But moving, moving hither,
> Came your son.
> Creeping, creeping hither,
> Came your Rata—
> Came in contact! Struck!
> There was no pity shown, indeed!
> But moving, moving hither,
> I your son have come!

Then fair Tahiti tokerau knew Rata for her son, they two embraced, and wept.

After they had concluded their lamentations Rata washed his mother clean in Puna's bathing pool, he took the lice from her hair, and he clothed her in royal tapa, whitest cloth.

Still all the people slept, for good Tavaka saw to it. And taking with him Puna's wife, not woken, and Tie maofe as well, Rata crossed the land to where his pahi lay. They launched that ship and sailed from Hiti marama, Horizon-of-the-Moon.

Then Tongahiti sent his storms, the wind and seas rose up; and Hiti marama went down, it sank beneath the sea. No man has seen that land again.

Before he set his course for Great Tahiti of the Golden Haze, big Rata accomplished one more deed for men.

'Steer for the shoal, Tavaka, steer for the fishing-ground!' he cried. Tavaka did so, and they anchored there. Then Rata took the rocks on which the seabirds sat, he threw them down that cave, the home of Puna's beastly sea-gods. Fish demons fought him, but Rata destroyed them all, the whole thousand of them. He closed that cave with rocks and sailed away.

Then Rata returned to his home, and great was his mana in the land. This was his dream: to stand up tall above the rest. His dream was to defeat—to destroy by Tane, lord in scarlet cloak.

Good Kui wept to have her daughter back, her son as well; and persons who had hated Rata once now came to greet him with respect. Old Puna's wife was well received. Her daughter Tie maofe became the wife of Rata, the mother of his sons from whom our chiefs descend. The sacred head of Vahieroa, son of great Tahaki of the Golden Skin, was dried and cleaned, and wrapped in perfumed tapa, and entrusted to the priests.

This story of Rata is concluded.

APUKURA'S MOURNING FOR HER SON, AND HER REVENGE

Here on Rekohu we tell of Apukura, how she mourned.
And how she ate the eyes of her who ate her son's.

WORD came to the many sons of Apukura that there was a beautiful woman living at Ta Uru o Monono who could not be approached. Her name was Maurea, she was the first-born, she was tapu. She was kept apart, to be the wife of one whom the chiefs of her land would choose.

When the sons of Apukura heard this word about Maurea they at once prepared to leave for that land. These were the ten sons of Apukura and her husband Rei: Tu whakararo was the first-born and the handsomest, his mother's favourite; next Pepemua, 'First Butterfly', and Pepetahi, Pepekonaki and Peperoto; then Tihangei te marama, 'Ring-round-the-Moon', Tihangei ra, 'Ring-round-the-Sun', and others who were named for the Nights of the Moon. There were also other children of Rei—forgotten, cannot be remembered. Sometimes they were called the Many-of-the-Moon.

With longing for the woman of whom they had heard, those sons made ready their mother's canoe to travel to Monono, land of the two chiefs Tupakihimi and Paparakewa. Their mother said to them: 'When you reach the shore of that land, do not hide the beauties of your eldest brother, Tu.' That mother feared that her younger sons might hide the handsome eldest from the woman of Monono whom they all desired.

They crossed the sea, they reached that land, the people of Monono watched them come. They dragged their canoe above the tide and went up to the village. Then Tupakihimi and Paparakewa asked them, 'Whose sons are you?'

'We are sons of Apukura and of Rei.'

'Is this all of you?'

'Yes, all.'

Those chiefs of Monono had seen the canoe come in and they said, 'There is another of you,' but the younger sons denied it. Then the chiefs asked them, 'What are those ornaments you hold?'

'They are our necklets.'

'We will count them then.'

'Pa-a! *His head was cut off.*'
A Chatham Island club made of whale bone

Those chiefs then counted up the whale-tooth necklets which the sons were holding. There was one for each man, but there was one left over.

Then indeed Tupakihimi and Paparakewa knew that their visitors were concealing one of their party. They left them and went with their weapons down to the shore, to that canoe dragged up. Beneath the flooring-slats they searched, they found there Tu.

Pa-a! His head was cut off.

The eyes of Tu whakararo were gouged out and given to Maurea, to be eaten by her. Then the chiefs returned to the younger sons and showed them what they had.

'See, the head of one of you!'

Then said Tupakihimi and Paparakewa: 'You may go. Take this left-over food back to your mother.' They threw Tu's head upon the ground before them.

Those nine sailed home, they took with them the head of Tu, and paddled to their land. Then Apukura watched, she saw that fine canoe of hers approach. Tu's paddling-place was empty. Did wail then Apukura, wail and weep, and call upon the gull that hovered over her. This was her wail:

> O son, O son of mine, O son!
> Hear me, bird, that flies up there!
> Have you seen dead my precious one,
> Who went among the thousands of Monono?
> > Feathers on your legs,
> > Feathers on your wing—
> > Your beak bends low.
> > *Alas, my son!*

> The canoe which I provided,
> The canoe on which the son embarked,
> The son so loved by me,
> Cast up upon some other land!
> > *O son, alas, my son!*

> *You are a moon that will not rise again,*
> *O son, O son of mine, O son!*
> *The cold dawn breaks without you,*
> *O my son, O son of mine, O son!*

Then landed that canoe, the sons came home. They gave their brother's head to Apukura, and their own heads they hung down. And Apukura wept, and said this word:

The embalmed body of Ti'i, a Tahitian chief

'Throw, throw away the left-over food of those warriors.'

Then Apukura asked her sons, 'What was the cause?' They hung their heads, they looked down. 'We hid our eldest brother, that was the cause.'

Then Apukura turned her back on them, she went into her house and wailed. This was her wail:

> Go bind my torches,
> Bind my torches,
> Lest I lose my way.
> Lest I be put off,
> Put off my purpose of revenge,
> Lest I lose my way in the parts of Havaiki.
> There were the Many-of-the-Moon,
> The many sons who went.
> There were those chiefs—
> He was not given for you-two!
> You were thought to be kindly men,

Tupakihimi and Paparakewa.
He was not given for you-two!

When she had ended her cry, Apukura took her torches and began her journey. 'I am going to seek for the land of your uncle.'

She arrived at the land of a people who asked her, 'Where are you going?' She put her basket down and chanted:

> I go to find my brother Whakatau—
> Whakatau far off,
> Whakatau where the heaven closes,
> Closes, closes down upon the earth.

She journeyed on, she went to the place which is beyond the horizon. She came to another people, and she said her chant of Whakatau again.

Came then Apukura to the country of the Ngunguwao. Those people of the forest are a silent race, they use few words. They told her, 'Go to that person over there. You see that small man starting toy boats—go to him.'

When Apukura reached him Whakatau looked at her and saw that their skins were alike. So also did Apukura.

'Who is the stranger?'

'It is I, Apukura. Who is the resident?'

'It is I, Whakatau.'

Then they-two had a cry, they said their lamentations there beside the sea. They said the karakia 'Tuturu te Rongo', and they wept. Then Whakatau began that chant, that wailing chant, and Apukura followed him. Then Apukura in her turn began that wail and Whakatau joined in. They cried on the ebbing tide, their tears ran outward with the sea; they cried there on the flowing tide, they cried until the edges of their cloaks got wet because the tide came in. Then they removed ashore.

They cried again, and Whakatau, hearing the weeping of his sister, asked her: 'What is the cause you come here to wail and sob?'

'Wait until I show you my love for the beauties of our first-born son, Tu whakararo.'

Then Apukura took out Tu's head and gave it to Whakatau. He said this word:

'Throw, throw away the left-over food of other warriors.'

Then dry-eyed Apukura handed Whakatau the tapu-ending food. She took the tuaporo from her basket and she said, 'Here is the cleansing offering.'

Her brother answered, 'Roast it for us two.' Apukura did so, and their tangi was ended.

Then Whakatau asked, 'Who killed your son?'

'Tupakihimi and Paparakewa.'

They-two then walked together to the house of Whakatau. He asked her, 'Was your son a warrior?'

'A warrior he was.'

'Was he handsome also?'

'His skin was like the skin of our mother Hapai.'

'Ah, wait then, wait until tomorrow.'

Next day Whakatau asked his sister how great was the strength of Tu whakararo.

He jumped, that short man Whakatau, he ran and sprang, and he said to Apukura, 'Was it like this?' Apukura made a face, saying '*Te-e-e*, that is *nothing!*'

He lit a great fire, and jumped over it, saying, 'Like this?' But Apukura replied, 'It is too small.' Many things did Whakatau jump over and ask his sister 'Was it like this?' but she always replied 'Too small, too small!' And Whakatau himself was but a small man, like a lark.

But now when Whakatau jumped right over the summit of Hikurangi, he went so far into the sky that Apukura could no longer hear the rattling of the paua shells he wore around his neck. She feared for him; but Whakatau lit safely on the other side of that mountain. When he came back over the summit, crying out, 'Like this?' then Apukura said to him, 'That is too great, indeed.'

Te Pou, a chief of Rarotonga

Then Whakatau said to his sister, 'You and your children go tomorrow.' She replied, 'We-two must go,' but he said, 'No, no, I will not go, but take your children.' Said Apukura, 'Then the death of my son will never be avenged,' and Whakatau replied, '*Your* children are of high rank. They will do.' And Apukura departed for her own land with her children who had come with her.

But Whakatau went also, he left after her, and by his swiftness he reached her home before she came. When Apukura arrived, Whakatau was there. His walking-stick was standing in the space outside the house of Rei, its owner was inside.

Rei and his people built a peepe, a great ocean canoe, to carry a war-party against Ta Uro o Monono, to avenge Tu whakararo.

They built that canoe and finished it, with finest work. They loaded it with weapons and with food. Then going to one people they got into the canoe ten, twenty men; of another people, two-score men. At length with seven-score warriors of all the tribes and Whakatau and Rei and the sons of Rei, that canoe set out and reached Ta Uru o Monono, rode at anchor off the shore.

When some young people of that land saw what was come, they ran up to the village shouting, 'A canoe! A peepe, riding outside here!' The elders said it was nonsense, would not believe it; but the young ones asserted it was so. Those old ones therefore came down to the beach. 'O-o! Indeed it is true.' Then all of Tupakihimi's people and all of Paparakewa's people came down to the shore, not one remained behind.

Tupakihimi and Paparakewa called out to all their men, 'Who is the warrior who will attack that canoe?' Mongouri tapiri and Mongorueke answered, 'Here are the warriors, we-two.'

Then were these two seen by those upon the canoe, plunging into the waves. Cried Rei to Whakatau, 'Warriors! Warriors!' Cried Whakatau, 'What kind of warriors?' Said Rei, 'Wading warriors, wading hither.' Called Whakatau again, 'What kind of warriors?' and Rei replied, 'Swimming warriors, swimming hither.' Rei called again, 'O Whakatau, they are close, they are near, they quiver.' Then Whakatau said this word:

'Allow, allow them to come on to the trembling, come on to the scattering. A face of speech, a face of rage! Be speechless, be silent! It is the hearing of a chief!' It was the first time in the land that this saying was uttered.

Then Whakatau dashed out. Two! He killed them both, and dragged them into that canoe. The shout rose from the shore, 'Killed! Killed! from there, from there. Ah! from here, from here!'

Tupakihimi and Paparakewa cried again, they called out to their people, 'Who is the warrior who will attack that canoe?' Taiki and Tainana answered, 'Here are the warriors! We-two.' They went into the sea in the same manner as the other slain, and Rei called out to Whakatau, and these two were killed by him. The shout arose upon the shore once more when this was seen, and now their head chiefs, Tupakihimi himself and Paparakewa also—they became annoyed and rushed into the sea, they waded, swam. When near enough, but safe, they called to Rei, 'You have a warrior, Rei?'

'I have no warrior.'

They cried again, 'You have a warrior, O Rei. What killed those?'

'I have no warrior, but indeed some thing just like a lark in size.'

They therefore turned their faces to return to shore; and Whakatau like a lark sprang on to Tupakihimi and Paparakewa. Pa-a! He tore the fat off their backs, brought it with him to the canoe. But those two chiefs escaped, they got ashore, and all their people with them fled.

When Whakatau landed, the waves broke waves of blood.

Afterwards the canoe returned out to the current and they waited until night. When it was dark they moved inshore; it was quite dark, and thoroughly dark; they paddled in and got very close to the land.

Then Whakatau said that he would go on shore: 'I will go to that land alone.' And he spoke to all his people in the ship:

'Be swift, be swift with what you do. Listen to my word to you, and be you prepared to take the news to Apukura: If Monono burns, it is they who have fallen. If it glares in the sky above, it is I who have fallen. Be swift, be swift with what you do.'

This was his word to the people who did not land but stayed to guard the ship. These words of Whakatau being ended he went overboard and swam ashore, and went in secret to the house of Maurea, that woman of his nephew's seeking.

Once there beside that house, he listened to the tone of Maurea's voice and made himself the master of it, in order that the Monono people might mistake him for that woman. When he had acquired her voice he went to look for the house of the chiefs.

He came to a house that seemed like theirs, and spoke through the doorway in Maurea's voice: 'Maii ma!'—that is to say, 'Old men!'—a greeting for those chiefs he sought. But a girl there, weeping, answered him: 'Oh, do not come to our house! There are no men here now!' For that was the house of Taiki and Tainana whom Whakatau had slain that day. 'Go you to the house of the *old* men,' said the girl to the person with the voice of Maurea. And so she directed Whakatau in darkness to the house of Tupakihimi and Paparakewa.

Then Whakatau dipped the edge of his garment in water, and when he reached the chiefs' house he made his voice again sound like the voice of Maurea, and called: 'Maii ma!' Those chiefs from

Carved handle of a paddle, Austral Islands

their sleeping mats replied, 'What do you come here for, O Maurea?'

'I have got wet with water.'

'O-o! Go back from this sacred place. This house is not for you to enter!'

'Then I will go over there,' said Whakatau in Maurea's voice; and those chiefs turned on their mats and slept again in the firelight, two chiefs back to back.

But Whakatau remained, he stayed in the dark space between their buttocks; the firelight did not show him, there. After a time he spoke this proverb to them in her voice: 'Throw, throw a bundle of your cracklers on to the fire, listen to the sound of the voice of the people which comes from the shore. Tomorrow will be waded the river of blood, and will rise up the warrior on the shore here.' It was the first time in the land this thing was said.

And they-two, sleeping, answered him, 'A small warrior, no bigger than a lark, can be hidden in the hollow of the hand.'

Twice Whakatau spoke his proverb again. And when he reached the third time he fiercely thrust his spear into the holes in their bottoms, the handle in Tupakihimi's, the point in Paparakewa's.

Then his call to his god sounded forth: 'O Maru! Break out an opening for me!'

Pa-a! It broke upon the roof of the house, upon the great roof of Ta Uru o Monono. A hole for Whakatau to leap.

And Whakatau sprang forth, and stood in the marae of that tribe, their open space. The great house fell, its thatch fell down into the fire, and all the people there were burned. Others with others also burned. All the houses of Monono burned, they were swept clear, and all of the people were killed. Then Maurea was fetched to be taken alive to Tu's mother—to Apukura, to be eaten alive by her.

Whakatau's canoe returned to Apukura's land, and she was filled with bodies of the dead. Whakatau gave portions to the stranger-people who had joined his party of avenging. To the people whose men did not come he threw the entrails. He said to those who came and helped him, 'See, this is for you, for your relatives and people to eat.'

When that canoe first touched the shore, Apukura rushed at Maurea and bit off her small finger. Maurea called out in pain, 'Aue! Aue!' and Apukura said, 'It was you who ate the eyeballs of my son, Tu whakararo.'

Then the oven was lit, and Apukura threw Maurea into the fire, into the oven. She sprang and jumped about. They threw her in the fire again, again she jumped out. And they roasted her alive, all the time still looking and not cooked. Apukura therefore ate her eyes raw.

This is the end of the story of Apukura and of Whakatau.

SEVEN AGES IN
THIRTEEN CHANTS

Priest's neck ornament, Tahiti

FOR THE ANOINTING OF A NEW-BORN CHILD

This is the purifier, the core of the mei'a,
Banana-tree of the gods
To pass over the smooth skin,
The tender skin of the child.

Anoint with sweet-smelling oil
The body of this child god.
Let it be soft, let it be glossy
With the sacred oil of the gods.

Squeeze dry, make soft with oil
　the spiral cord;
Be dry for a neck-wreath for the child.
Let the cord lie round the neck
As a garland, a pledge of long life
For the child god here present.

BAPTISMAL CHANT FOR A CHIEF'S FIRST CHILD

Bathing the skin of this child of the gods,
Bathing it in the Living Water of Tane—
Listen to the wind the gods have sent,
The soft wind from the east,
Which is blown this way
To give feeling to the skin of the child.

Arise, Tangaroa! Arise, Atea! Arise, Tane!
Arise the host of gods!
This child will lay hold of fugitives behind,
Of fugitives in front—
The fort above as well,
While the skies cry out.

O gods, a warrior accomplished, this!

CHANT FOR THE CUTTING OF A NEW TOOTH

*W*HEN *the loose tooth has been thrown on to the roof-thatch where the rats nest, these words must be said:*

> Big rat! Little rat!
> Here you have my rotten tooth,
> Give me now a new one.
> Give me now a new one.

LAMENT ON LOSING A KITE

Aue! Aue!
My kite-string's bust!
My kite's gone off,
It's lost in space,
It's gone for good!

    All right, kite:
    Fly on to visit.
    Visit here and visit there—
    Old Wind has got you now.

    And where have you gone—
    To the home of the stars?
    Where are you clinging—
    To the breast of the sky?

Aue! My kite's flown off,
It's tangled with the far side of the sky.
Its head is hanging down
All drooping in the wind.

Aue! Send back my kite,
I want it back!
Make it come back to Akaria.

    But Akaria only reminds me—
    Sad thoughts make more sad thoughts.
    I think I'll go to Rama;
    I do not like Akaria.

That string snapped in my hands,
Snapped under my foot—

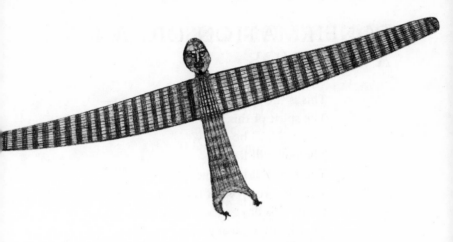

A Maori kite, eight feet across

Useless end of string!
Now I'm starting to cry—
I sound like a startled duck.

It is *lost!*

CONFIRMATION OF
A WARRIOR

This is the spirit, the spirit is present—
The spirit of this tapu.
The boy will be angry,
The boy will flame;
The boy will be brave,
The boy will possess thought.
Name this boy:
That he may be angry,
That he may flame—
To make the hail fall.
Dedicate him to fight for Tu.
Ward off the blow, that he may fight for Tu.
The man of war jumps, and wards off the blows.

SONG OF A LOVER TO A GIRL WHO LEAVES HIS ARMS AT DAWN

O Miru girl, you are dampened to the bones by morning dew,
By the dew of the Rano aroi.
You will not be dry when you go down to the shore to soak
  aute
To make tapa for the ribbon of your topknot.

POEM OF A GIRL WHOSE YOUNG SISTER LOVES THE SAME MAN AS SHE DOES

O Mea, for your body the little one and the big one
  are fighting.
It is winter, my friend, the flower gives off its
  perfume,
The flower is very fragrant.
It is summer; the flower, my friend,
Is withered on my breast. Aue, Aue!
The older girl, she feels afraid.
Here is the wreath to hang an ornament—
The ornament is your face,
O my brother Mea.

CHANT TO DUMP A SURFER

There's a young man riding on the wave-
    crest,
Now he's rising to the sky—
The sun! The foam!

Ruahie!
The wave folds down,
It's flat,
It's lost its force.

A BOASTING CHANT IN WAR

Clap hands on thighs!
Rush headlong like an angry boar!
Should I flinch at a fly like you?

   A whirlwind is anger, O Te Ahoroa;
   A rock-breaker is anger;
   A strong north wind is anger
   That blows away the grass.

Give me the fearless warrior
With rage and strength!
This is I, Huriaau!
My father was a better warrior than yours!
You cannot even lift my spear.

CHANT ON THE DYING OF
AN ONLY CHILD

Spring up, spring away, to the stars, to the moon!
To the sun, to the gathered clouds, to the parting clouds, Aue!

Tahitian priest in mourning robes

The heaven stricken by Tu, devoured by Heuoro.
Ascend direct, ascend there straight,
Ascend to the Morning-of-Heia, to the breaking morn;
Gather together the Morning-of-Heia,
Gather the morning beyond the edge of sky,
Ascend direct, ascend there straight.
Ascend to the first horizon, ascend to the second horizon,
Ascend to the third horizon, ascend to the fourth horizon,
To the edge beyond, to the edge without, to the horizon of the
    gentle air.
To the horizon of Wairuarangi's gentle air, ascend direct.
Rise up in Tupuaki o Hiti, rise up in Tupuaki o Tonga;
Rise up in the crown of the Gathering of Happy Heavens,
    ascend direct.
To the source, to the hundreds, to the innumerable—
For you, my son, the only child, are lost now to desire.

TONGA'S LAMENT ON BURYING HIS DAUGHTER WHILE AT SEA

I have lowered you below,
Below the ocean road,
My loved one, O my child,
> *E te ipo, tuku au*

Our precious daughter Tepeiru,
You who plaited precious things—
Far out at sea you died,
My loved one O my child,
> *E te ipo, tuku au*

My fishing takes us far from land,
Too far, when troubled, for the gods to hear—
So you are lowered down, my child, below,
> *E te ipo, tuku au*

A WIDOW'S FUNERAL CHANT

Aue! Aue! Alas for us!
Alas for us, father who brought much food.
Many fish, many yams, many kumara;
Many crabs, much sugar cane, many bananas.
O father who did not go begging to houses of others—
Now you are lost by us.
O father, great fisherman—your taut line sang.
Aue, Aue! Alas for us two!

Rei miro, a wooden neck ornament of the Easter Islanders

ONOKURA LAMENTS THE OLD AGE WHICH HAS OVERTAKEN HIM AND HIS WIFE

Alas, we are growing old, my love,
We two—

We two indeed together, O my love,
When we were children!
When we played together in the sea!

We two indeed together, O my love,
When we went inland—Oh yes, inland!—
In our years of growing wise.

We two indeed together, O my love,
When your girlish breasts were firm,
And when in motherhood they drooped.

We two indeed together, O my love,
When long hair floated down your back
And springy strength was in your arms.

We two indeed together, O my love,
When we both grew old and thin
Like two grey flatfish resting on the bottom.

We two indeed together, O my love,
When grown so frail, we sit apart
And only rest the hours away.

We two indeed together, O my love,
When our dim eyes stare at misty skies
And no more know their splendour—

Ah! Where is the god taking me?

THE MARQUESAS, AND MANGAREVA

Marquesan canoe ornament

KAE AND THE WHALE

IN Vainoi there were no men. Only women by themselves lived in that land. Their husbands—they were pandanus roots!

When a woman was to have her child and the time had arrived, certain experts came and cut her open. This caused her death. So it was always in Vainoi. When the women had children they were always cut open by the tuhunga, and they died.

Into that valley of Vainoi came Kae; he was a man of Vevau. He saw this good valley with only women in it and not a husband between them, therefore he hid himself at their bathing place. The women's custom was, they went to that place each day and had their pleasure with the pandanus roots, then they bathed.

Some women came down from the valley when Kae was hidden. They were calling out to their chiefess, their peiu: 'E Hina, come down to the sea to our work.'

Their peiu answered, 'I am coming; you go on', and they came and lay with their husbands. When they had finished their play with the pandanus roots those women had their bath and dressed themselves again, but their peiu stayed, she remained to bathe alone. Then Kae came out from where he was.

Now when that chiefess saw Kae and what he had she was delighted with this man, she said, 'A question, man: who are you?'

Said Kae, 'That is for me to ask. I am the stranger, you the resident.'

'I here am Hina i Vainoi.'

'I here am Kae.'

Said the peiu, 'You are my husband.' Said Kae, 'You are my woman.' Then he took her.

Then indeed was that chiefess delighted with her husband,

more than with pandanus roots; she took him to her house and kept him there, she did not reveal him to the rest.

Each day the other women went down to their play with the pandanus roots, they called out to their peiu, 'Hina i Vainoi, come bathing.' But Hina opened the door of her house and said, 'You all go without me, I am sick.' Three days it happened thus—'I am sick.'

This made those women think. One said, 'Perhaps it is a man with our peiu.' Another said, 'How would a man come here?' Then certain women said, 'There are scratches on our peiu's cheeks; we have seen them.' Therefore they went to Hina's house and asked her, 'Tell us, O peiu, is there a man here sleeping with you?'

She said that there was not, and so they asked her, 'Then who has been scratching you?' 'I scratched myself on the pandanus spines.' But the women said, 'Pandanus pricks are not like that; those are nail-scratches.' They did not believe their peiu.

One day a young woman came to the house of the peiu and said, 'Come up to the old woman's the day after tomorrow. She is ready to be cut open.'

When this messenger had gone, Kae asked Hina, 'Why do you cut open a woman's belly?' Said Hina, 'To get the child out.' 'And when the child is out what happens to the mother?' 'She dies. With us in this land it has been like that always, O my husband.'

Kae said, 'Well then my woman, you will have to get rid of that. With us the woman is not cut, she is caused to give birth.' Then he said to her, 'Tomorrow when you go up-valley tell the women to break off nono leaves and bind three bunches of them round this woman's waist. Then two must hold her knees and one must stand behind her. Then tie the rope to the top of the house-post, for her to pull on. After the waters, the child will come. When the child comes, bite the cord. Then push the stomach, make the rest come out. After that, mash up some shrimps with coconut cream; give that to the child, it will empty him. Then mix up some breadfruit paste and heat it, give it to the woman.'

Said Hina, 'Very well.'

Then those two gods Pohihia and Pohahaa arrived to cut the woman with the shark's-tooth knives, her relatives were wailing where she lay. But Hina went there also and she told them they must do all those things which had been told to her; and those two gods knew what Hina was doing, and how she knew of it.

So the women gathered nono leaves. 'What are these for?' 'Tomorrow we shall see.'

At dawn those tuhunga were ready with their knives, but Hina said, 'You-two are not to cut this woman; stand aside. One of you others is to stand behind her and two of you in front. Put the nono leaves in her bottom there, beneath the place. Now tie this rope.'

Then Hina said to the woman with child, 'Now pull, pull hard.' That woman did so, she pulled on the rope. Said Hina, 'After this pain the water will come away, then the child.'

And she said to Pohihia and Pohahaa, 'You-two are evil men.' They were ashamed, and ran away from that place for ever. Then the chiefess showed those women how to do this work.

One woman husked a coconut, she brought shrimps, and mashed them up with cream of grated nut. They made it warm, gave it to the child. Then for the mother they mixed up breadfruit paste with certain juices. Said Hina, 'When the cord drops off, stop giving shrimps.'

Said the women, 'We will do as you have said.'

Then Hina returned to Kae and said to him, 'But for you, O my husband, that woman would have died, cut open by Pohihia and Pohahaa.'

Afterwards some of the women saw their peiu's husband, then they understood; they said to her, 'There is the man who has been sleeping with you, telling you things. It would be well, O peiu, if you would let us all sleep with your husband.' Said Hina, 'I will not.'

'Only a little?'

'I absolutely do not wish it.'

Afterwards when the women of Vainoi were giving birth they used the rope. They never again sent for Pohihia and Pohahaa.

One day Hina i Vainoi said to her husband, 'Do my hair.' While Kae was picking out the lice he said, 'Your hair is turning grey.' She answered, 'Never mind, when that happens I know how to make myself like a young thing again.'

Then she said to her husband, 'Let me do yours,' and on Kae's head she saw many grey hairs. Said Hina, 'You are growing old, husband. Tomorrow, we-two will go out surf-riding.'

In the morning they went to the beach. Kae said, 'You go first.' Said Hina, 'No, you go first, my husband; then I can see how you do it.'

After Kae had come in on three waves he looked the same as he was before, he had not changed at all. Then Hina rode. After riding in on three waves she came out looking as fresh as a shrimp that has just been shelled.

'See, husband! Do I look the same?'

Said Kae amazed, 'No, no, my wife.' Then Kae was much ashamed, for it was Hina who had youth. After this Hina became pregnant. Kae longed for his own land of mortals.

When six moons had passed Kae said, 'It is time now for me to go and prepare for our child.' It was Kae's duty in this land to plant one breadfruit tree for the child, and aute trees for its tapa cloth; and to provide pigs, and make a bathing basin near the stream, and other matters. Therefore he said to Hina, 'I shall go to my land now. If you have a boy, you are to name him Te Hina tu o Kae.' But Hina said, 'Not yet, husband. Wait for three days; then my brother Tunua nui will take you on his back.'

So Hina called her brother from the sea and that great whale came up to her. Said Hina, 'Take your brother-in-law to his land.'

'Yes, yes, I will do so.' Then Hina said to Kae, 'When you come to Matafenua give a kick to each of the islets that you pass. Kick Motutapu, Motutomotomo, Mataukaaea and the other islets, kick them all. That will make Tunua nui turn his head towards Vainoi, then he will return here when he has put you ashore.'

Therefore Kae climbed on Tunua's back and this great fish carried him to Vevau here. But when they were off Matafenua, Kae did not kick the islets Motutapu, Motutomotomo, Motuofio and the rest.

In Vainoi, Hina knew it. She said, 'You bad one, my husband. You have failed to kick the islets. Now your brother-in-law will die, because of you.'

Tunua nui went up on the beach at Taaoa, here in Vevau, to let Kae off; but then he could not turn around again because of what Kae had done. He was stranded there, that great whale, and the people came to cut him up.

His blood touched Hina's breast; in Vainoi she felt his death. Then Hina wept, she wept for her brother, crying, 'You are a bad man, O my husband. You did not listen to the word of Hina.'

Kae said to his people here in Vevau: 'Make a bathing pool for my child that is to be born.' To others he said, 'Feed and breed pigs; plant sugar-cane; plant bananas; cut down the old coconut trees; feed chickens; plant aute for making tapa.' So the people did these things as Kae had told them.

Then Hina i Vainoi gave birth to her child, she had a son, and she named it as her husband had told her. That child grew and grew.

One day Kae's son had a quarrel with another boy. This boy teased him, made him angry, then the others said, 'Who are you to talk to us? *Your* father is just some foreigner.'

Kae's son wept, he went to Hina, said to her, 'They are teasing me, they say my father is a foreigner. It is time you told me where he is. What is my father's name?'

Now Hina i Vainoi was still angry with Kae because of her

brother killed, and she replied, 'You have no father. I am your mother, that is all. In this land there are no fathers.'

He replied, 'Do not hide it from me, my mother. Those boys say I have a father and that he is some foreigner.' He kept on crying, he would eat no food. In the end Hina said to him, 'Enough, now, of that crying. This is your father's name: Kae. He is at Vevau, that is your father's land. Now eat your food. Tomorrow you can go to him; Tunua iti will take you.'

In the morning Hina called to her younger brother in the sea, Tunua iti. Said Hina to Small-whale, 'Take your nephew to Vevau.' 'Yes, yes, I will do so.' Then Hina said to the child this word: 'Now when you and your uncle go past Matafenua, you are to kick all the islets there. Kick Motutapu, Motutomotomo, Motuofio, Kahena te tupuna and all those islets. You are to do this so that Tunua iti will turn round and come home again. When your father went there on Tunua nui he did not kick those islets and for that reason Tunua nui could not turn round, he was stranded and was killed by the people of your father's land.'

The boy said, 'I will kick all those islets, my mother,' and Hina i Vainoi embraced her son and wept over him. Then he climbed upon Tunua's back and rode away.

When they-two passed the islets off Matafenua the boy kicked all of them and Hina i Vainoi wept with gladness; the sound of the kicks had come into her ear. Then the head of the fish was turned toward Vainoi and its tail was toward Vevau; and Tunua iti went ashore tail-first and set his new nephew down at Taaoa, in Vevau here. The nephew got off and pressed noses with his uncle, then he walked on the beach.

When the people saw the tail of that fish on the sand they thought of their last great feast of whale, therefore they all rushed down, that tribe, and seized the tail to pull it up. But Tunua iti made off quickly, he dragged them into the sea, they all perished. Thus was the death of the older brother avenged.

Kae's son went up-valley, saw his bathing basin there; he therefore bathed in that pool. Then he made the poko with his hand, held his elbow against his side and clapped his palm on the hollow place. This loud noise made the people angry. 'Who is that making the poko in the sacred basin built for Te Hina tu o Kae?' So they rushed after that person with sticks and he ran away.

Then he saw some ripe bananas that were planted for him and he tore them down, tearing, tearing, tearing. Again the people came after him, therefore he stopped, went away. Next that boy saw some sugar-cane growing, it was his. He tore it all up, tearing, tearing. Then the people grew very angry with this boy who ruined everything, they caught him and took him to the old tuhunga to strangle. These two old men put him in a hole as prisoner, to keep him there for three nights, then strangle.

After three nights they-two put the cord around his neck, and all the people came to see it. The boy then chanted from the pit:

> 'Oe oe oe oe oe oe oe,'
> Answered my mother, Hina i Vainoi.
> 'That is your father:
> Kae at Vevau.'
> Are you laying hands upon
> Te Hina tu o Kae?

He chanted this three times. Then those two tuhunga stopped and sent a messenger to Kae. 'There is a boy in the hole at the tuhunga's; to be strangled today. He said a chant, it had your name in it.'

'Let me hear that chant.'

The person said the chant to Kae.

Then stood up Kae, he took his club and strode. When he reached that place the people saw the tears in his eyes and they were afraid, because they knew that the child in the pit was his first-born child. Said Kae to the tuhunga, 'Take the child out of the pit.' Then he asked the boy his name.

'I here am Te Hina tu o Kae.'

Then Kae took him on his sacred head; to consecrate the boy and make him tapu he placed him on his head. Then the two tuhunga said, 'Now, sir, we shall perform the naming ceremony for this little child.' Said Kae, 'That is good. Let all the proper things be done correctly for the child.'

Then the tuhunga consecrated Te Hina tu o Kae. Many pigs were cooked, the cane was cut; bananas were gathered, coconuts were split, aute was collected and fine tapa made. The tapa makers wove a chiefly girdle for the son of Kae. A great feast was held in the land.

When all these matters were completed, the child lived here in Vevau with his father.

TAHIA THE FRAGRANT GIRL

THIS girl was the daughter of Tuapu and Hina te ii, but when she had been growing in the womb three months her father Tuapu went away, he went to another valley and took a new woman.

Hina gave birth, she called her daughter Tahia noho uu, and that girl grew in beauty most uncommon. Her body was sweet-scented entirely; her hair was sweet-scented, her breath was a perfume, even that which came out when she squatted was sweet-scented. Therefore as soon as she was comely all the young men of Hiva Oa wanted her, they sought Tahia because that girl was like the scent of all the flowers in Hiva Oa.

The good word concerning this girl went throughout the land, it reached that valley where her father was. And when he heard about the perfumed girl, Tuapu had desire. He did not know that she was his daughter.

Tuapu went to see this girl, he went back to Hina's valley to look at her. It was in a time of famine that he went. The gardens and the breadfruit trees all were barren, therefore the men of Hina's valley had gone up in the mountains to look for food. The young men were on the ridges gathering wild yams and fern-root; the old men were in the valleys collecting ihi leaves. Tahia's mother Hina with her brothers Tika'ue and Namu was up on the ridges also, they were away from home for three nights. This was the time when Tuapu returned—when the mother and the uncles were away, and Tahia was at home in charge of children. That girl did not know him when he came, not know he was her father. She let him take her.

After the man was gone, Tahia's mother came home, and Tahia

Patini, a chiefess of Nuku Hiva

spoke to her of what occurred. She described that man she had and how he did it. Said the mother, 'Did he thus and thus?' and 'Did he so, then so?' and Tahia replied, 'He did. And then as well did such, and such.' From this that mother knew what man her daughter had had, and she was angry, was disgusted. Said the mother to the girl, 'You *sleeping-mat!* You *loin-cloth!* You diseased and scabby head!' And she turned away in anger, took her clothes and went to bathe.

After her bath Hina wound her best kahu around her and put on her finery. She placed a scented garland round her neck, she put on her tortoise-shell crown and her ornament of white hair, she took her fan that was like no other. Then went she in anger to that valley where Tuapu lived, and called out 'Husband! Husband!'

As soon as he heard the voice of Hina calling 'Husband' Tuapu desired her, and he came to her like that. But Hina was angry with that man, she said, 'You sleeping-mat! You sanitary towel! You stench! What filth of yours is this, sleeping with our daughter?'

Tuapu said, 'O *paa, paa, paa*—silly woman!'

The woman shouted, 'Don't talk back at me!' and she went for him with her fan.

He ran off; but Hina caught him, and they-two came back to Hina's house in this valley. Then was Tahia afraid, because she knew this was the man she had had in that house. When her mother said 'Here is your father', Tahia hid her face, she was ashamed.

They all dwelt quietly together there. The father and the mother slept in one half of the house, the girl and her uncles slept in the other half of the house.

The girl never came outside, never was her skin allowed in the sun. She had no food also. The wind alone was her food. After she had dwelt thus in the house some time, and the hot sun had not been on her, the skin of Tahia was fair as flesh of coconut. She was white all over, that fragrant girl.

After this it was the work of Hina's brothers to find a husband for their niece. They were searching everywhere, searching, searching. Not one man fit for Tahia could they find in all of Hiva Oa.

One day Tahia heard this news: the chief Tu Tona was making preparations for a voyage to Nuku Hiva. She said to her uncles, 'Why do not you-two go to Nuku Hiva with Tu Tona, find a husband for me there?' They replied, 'Yes, yes,' and so Tahia said to them:

'Prepare all the scented things for me—red pandanus seed, some niapa, pua flowers, gardenia, mahatuhi and mahapoa leaves, wild ginger—all those sweet-smelling things.' Then she made them climb for coconuts, and when they had brought two nuts she told them to put the scraped-out meat of one nut with the scented things.

They-two did all this, they gathered flowers and perfumed seeds and stems, until they had every kind of scented thing that is; then they put them all inside a gourd, and closed it well.

Then said Tahia, 'Here, Tika'ue. Get Namu to bring the other coconut.' When Namu came she said, 'Now split the nut on Tika-'ue's head.' So Namu tried. Once, twice, he tried to split the nut upon his brother's head. It would not split; but Tika'ue's head was aching! Therefore Tika'ue said, 'Now let me try,' and at one blow he split the nut on Namu's head.

Then Tahia took one half, and held it to her well-bleached skin. 'When you-two find a half that is as white as this,' she said, 'that is my better half!' Then those uncles knew her meaning. They took the white-fleshed nut, to find a man as fair.

Then Namu and Tika'ue were ready for their work, therefore they went to Tu Tona and asked him whether they might go with him to Nuku Hiva. Tu Tona said, 'Yes, yes. Get your things ready.' They answered, 'Our things are ready now. When shall we be leaving?'

Tu Tona said, 'We will leave on the fifteenth night of the moon.' Therefore the uncles told Tahia, 'The chief wants us to go with him. We leave on Hotunui.' That girl was pleased.

When Hotunui came, Namu and Tika'ue went to Tu Tona's, they joined the party who were going with him to Nuku Hiva.

That chief had his reasons for the journey; the uncles had another reason!

They sailed from here at evening, at the time of fires. They put the mat sail up, the night was calm, the stars were good; but Tahia noho uu by her mana raised a steady wind to speed them on, and in a single night that canoe reached Nuku Hiva.

At daybreak certain Nuku Hiva people at the beach called out, 'There's a foreign canoe coming in—with seven-score men!' Others who came to look then said, 'That is Tu Tona's canoe, from Hiva Oa.'

Their chief was pleased, and the people too, they all began preparing for their guests. They collected breadfruit, and brought out breadfruit paste from the storage pits; they killed a score of pigs, they sent out men to fish; the women cooked poke, they made popoi.

The invitation went to Tu Tona and his party at the beach, the word went out to all the land, and so they all assembled at the chief's place, they exchanged their gifts and feasted on the food. Tu Tona and all of his people were living in the visitors' house, they slept together there and had their pleasure of the food; but the uncles of Tahia were thinking always of another thing. Their work was looking for a man for their niece, a handsome husband with a skin as fair as flesh of coconut. Not one man did they see among the people at the feasting.

'Then we shall have to try again on the night of Tua,' Namu said. 'On that day they are to show all the tattoo designs, and we will see everyone.'

The Nuku Hiva people were enjoying themselves being tattooed, and Tua the second night of the moon was the time for seeing all the patterns. Therefore on that day when the third cock-crow was heard in the valley, the people who had been tattooed went down to the bathing ceremony, and Namu and Tika'ue watched them, watched them all the time. As they bathed those Nuku Hiva people made the poko loudly, slapping their wet hands in their elbows by their sides. Namu and Tika'ue watched them, but they saw no lightning there—not one who was as fair as flesh of drinking-nut.

As the dawn broke, they-two heard more poko noises and they went to look. Then saw they lightning! There was a handsome young man, a true poea! Tika'ue said to Namu, 'Bring the coconut of Tahia, get it quickly.' Namu did so, and they-two went to look at that poea, that handsome fair-skinned youth.

'Who are you two?'

'We are two of the men from Hiva Oa.'

'And what are you wanting?'

'We came to look at you. We could see that you are handsome—you are poea.' Then said Namu to Tika'ue, 'Here!' and he took the nut, and struck it on Tika'ue's head; once he struck it, twice he struck it. Still the nut would not split.

The poea watched them at this work and thought, 'They must be fools, these two. Why do not they use a stone?'

Very sick was Tika'ue's head, it ached and ached! And that poea laughed at them.

'Let me try then,' said Tika'ue; took the nut and with one blow he split it on his brother's head. Then indeed they held the white flesh of the nut beside the poea's fair skin: just alike were the two in whiteness.

'All right, then,' said the poea. 'And what of that?'

They-two replied, 'This is the likeness of your woman.' Then indeed was that poea much surprised and pleased, that these two knew so fair a girl. He said to them, 'If she is white like that, she is for me!'

Then Namu and Tika'ue put away the nut and opened up the gourd, the gourd filled with scented things of Hiva Oa. At once the perfumes spread throughout the land, through all of Nuku Hiva—went into the flowers of that land. Before that day, no sweet scents such as those had grown in Nuku Hiva, only Hiva Oa had them. But from the opening of that gourd the perfumes went to

Tattooed girdle of a chiefess of Nuku Hiva

all that land, they have since grown there.

Then Namu and Tika'ue made a present of the gourd, they gave it as a kaoha to that fair-skinned youth, and all the people gathered round to see his gift.

The Hiva Oa party came. Tu Tona smelt the perfumes of his home and said, 'Does that thing belong to Tahia noho uu?' The uncles said 'Yes, yes', and the chiefs of Hiva Oa and Nuku Hiva talked together. Said the Nuku Hiva chief, 'Now we know what a lovely perfume it is!' And he turned to his people, saying, 'This visitors' house where our guests are staying—let it be divided. Put in a tapa screen, and let half be for this poea and his friends, the rest for the strangers.'

Next day Tu Tona's party put on all their finery and went to see the feast at the dancing place, the feast after the tattoo showing. The drums were beating rhythms, the people were singing pue and dancing haka, more visitors were arriving; but Namu and Tika'ue and the poea were late, they still were in their room in the visitors' house, powdering themselves with turmeric and arranging their scented garlands.

The father and the mother of the poea had come to the feast to see their son, but he was nowhere to be seen—he was still inside, with his friends from Hiva Oa.

Then they came out at last, those three—Tika'ue, Namu, and the youth, all brightly garlanded and oiled and coloured up. Then indeed did everyone perceive that youth, his beauty, and the fairness of his skin. He was indeed like lightning, handsome beyond all, and full of perfumes never known. All his dress was heavy with the scents of this land, Hiva Oa.

When he stepped out on the dancing space the people came from above, they came from below; the drummers stopped, they could not continue; all the people at the feast stood still, they could not think of anything but this youth, this poea so fair. The women—they desired him!

Just two haka, only two, did this poea dance for them. He danced along one side of the dancing floor, then along the other, that was all. The people gazed, they could not speak. Then he came off, to his friends from Hiva Oa. And Namu and Tika'ue said to him, 'Let us three get ready now.'

When the poea was gone, all the pleasure left the people. 'What is there to look at now?' So they all went off to where the food was—left the dancing, went to eat.

Then did Namu and Tika'ue by their powerful mana cause the wind to swing about. The tokerau came up, it made a rattling in the coconut trees, it started flurries up the valley, which could be seen far off. Then said Tu Tona, 'This is the wind to get us home! It would bear us straight to Hiva Oa!' And the people of his party all agreed with him. 'Then all make ready,' said Tu Tona. 'The food is finished—let us go. Get the canoe down to the beach and put everything ready to-night. We will leave at first light.'

Then Tu Tona's people began gathering up their gifts from the Nuku Hiva people, and all their belongings; and Namu and Tika'ue, behind their tapa screen, got ready the belongings of their friend. The main party were always doing one thing, these two were doing another thing—always thinking of something else!

By the time of fires the Hiva Oa party were all packed up, they were ready to sail at first light. Their speeches of farewell were made; they all lay down to sleep.

After they had been sleeping for a while Namu went outside in the coolness, and with his lips he made the call of the koma'o, the bird that cries before the dawn. The rest turned over on their sleeping mats. Said some of them, 'It is time to be moving.' But said Tu Tona, 'It is only evening yet.'

'The koma'o did call out,' said some of them; but Tu Tona did not move.

Then Namu came inside and Tika'ue went out. He walked away a little distance, then he crowed like a rooster. It was a real rooster's crow! 'There is no mistaking that,' said those who were sleeping near Tu Tona. 'Come on. Let us go.'

In this way, Namu and Tika'ue caused the Hiva Oa people to get up and leave while it was still dark. Then they whispered to their friend, 'Come now. We will hide you beneath the flooring slats before the rest get down there.' So they three went, and no one saw them. And the uncles hid the poea beneath the slats, and put their mat-rolls over him.

Then all the rest came down, they loaded up, they pushed off in the dark and paddled out. They unrolled their sail, and took their bearing from the stars, they rode before the northwest wind toward this land; they sailed with a fair wind on a flowering sea.

It was not yet day when that canoe reached Aihoa here, on the north side of Hiva Oa. Then the wind dropped, fell away; the paddles were brought out, and by the early light they started bailing out the bilge-water from the bailing-place. On that water there was yellow stain floating!

'Look at this!' said the man with the bailing scoop. 'We have a dancer stowed away, I think.' Then did Tu Tona see the turmeric and oil that floated on the bilge.

'E Namu! E Tika'ue!' said that chief. 'What is this? And where is that new relative of yours?'

They-two replied 'Yes, yes', and looked ashamed, folded their hands. Then was Tu Tona angry with them. 'And why have you concealed him, this husband of your niece?' They-two had nothing to say, they looked downwards.

Then Namu and Tika'ue moved the baggage, revealed their relative, he came out from his hiding-place. And all the party were amazed, the paddlers stopped and gazed at him, that fair poea, fair as flesh of coconut. They could not continue paddling.

Tu Tona ordered, 'Paddle on,' and in an instant they were round the point and off the beach at Atuona here. 'Stand up now,' said Tu Tona to the handsome youth. 'Do you see that whiteness beyond the beach? It is your woman.' Then the poea shone like lightning, and the woman on the beach shone also.

In one more stroke of the paddles they reached the sand at Atuona. Namu and Tika'ue sprang ashore, the poea walked before them. Old Tu Tona came behind him crying 'He Tuia! He Tuia! The betrothed! The poea from Nuku Hiva for Tahia noho uu!' With shouting then they went up-valley to the house of Hina—for the two women had gone to that house.

As they approached that house the poea saw two women sitting there; both white, both beautiful. He did not know which one was his. Then called out Hina, 'Come here, my son-in-law.' And Tahia, the other one, stood up and embraced her husband, they pressed noses. And they all went together into the house.

There inside the house Tahia took the half-of-coconut which Namu had, she touched her husband with it, matched the fairness of his skin; then she was pleased. Exactly like the half-nut was that mate.

Back on Nuku Hiva was there searching, searching for the handsome youth. Everywhere on Nuku Hiva was his father searching for him, and the people said, 'Your boy has been stolen. Those two from Hiva Oa, they have taken him.'

Here in Atuona this handsome poea dwelt with his wife, with Tahia noho uu who was all the perfumes of this land. But after six moons, grief came on him for his parents, he was homesick, said to Tahia: 'Time for me to go to Nuku Hiva. I long to see my parents.'

Said Tahia, 'I am willing for you to go; but you must return within one moon. Should one night pass beyond one moon and you have not returned to me, my husband, I shall die.'

That husband said 'Yes, yes', and went to Nuku Hiva. Gladness in Nuku Hiva—gladness of his relatives to see their son! They gathered round and asked him, 'What is all the news from Hiva Oa?'

Said that poea: 'I have found a wife so beautiful, there is not a woman like her in all of Nuku Hiva here.' He lived quietly with his relatives in Nuku Hiva.

Here on Hiva Oa, Tahia noho uu was counting all the nights. The thirty moon-nights passed—this husband of hers did not come back! She wept for him, the people saw her weep. She said, 'This husband of mine does not come back!' and went on with her weeping.

One day that grieving wife said to her uncles, to Namu and Tika'ue: 'I wish you two to climb for nuts. One climb one tree, the other climb another, bring me two coconuts. One is to make pani for my head. The other is to make hoho for my body.'

They-two therefore did as Tahia asked them, brought the nuts. Said Tahia, 'One scrape one nut, one the other,' and they did so. Then she dried the flesh to get the oil, she took perfumes, she took sandalwood and flowers, and she made pani for her hair and hoho for her skin. Then she said to the uncles, 'I have a craving for some crabs.'

So they-two thought, 'Our niece is pregnant, then.' They went away to get the crabs she craved. But this was not Tahia's thought—

she only wished her uncles to be absent, while she hanged herself.

Therefore Namu and Tika'ue went to catch crabs. On their way to the place, Tika'ue stubbed his toe against a stone. Said he, 'This sign is evil; let us go back. Our niece has strangled herself.'

When they reached the house those uncles found the girl was dead. *Aue!*—much grief was theirs. They in their grief remembered words of hers, they went and climbed two leaning trees, one each. Then down they threw themselves, like drinking nuts. Wishing to die! But when they fell they did not die. They climbed again, dived again. No death! Three times those uncles flung themselves. They did not die!

Now three nights after the death of Tahia noho uu, her ghost went to her husband in Nuku Hiva. When the ghost came to him in his sleep, he wept and wept. Said the ghost, 'You are weeping much for me, my husband!' Then he awoke and saw her; they embraced, they pressed noses, they wailed together.

Said the husband, 'How do you come to be here?' Tahia answered, 'I who am here, O my husband, have died. I have died of grieving, that you did not return.'

Then was the husband seized with fear. '*Not* dead! You are not dead! Your body is good.'

'Even so, I have died. But you must tell your family, O my husband, this: they are to collect coconuts and scrape wild ginger, scrape the meat of the nuts and go out gathering kaupe flowers and kokini berries; then put all these good things together, press their juices in a food-trough.'

The husband rose, he spoke to his relatives, and when all had gone away to get those things the woman said to him, 'Now you are to close off our room with a piece of tapa, hide me from their sight. And tell them—in three nights they are to take away the tapa curtain.'

The husband did this as his spirit-wife had said, he put up tapa, made the place tapu to his relatives. And when three nights had passed, the cloth was taken down. Then all the family saw this girl, alive again.

'How did this woman reach this place?'

'That was my work in the three nights when I made this room tapu to you.'

Then the relatives all marvelled—marvelled greatly at the beauty of this girl, and they were pleased indeed; they knew that the woman of Hiva Oa was truly a great beauty.

Chief's headdress from the Marquesas

Tahia and her husband dwelt quietly together there in Nuku Hiva. In one month a child was growing in the womb, in nine moons it was born—a boy. Tahia named him Tuapu, the name of her father and the man she had. Another child grew in the womb, a girl was born. Tahia named her Hina te ii, the name of her mother. Another child, a boy: she named him The Poea of Hiva Oa. Another girl: the mother called that girl Tahia noho uu, from herself.

Here on Hiva Oa, five years passed since the day when Tahia noho uu hanged herself. Namu and Tika'ue were making a stone paepae in which to place her bones; they were down at the sea looking for turtles, for sacred offerings.

Now the soul of their girl who was dead saw them at this work, saw them from Nuku Hiva. Then said this ghost to her husband, 'The time of my death is approaching.'

'What makes you know your death is near?'

Tahia said: 'I looked, husband, and I saw Namu and Tika'ue seeking turtles, I saw them building a paepae to put my bones in. The time of my going from you is near.'

When the paepae at Hiva Oa was finished and the turtles had been caught, the ghost of this woman long dead spoke to her husband, she said this word: 'In three nights I am going to die. When I am dead, bring my first-born child and put in his hands a piece of kava root and a pig; bring the girl, and give her two pieces of fine tapa to dry their tears for their mother.'

Then the husband wept, for he knew that Tahia had taken no sickness, her body was firm. He wished to know what this was about, this dying in three nights' time.

On the evening before she was to die the woman said to her husband at the time of fires, 'Gather around me, all of you; two children at one side, two children at the other; you, my husband, at my head.' Thus they all attended. The woman lay down; the family were wailing. All night they wailed.

When the first cock crowed in the valley, the feet of the woman disappeared. She said to her husband, 'My dying is near. Take my legs.' When the husband and the children reached for the legs of Tahia, there were no legs. At the crowing of the second cock, half of the body of Tahia disappeared. When it was nearly light the rest was gone, only her head remained.

Said this head: 'Enough. Let us make the hongi.' Therefore the children pressed noses with their mother's head, and the husband did also. Then that husband twisted the hair of his wife around his finger to hold it, but the head said, 'I am going to die. You cannot hold that hair.' Then she died; the head flew up into the rafters like a young green bird, and it chanted there, sang this:

Oe oe, oe oe, oe oe oe,
The seeking here of Namu and Tika'ue,
The seeking for the spirit of their niece.
Tahia noho uu.
Doing my work,
Looking for my turtle,
Building my paepae,
Carrying my body far.
O my husband—Kaoha!
Kaoha to you and to our children!

Then the bird flew up to the ridge-pole and it cried again
'Farewell!' They were all wailing, wailing. They wailed indeed
because they would not see the spirit any more.

After three nights, those children departed from Nuku Hiva.
They had with them the pigs, the kava, their mother's garment,
and the tear-drying cloth. They left Nuku Hiva early in the morning, they reached Hiva Oa on the same morning.

At Hiva Oa no one knew them, no one knew where they were
from. They went directly to the paepae, the sacred paepae built
by Namu and Tika'ue. As they went up on that sacred place the
sister loudly wailed, 'O my mother, Tahia noho uu! Ee-ee-ee!'

Namu and Tika'ue were in a house, they-two were at their work.
They heard this noise, heard this wailing; they looked out, saw a
girl-child climbing on the paepae, the paepae intensely tapu to
females. That girl was standing on it, wailing!

Then were Namu and Tika'ue very angry; they took the stranger-
children, threw them off with angry words. But the children kept
climbing back. Even though the uncles had thrown them off the
paepae, they wailed and climbed again.

After they had been thrown off three times the children stopped,
they said to the uncles, 'Why do you throw us off this place?
I here am Tuapu and this is my sister Hina te ii. We-two are the
children of our mother who is buried here. We are bringing the

gifts—the pig, the kava, and the tear-drying cloth.' Then they wept again.

Then did Namu and Tika'ue know the children; they took them up and placed them sacred on their heads, and wailed. Then they carried those children to their grandmother, to Hina te ii.

It is concluded.

'*They took them up and placed them sacred on their heads*'

KUIKUEVE

KUIKUEVE was of both worlds, she was a woman of this world and also of the world below. Her husband's name was Tu. Kuikueve lived in his house and two children were born to them, but after a time Kuikueve grew tired of her human husband and left this world. She went down to her other world, Te Po, and left her children with their father.

After he had finished sorrowing for Kuikueve, Tu took another wife, whose name was Ruaia. This Ruaia was greedy, and she was unkind to her husband's children. When he was at home for meals she would give them their share of the fish, but when he was away she gave them nothing. One day they-two were sitting beside a spring and crying because they were so hungry. They cried 'Me ko to taua kui i ara ra ko Kuikueve, e makona taua', which means, 'If it were our other mother, Kuikueve, we'd have things to eat.'

Now the spring-water carried their voices to Kuikueve in the world below. She heard them crying and heard what they said, and she came up bringing food for them. She came up through the water of the spring from the darkness below, bringing fish and popoi, and lizard, and puputa. And they ate up all these good things, and went home with cheerful faces.

Their father had grown used to seeing them sad. When he saw their cheerful faces he asked them what had made them happy, and they told him. Then Tu, as well, wanted to see Kuikueve again. He asked them to help him catch her and bring her back, so that they could all be together again. 'Next time,' he said, 'you two wait here beside the spring, and when she comes out, get her to put the food as far away from the pool as you can.'

So the children went to the spring when next they were crying with hunger, and they cried and waited, and their mother came, and they did as Tu had told them; and Tu was hiding in the bushes. Their mother came out, shining from the water, carrying baskets of good things for her children, and they tried to coax her from the spring. But Kuikueve would not come. She remained there, saying, 'I can feel your father's influence and I am afraid of him.' So the children went on crying, out of hunger, and would not take the food from Kuikueve's hands; and so at length they made her come right out. Then Tu dashed into the spring, to prevent her escaping.

When she saw what had happened Kuikueve dived back like a bird, but her husband caught her in his arms and they-two struggled in the water, and Tu was laughing. He made it seem a joke and the children called out to him to hold their mother; and Kuikueve at length gave in, and she agreed to remain here in this world.

Therefore Tu went home alone, leaving his children and their mother at the spring. And he took Ruaia out in his canoe, to go fishing. They paddled over to Marutea, where certain fish are caught that are tapu to women. And Ruaia was very greedy as always, and wanted to eat those forbidden fish where no one could see her do so except her husband. Tu therefore gave her urua and pu'i, that is cavally and sea eels, and she was so greedy, she ate till she was filled.

That woman died of eating tapu fish. In this way was Ruaia paid for her greed, and from that time on Tu and Kuikueve lived happily together with their children.

Figure of a god, from Mangareva

A MOTHER SHAMES HER SON, MAPUKUTAORA

On his hesitating to follow out to sea his chief, Tupou, who has had to sail defeated for some other land. To remind him of his honour and make him leave, she speaks these lines in earshot of her son:

O Tupou! O my chief!
The sea is moaning on the reefs
Under the wind behind Hararuru.
It is for you that they are moaning,
O Tupou, O my chief!

With your seven rafts you have taken to
    the open sea,
O Tupou, O my chief!
But one canoe remains behind:
Mapukutaora's—my son's!
What will *he* do,
O Tupou, O my chief?

EASTER ISLAND

*Stone figure from
Orongo village, Easter Isl*

HOW HOTU MATUA
FOUND THIS LAND

We of the Navel of the World narrate the deeds of our
ancestors. How they came to this land, and how the
quarrels were resolved.

OUR homeland Marae renga lay a distant journey to the west.
There Hotu matua our king was one of the chiefs: Oroi was his
rival. There was war between their tribes.

Hotu matua's tattooer called Haumaka had a dream: that he
went across the sea to a land with holes, with beaches also of fair
white sand. There were six men in the dream who landed on that
place. Haumaka told his dream to Hotu matua.

Hotu matua thought, 'There is a promise in this dream of
Haumaka's.' He therefore sent away six men to find that land.
'Look for a handsome country with sand for the king to live on.'
They came, those six, across the sea in their canoe Te Oraora
miro, bringing with them yams and breadfruit, coconuts and other
things to plant. They found those rocky islets off the western
headland, saw them first; jumped upon them, jumped off, came
to this land here and landed at Te Pu.

They searched the land, they looked for what the king desired.
They found this open land of waving grasses, grasses rolling like the
sea. There were no tall trees, nor any streams. They climbed
the rocks, they came to Orongo. They came to Ana marikuru on the
slopes of Rano kao and there they dug the ground, they mounded
earth to plant their yams. When they had finished this work they
climbed up Rano kao, they saw the crater there. They said, 'This
is Haumaka's hole—the hole of which Haumaka dreamed.'

They came on again, they came to Te Manavai, to Canoe Bay,

to Anavaero and all those places along the south coast. They came
to Onetea where the white sand is, and said, 'This is the land for
the ariki to live on.' But one said, 'No, this is poor land, our breadfruit and our coconuts will not grow here. Let us search, let us
go.' Therefore they came on, they came to Anahavea, to Tongariki,
to Big Bay, to Mount Parehe and all those places. They came around
the eastern headland.

They saw the fair sand of Taharoa. Said one, 'This is the king's
land, here.' But the rest said, 'No, this land is not good.' Therefore
they continued until they saw the good fair sand at Anakena;
it was like the beaches of the homeland. Then all those young
men said, 'Here the king will live in a handsome place.' They
rested in the dry cave at that place and therefore called it Anakena.

On the sand at Turtle Bay they saw a turtle sleeping. Those
six young men came on, they arrived at the turtle, they seized it.
The turtle struck with its flipper, one was wounded. They carried;
the turtle escaped. They carried a man instead of the turtle!

They found the cave called Ihuarero and carried the man to that
shelter, to wait for his wound to heal. The five kept watch—one
day, two days, three days. They were ashamed to leave that man.
One man grew bored. He said, 'What do you say, that we go on
and leave this person?'

So the five built cairns of stones. Each man brought stones, they
built five things like men in cloaks outside the opening of the cave.
They then said to the cairns, to the five things of stone like men:
'If the young man asks you questions, tell him lies, you five.
If he asks again, tell him only lies.' Thus they left him cared for.
They came out and went away, the five.

They came to Rapanga, to Ira, to Ringiringi and all those places;
and so they came to Mataveri. At Mataveri they met a young man
in the middle of their way, and so again were six. They now had
come around the land, completely round. Therefore they climbed
the slopes of Rano kao to where their yams were planted. The
grass was tall again, the place was full of weeds, of waving weeds

like waves upon the beach. They said this word: 'Poor land, covered with weeds there.'

They came on again, they came once more to Orongo—and on the sea they saw the king! They saw the double canoe of Hotu matua. There were two canoes—that of Hotu matua the ariki and that of Tu'u ko ihu the priest. When they came in close to shore the bindings that tied them were cut.

Cried Hotu matua the king: 'What is it like inland?'

His six men answered him: 'It is a poor land, mostly weeds and grass. If it were cleaned it would be clean. If it were weeded it would be weeded.'

Said Hotu matua about those grasses waving like the sea: 'A poor land this. When the tide is low we die few. When the tide is high we die many.' This was the first occasion of the saying of those words.

Then one of the six called out. 'Why do you speak that bad news over the surf, Hotu matua? Because of this there will be bad luck for us.'

Then Hotu cut the bindings of those two canoes. His ship went along the south and his relation Tu'u ko ihu went to the north, they both went round the land. When the king's ship came again and passed the headland Vai mahaki, Hotu matua saw the navigator's ship at Veronga. Tu'u ko ihu was going to land at Anakena, to be the first chief to stand on this land. Therefore Hotu matua said a word which made his own ship speed to shore and Tu'u ko ihu's be delayed. This was his word, his word that was filled with the mana of Hotu matua: *Ka hakamau te konekone!* 'Stay the paddling!'

Thus the canoe of Hotu matua came on and was the first one to touch this land. As it was being beached at Hiramoko the child Tu'u ma heke, son of Hotu matua, was born. The mother gave birth there at the beach. The ship of Tu'u ko ihu came on also, and as it was beached at Hanga ohio there was born the girl Avareipua, daughter of the priest and navigator Tu'u ko ihu.

Then Hotu sent a messenger to his relation Tu'u ko ihu: 'Come and cut the son's navel cord. Make ceremonies for this chief Tu'u ma heke.'

Tu'u ko ihu came, he spoke the chants, the red chiefly halo then was around that child's head. Then Tu'u ko ihu bit the navel cord, he cut it with his teeth. It was placed in a gourd and sent out to sea. When this ceremony was properly concluded Tu'u ko ihu returned to his own people at Hanga ohio, tied the navel cord of his chiefly daughter Avareipua. He bit it, he sent the cord to sea, he finished.

Then all the people came ashore; they landed from the two canoes, and stretched their legs, and rested—Tu'u ko ihu's people at Hanga ohio, Hotu matua's at Hiramoko.

There came to this land on those canoes the man, the fowl, the turtle, the banana plant; the aute tree whose bark gives tapa cloth; the crayfish, the gourd, the kumara and the yam. These things all came with Hotu matua the king. Hundreds and hundreds were the people, the mahingo who came to this land on that canoe of Hotu matua the king.

THE FIGHT WITH OROI AND THE KILLING OF OROI

IN the homeland Marae renga, Oroi was full of hate for Hotu matua; he killed the children of that chief.

When Hotu matua the king and Tu'u ko ihu the navigator came in their canoes to this land, Oroi hid himself beneath the cargo of the priest's canoe. They were large canoes, those ships; their hulls were as long as fifteen tall men swimming head to foot; one tall man standing up inside could not be seen. Oroi concealed himself beneath the yams and taro, the sugar-canes, banana stems, and other plants.

The ship of Tu'u ko ihu came to shore, the people sprang out to stretch their legs. Oroi remained concealed. At night he came ashore and hid.

When the children were born—the new-born son of Hotu matua and the daughter of Tu'u ko ihu—their navel cords were cut. Tu'u ko ihu bit them off and said the chants. Then was held a gathering of all the people—Hotu's people, Tu'u's people. They held a gathering and feast to mark the cutting of the cords. Oroi stayed, he remained hidden.

The people lived quietly together. Again children were born to Hotu matua the king; they grew well.

These six children of Hotu matua went down to the beach to bathe, at Rotokahi—that was the bathing place of Hotu's children. They bathed in the sea, they came out on the sand, they lay with their backs in the sun to warm themselves, grew drowsy, fell asleep.

Then came Oroi from his hiding place, came to the beach where Hotu's children were in the sun. He brought his crayfish tail, he put it into the holes in their bottoms and drew out all their guts.

Oroi pulled out the intestines of all those children with his crayfish tail, he left them lying there. Those sons all died, Oroi killed them with his crayfish tail.

In the evening Hotu matua was looking at the rocks of Roto kahi pahenga; he thought they were his sons coming out of the water. He went to meet them on the beach, came there, saw. They were seen at low tide only, those children-rocks. All were dead with their intestines pulled out from behind. Then Hotu matua knew the work of Oroi. Bad was his stomach with passion against that man. Again he spoke his word. 'When the tide is low we die few. When the tide is high we die many.'

Hotu matua did not know that Oroi was in this land, he thought that person was left behind in Marae renga. But he knew what work was done by Oroi with a crayfish tail; he had seen the pulled intestines in the distant land. Then his heart grew bad with passion against that person. Said Hotu matua the king:

'O, Oroi! You are going on with our quarrel, from abroad to here!'

Then Hotu cried, he wept on the beach for his children who were dead, they now were rocks.

Oroi stayed concealed at Turtle Bay; twelve moons went past. The king made his inspection of the land, he saw the people in the koro houses—at the paina feasts, at the houses where they taught the rongo rongo; at the houses where they studied the signs of reckoning, at the houses with the writing about the dead; at the houses where they studied the inscriptions concerning the serfs; at the houses for the prayers to Rarai a hova.

Oroi saw the king, he watched him going to the four parts of the land with Tu'u ko ihu the priest. Oroi twisted a long rope to catch the person of the king. He made a noose, he took his rope and put it in the middle of a path, and covered it with earth and grass.

Came Hotu matua along that path. Oroi said within himself, 'You will be killed by me, O Hotu matua!'

Ceremonial paddle, Easter Island

Hotu matua saw the thing hidden by soil and long grass; the king knew what it was, he walked slowly, stopped beside the rope, stepped here, stepped there. Oroi pulled, he tugged his noose with mighty force, but the foot of Hotu was not taken in that noose. The king went on. He said within himself, 'O Oroi, some day you will be killed by me.' He also spoke his word about the weeds, the height of their tide and the dying.

Hotu matua went on, he came to Ruahaua, and to Orohie. He visited the people at Hanga te henga; then he returned to his home.

While the king was away Oroi put his noose inside that house, within the house of Hotu matua the king. The rope was long; the noose lay in the entrance-way. The king came by, he saw Oroi's noose. He raised his foot, trod on the rope. Oroi pulled, he tugged, and Hotu matua fell down, he lay as if his foot was caught.

It was not caught, the foot of Hotu matua! Oroi ran to seize his man; his man sprang up—he seized, he killed! With his club he split Oroi's skull. Oroi was killed by Hotu matua the king.

Thus died Oroi, a chief from abroad, from Marae renga.

When the corpse of Oroi was put in the earth-oven to cook, it came to life again. Oroi looked, he saw. Therefore they had to take him over to the far side of the land, to the ahu that is called Ahu oroi. There he was cooked properly. They ate him.

When he was old Hotu matua divided the land between his sons, and he named as his successor Tu'u ma heke, his first child of this land. So it became the custom of this land that the new king should be the first-born son.

The king grew old. He became blind, his breath was leaving him. His elder sons came to see him, but Hotu matua kept asking for his youngest son, his favourite Hotu iti.

There came to him Marama, stood beside his sleeping-mat. The king felt the calf of his leg and said, '*You* are not Little Hotu, you are Marama. Where is Hotu iti?' Next Koro answered his father as if *he* were Hotu iti: 'I am here.' But Hotu took Koro's leg and knew he lied. 'You are not Hotu iti.' The same thing happened with Ngaure, with Raa, with Hamea and the others. At last came Hotu iti, and his father knew him by the slightness of his leg.

Then he was angry with the other sons and he said to his last-born, 'You are Hotu iti of Mataiti and your descendants shall thrive, and outlive all others.' And he said to Kotu'u, one who lied: 'You are Kotu'u of Matanui and your descendants shall multiply like the shells of the sea, like the reeds of the crater, like the pebbles of the beach. But they shall die and not remain.'

When he had said this thing, Hotu matua the king went out of his house, his sons assisted him. He went along the cliff to the place where the edge of the crater is narrowest. He stood beside it on two stones and looked over the islet Motunui toward the homeland Marae renga; and he called out to these four gods in his homeland: 'Kuihi, Kuaha, Tongau, Opapako, make the cock crow for me, for Hotu matua.' Then the cock crowed in Marae renga and Hotu heard it over the sea. He therefore knew it was his time to die, and he said to his sons, 'Take me away.'

They took him to his house to die. Thus died Hotu matua the first king of this land, and he was buried at Akahanga.

'They were like men who are dead, with their ribs showing.'

THE STORY OF THE WOODEN IMAGES

TU'U KO IHU the priest and navigator was the tahunga who first carved images in this land. When he was living at Ahu te peu this chief decided to go to the house at Hanga hahave called the House of Cockroaches. He therefore left in the early morning and climbed up to Punapau. In front of the red cliff there he saw two spirits, sleeping. They had no flesh, those spirits, their ribs were showing. Their names were Hitirau and Nuku-the-Shark. Tu'u ko ihu did not stop lest the spirits should know he had seen them. If they did he would die. He went on his way toward the House of Cockroaches, but another spirit, Ha uriuri, saw him, and he cried out to those others, 'Wake up! The chief saw your ribs.' They woke up with a start and saw this human, they saw his back as he walked up the mountain. Therefore they quickly climbed and crossed the way in front of him. They asked him :

'What do you know?'

Tu'u ko ihu answered, 'Nothing.'

They said again, 'Perhaps you noticed something,' but Tu'u answered 'No.' The spirits disappeared.

Tu'u ko ihu went on his way, but the spirits appeared in front of him again. They asked him, 'What do you know about us, O ariki?' He answered still, 'I know nothing.'

The chief went on, the spirits met him again at Pukurautea.

'What do you know about us, O ariki?'

'Nothing.'

If Tu'u ko ihu had told those spirits he had seen them they would have killed him. His priestly wisdom held him safe. They left, they disappeared. Afterwards they prowled about his house with their hands up to their ears, listening to hear if he gossiped of what he had seen; but the chief held his tongue. He spoke to no-one of what he had seen.

When Tu'u ko ihu went down to the House of Cockroaches the people were taking the stones from their earth-oven and were throwing out the ends of burning wood. This wood was toromiro. Tu'u ko ihu took two flaming pieces of the wood and carried them into that house, into Hare koka. He sat there, and with his sharp pieces of obsidian he carved them into moai kavakava. They were like men who are dead, with their ribs showing. They were likenesses of Hitirau and Nuku-the-Shark. Tu'u ko ihu spoke to no person of what he had seen.

After he had made these male images Tu'u ko ihu fell asleep and dreamed of two women. Their names were Pa'apa ahiro and Pa'apa akirangi. In his dream he saw that they were hiding their Things with their hands, they were covering them with their fingers; therefore as soon as it was daylight he got up and carved two flat images exactly like those women. When he had finished, Tu'u ko ihu loaded all the images on his back—the male images with ribs and the moai paepae with their fingers in a certain place; and he returned to his house at Ahu te peu. He left all the moai standing in that house.

Tu'u ko ihu dwelt quietly in his house for some time, and the people saw what he had done, they saw his work with the wood. Then they all went to this chief with pieces of toromiro to be carved. They wanted moai kavakava, they wanted moai paepae. They lit their earth-ovens and cooked for him many good things: seabirds, fish, yams and kumara. They brought this good food to Tu'u ko ihu so that he would carve images for them.

The people got the moai when they offered an umu to the owner. If there was no earth-oven, he kept all those that he had made. He kept their pieces of toromiro.

One day all the men who had given wood but got no images went to Tu'u ko ihu and said, 'O chief, give us back our images.'

'You wait.'

Moai paepae (female figure) from Easter Island

Then Tu'u ko ihu went into his house and made all the images walk. They walked about inside the house! After this the people called that house the House of Walking Images. The images walked, they made turns and turns—karari-karari, karari-karari, all about the house.

Their owners saw them doing this and said to one another, 'See—these images are moving in the house! What good fun this, the images that move!' They saw it, they were amazed, they were filled with admiration. 'How funny are these walking images!'

In the evening those people who had made no ovens returned to their houses. Tu'u ko ihu did not give them their images.

HOW THE SHORT-EARS CONQUERED THE LONG-EARS

THE Long-ear people were strong, they ruled. They lived out there on Poike, the headland, where the ground is not covered with heavy stones. They stretched their ears with ornaments, those people, they made them hang.

The Short-ears lived on poor land that has many stones. The Long-ears wished to build more ahus near the shore, more ahus for the gods. They said to the Short-ears, 'Come and carry stones with us to the place for the ahus, this will make your ground clean.' The Short-ears would not do it. They were afraid that the Long-ears would take their land when it was made better.

'We do not want to carry the heavy stones. Leave them on the ground for our food plants, to make them suffer—for the kumara, the banana trees, the sugar-canes, to make them suffer and grow.'

The Short-ears would not work for the Long-ears, they did not carry them, they left the stones. The Long-ears carried all the stones to build their ahus, angry with the Short-ears.

They built their ahus. They also thought evil against the Short-ears. They dug that long pit which stretches from Potu te rangi to Mahatua; the long pit like an oven. They dug it, they brought firewood, they strewed the whole pit with firewood. The Short-ears did not know for whom the Long-ears were making that oven.

There was a woman of the Short-ears who had a husband of the Long-ear people. She lived at Potu te rangi; that was where she had her house, at that end of the Long-ears' pit. One day her husband in anger said to her: 'This pit that is being dug is for all you Short-ears!' He went away angry, left that woman.

Then that woman knew, knew for whom the pit was made. She waited. At night she went to her people, went to the Short-ears and told them:

'Watch my house. Watch it for the sign that I shall give. On the day after tomorrow the Long-ears are to light the oven for your corpses. Form yourselves into a line, make everybody join it, come there, make a circle round the Long-ears, round their land of Poike. Start killing them. Throw them into the pit, change that oven to your own and cook the Long-ears for yourselves.'

Before the dawn that woman went back to her house at Potu te rangi. She said to her people, 'Be quick and do.' Then she went to her house and stayed there, plaiting a basket in the doorway. She was plaiting a basket with her eyes on the Long-ear men. They were filling their oven with firewood.

When it was sunset the Short-ears gathered. It was already dark; they gathered, they came; the first men hid in the house of the woman who was plaiting the basket. The rest concealed themselves behind, they formed a line, they waited. The woman who was plaiting told them where the Long-ears were. They were in their houses. Therefore the Short-ears went around Kikiriroa and Mount Teatea. They drew up all in order, they marched in the night, they came down to the point of Mahatua. They remained there, they slept, they hid themselves. And at the first light all those Short-ears rose up, they rushed out with their spears and surprised the Long-ear people, they were all still resting in their houses. They rushed and chased, those Short-ear men, they chased the Long-ears out. They made them all run to the ditch which they had dug themselves. They lit the fires.

When the Short-ears rushed upon them the Long-ears dashed out of their houses, they all ran away, they ran toward the ovens. No other way could the Long-ears run, the Short-ears were behind and all around them. All the wives, all the children of the Long-ears ran, they rushed toward the pit. The men, the women and the children arrived at the pit, stopped there. They were afraid of the flames. The war-party of the Short-ears came behind them with their spears. Which way could the Long-ears escape from the heat of the fire? There was no way. The war party of the Short-ears came on, they yelled at the Long-ear people.

Then all the Long-ears began jumping into their earth-oven, jumping into the flames. In the flames they jumped, they went

Human effigy covered in tapa cloth, Easter Island

on jumping. Their hair was burning, the Long-ears went on jumping. The men, women and children—all were burned.

Two of the Long-ear people stepped over the bodies; these two men jumped and fled across the land. The Short-ears went round the pit and chased them. All the way to Anakena they chased. They arrived at Anakena, those two Long-ears, they ran into Anavai—the cave that has fresh water. They hid themselves in the darkness there.

The Short-ears brought a long stick and they poked it at those Long-ears hidden in the cave, poked and poked. The Long-ears became mad, they showed their faces and jabbered: 'Ororoin, Ororoin.' It was finished. One of those two died. The other lived, came out; he jabbered. Said one of the Short-ears to the chiefs:

'Important men, let us spare this man who is now alone. Why kill this person? Leave him.'

The war party returned to Potu te rangi, they looked at their oven to see whether any of the Long-ears were still living. None remained. All of those people were dead. The Short-ears took as much as they wanted; then they covered them with earth. They returned to their homes.

He remained, that one man of the Long-ear people. He joined the other people and lived at Turtle Bay. He took a wife and made children. He was the jabbering man of whom they said 'Ka hakarere mahaki etahi'—'Let us spare this one man only.'

I know an old man called Arone arapu; a man of the blood of the Long-ears. The war was in the time of Hotu matua's children.

There are today two men alive who are of that blood; one lives at Hangaroa and one is where the lepers are kept; children of the blood of the Long-ears.

HAWAIIAN ISLANDS

Figure of the Hawaiian god Ku

THE ERUPTION OF PELE'S ANGER

*We of the land of flaming mountains tell of Pele, fiery
goddess, and her glowing wrath.*

IN the time of the chief Kahoukapu the great festival of Lono
makua was being held at Puna on this land Hawaii. They were
carrying the god about the land and taking in the offerings of
chiefs. Much taro and kumara, many fowls and pigs, red feathers,
garments, mats, dried fish—these things were all collected for the
god and laid upon the ahus, and there were boasting contests,
hula dancing, sport of many kinds. All the dancers and the drummers came to their work, the strong men fought with fists and
wrestled, the chiefs who were skilled slid down the hill on papa
holua, the risky sleds.

It was Kahawali, that handsome chief of Kapoho, who was riding
down the slope we call Ka holua ana o Kahawali. He was racing
with his sled down Kahawali's sliding-place, his friend Ahua was
against him, they competed in the race. Kahawali ran to the track
with his sled in one hand; he took the left rail with the other
hand, he threw his body on the sled and dived. The people all
applauded, shouted, when Kahawali came down whizzing like a
surfer on his well-oiled papa holua. Strong men have died from
their hurts in holua; not Kahawali. The people all would watch
that man, he slid the furthest. Ahua his friend slid well indeed,
but Kahawali was the winner.

The great noise of the people caused Pele to descend from Kilauea to watch the games. That goddess left her home in the burning crater, stood near Kahawali's sliding-place, admired his skill.
Pele-in-the-form-of-a-woman watched Kahawali, challenged him

The pali, the volcanic cliff-formation behind Honolulu

to race with her. A woman broke the tapu of the chiefly sport, the sport of chiefs alone!

Kahawali let this woman ride the track. She did not know the skill. He defeated her, he made his sled go further; all the people applauded him.

Jealous Pele asked that chief, 'Then let me try your sled, your papa holua whose runners are more oily.'

Said Kahawali crossly to this person, '*Aole!* Do you think you're my wife, that you can use my papa holua?'

He took his run, ran past that goddess, leapt on his sled and raced downhill.

Then Pele stamped her foot, the whole land shook; it quaked, the people cried in fear. She said her word, she called her word to Kilauea and all the burning rock came out, the fire and lava, the mountain's blood.

Then Pele changed, she changed from woman into akua again, came rushing down the sliding-place with all her fiery creatures. Roaring thunder, leaping rocks, streams of burning lava followed Pele down that hill.

When Kahawali reached the bottom of the slope he looked behind, he saw the anger of Pele pursuing from Kilauea. The people fled with screams, they scattered, ran. Then Kahawali took his spear which he had planted in the ground before the race, he ran as well; with Ahua his friend, that chief made off.

The burning lava came from Kilauea; it poured upon the people, burned them all, that lava-flow. Came Pele in fire-form riding on its wave, her anger showed. The singers, dancers, drummers, all were devoured by Pele.

Kahawali and Ahua came to the high ground of Puukea, to Kahawali's house and family. That chief threw off his cloak to run more quickly, met his favourite pig Aloi pua'a; they-two rubbed noses, made the hongi. Then Kahawali ran to the house of his mother at Kuki'i, made the hongi with her: 'Compassion great to you! Close here perhaps is your death. Pele comes devouring.'

Then Kahawali, having said this last thing to his mother, came to his wife—her name forgotten, cannot be remembered. They-two made the hongi, said farewell. Cried the wife, 'Stay here with me! Let us die together!' But Kahawali answered, 'No, I go. I go.' Then he made the hongi with his children Poupoulu and Kaohe, and said to them, 'I grieve for you two.'

The lava came on, Kahawali ran, he came to a deep ravine, could go no further. That chief stretched out his spear with a powerful word, he made it stretch the chasm, laid it down, walked across. Came Ahua behind and Kahawali held the spear, his friend took hold, was drawn across.

Came Pele speeding with her fire to eat that chief. He came to Kula, greeted there his sister Koai, had no time. Could only say to her 'Aloha oe!'—then he ran down to the sea.

Kahawali's youngest brother came with his canoe from fishing out at sea—saw Pele's anger, Kilauea pouring fire. They-two sprang off in that canoe, and with his broad spear Kahawali paddled fast, they left the land. Came Pele flaming, saw them get away. She hurled great stones, great burning rocks from Kilauea's hole. They fell around, they singed the sea, they did not hit the canoe of Kahawali.

When Kahawali had paddled a certain way the east wind blew, it drove them from Pele's anger. Smoke and ash came after them. Therefore Kahawali set his broad spear upright as a sail, it carried them across the sea to Maui. On that land this chief rested for one night.

They sailed again to Molokai, afterwards to Oahu, where Kahawali's father lived, Kolonohailaau; and his sister, Kane wahine keaho. There with his sister Kahawali afterwards remained. They dwelt quietly in their homes.

LONOPUHA, OR THE ORIGIN OF HEALING: AND THE STORY OF MILU

IN the time when Milu was living in this land Hawaii and was not yet lord of The Below, a party of god-like persons came across the sea from Kahiki. They landed at Ni'ihau, crossed to Kauai, came to Oahu, came to Molokai, to Maui. They arrived on the south side of this land and went to Puna, went to Hilo. Then they settled at Kukuihaele. These are the names of those people: Kaalae nui a hina, Kahuila o ka lani, Kane ika ula na ula, and many others.

They brought sickness to the land, those spirit-persons. Wherever they arrived, the people had headaches and fevers, shiverings, pani and all those troubles. The people died. The strangers brought death with them.

A person followed after them with healing powers. Kamaka nui aha i lono visited all the places where those akua made the people sick, he arrived at Kau, stopped near Waiohinu, where great numbers of people were living and Lono was their chief. This stranger sat on the hill where visitors wait; the people went to see him there.

Kamaka saw the redness of the skin of one of them and said, 'Oh, the redness of skin of that man!' So they told him, 'That is Lono, the chief of this land. He grows food. See his digging stick.' Kamaka spoke again of the colour of Lono's skin, said to the people, 'That chief is sick.' They replied, 'He is a healthy man, but you say he is sick.' Then Kamaka went on his way.

Some persons told the chief what was spoken by the stranger. Lono was angry, he raised his digging stick and said, 'I here have no sign of disease, yet that man says I am sick!' He thumped his digging tool. The point went in his foot and made it bleed.

Much blood came out, the chief fell down, he fainted. Therefore one of his people seized a pig and ran after that stranger.

Kamaka heard the pig squealing, turned round, saw the man running with an offering. The man put the pig before him and asked him to return. 'Lono's foot is injured. Come back and heal it.' Kamaka therefore turned back, and on his way he gathered the seeds and leaves of young popolo. He asked the people for sea-water, and they brought it. He pounded up the popolo with salty water, placed it in the wound, covered it with coconut, said chants for healing. The blood stopped coming out. After waiting there some days, Kamaka went on his way.

Someone breathing heavily behind him caused that kahuna to stop; this person was Lono. Said Kamaka, 'Lono! It is you! Where are you going?' That chief replied, 'You healed me. As soon as you were gone I therefore gave my powers to those who will succeed me, and have come, that you may teach this thing to me.'

The kahuna then said to the chief, 'Open your mouth,' and he blew spittle into it, which gave the chief his sacred powers, his work of healing.

They-two went on, Kamaka and the chief called Lonopuha: Lonopuha was his name after that time, because of his swollen foot. They went through Kau, through Puna, through Hilo. While they were going, Kamaka taught Lonopuha the plants that possess the mana for healing. They went to Hamakua, as far as Kukuihaele. Said Kamaka when they reached that place, 'We-two had better be apart, lest your work not succeed. Live elsewhere, let your own skill be your own.'

Therefore Lonopuha went on to Waimanu, Kamaka remained at Kukuihaele. And the good word came to Kamaka of Lonopuha's work, his skill, his healing mana. But Kamaka never revealed his teaching of Lonopuha, his secret rested. It was never learned by all those spirit-visitors who came before, what Kamaka had done. He taught the art to Lono of this land.

A Hawaiian chief in his house

These things happened in the time of Milu, before that king became the Lord of Below. It was the time when Kaalae nui a hina and his foreign party were looking for a way to kill Milu. Through the evil work of those akua, Milu was sick.

The word came to Milu, 'Lonopuha heals. His mana will send this thing out of Milu's body.' Therefore Milu sent his messenger to Lonopuha, Lono came. Milu was felt by Lono, Lono felt his body, said: 'This evil thing will go away when you have done what the gods expect.' Then Lonopuha said his chants, put on wet poultices of certain leaves. After a time Milu was well. Said Lono then: 'I have done this. You are well within. But now you are to rest in a house of curing, remain within the pipipi for one whole moon.' Therefore a house was built, of ti leaves entirely. Milu went within, lay.

Said Lonopuha, taught by Kamaka: 'O King! You are to rest

inside this house for a certain time. Remain here quietly. Should crowds applaud the sports, do not loosen the leaves of the house and look out, but remain here quietly. Should you look outside to see the cause of shouting, you will die.'

When a certain time had passed there was a great noise of the people. The cause of it was, two birds were playing in the air, and all the people watched them, cheered and shouted all day long. The king remained, he did not open the leaves of his house.

When the moon was twenty nights old this cheering was again being heard at Waipio. The cause of it was, a large tropic bird decorated with beautiful feathers flew out of the clouds, it soared above the pali cliffs of Koaekea and Kaholokuaiwa, it hung above the people, hovered there. They shouted, cheered, ran after it. Then Milu was careless of Kamaka's word, he lifted up the leaves of his house, he looked to see the cause.

That bird sprang down, it made a dive at him, thrust in its beak below his armpit, seized his liver—snatched the liver of the king! Thus Milu's life was taken, he was dead.

The kahuna saw the bird flying with the liver of Milu. He followed after it. The bird saw Lono chasing, dived; it entered the rock at the foot of the pali called Koaekea. As Lonopuha reached that rock he saw the blood spattered around where the bird had gone in.

He took a piece of his garment and soaked it in the blood; took back the blood to Milu's body in the house of leaves and pressed it in the wound; put healing leaves on top. Milu recovered, was alive again.

That place at the foot of this pali Koaekea has ever since been called Ke ake o Milu, 'Milu's Liver'.

A long time afterwards, when the death of the king was as nothing, Lonopuha his priest warned him, saying: 'You have escaped from this death; there remains for you one other. Do not disobey my word again. If the crowds cheer the surf-riders, remain within.'

One day the surf at Waipio was high. Great combers rolled upon the beach and many young chiefs had their surf-boards out, the common people also. The crowds were crying, cheering when the surfers rode. The riders said their chants for great waves from Kahiki and the gods replied with combers, long slow-rolling combers good to stand on.

Was tempted Milu then. He left his healing house, he lifted up the leaves, came out. He went to where his board was kept, his chiefly oro made of wiliwili.

This board of his he took, his surf-board that was larger than are two tall men—well stained and oiled, that shining board. Milu took down his board from the rafters, unwrapped its covering of tapa, ran to the beach, swam out.

'Here is Milu! Here is Milu the king with his oro! Let us watch him.'

The people watched their king seek out the place. He swam beyond the low surf, through the high surf, found the place; he waited. Then Milu let the first great wave go past, he let the second go. He saw his chance, he started on the third, a beauty!—caught the crest. His chiefly board held up its head and handsome Milu stood, the king stood up and rode that rolling crest. The people cheered, they shouted, cried: 'Here's Milu! He's recovered! He is riding on the surf!'

The king rode in and landed on the beach. He turned about, pushed out his board again, he found the place. He waited for his chance, it came, and Milu stood up on his board and proudly rode the curling whiteness to the beach.

But where the rollers finish as they break, and lift the sand, there Milu's board this time slipped out from under him. He fell, was thrown with force in the frothing waves. The people in amazement cried, 'He's gone! Our Milu's gone!' Then all the people rushed to look for him, in vain. Was never found, the body of the king.

This concludes the story of Milu's disobedience in this world. Afterwards he was below.

AHU ULA: THE FIRST FEATHER CLOAK

KAKAALANEO, the high chief of this land Maui, had runners in his service at Lahaina who would take his messages across the land as straight as birds. Swift men, these kukini. Up the mountain; over the rocks; down the cliffs; through the streams, through the bush; straight, direct. The ariki valued them, rewarded them well with food and garments. Among our people it was said: Send a kukini of the chief to Hana and he will be back before a fish in the umu is ready to be turned over.'

Eleio was the swiftest runner Kakaalaneo had. He could run round Maui three times in a day. If he was sent to Hana on the far side of the land the people said, 'He will be back before a fish is cooked on one side.' He was therefore sent away for kava when the meal was to be cooked, he chewed the kava on his homeward journey. Yet if Eleio was delayed, then his chief, who expected much, was angry, threatened death.

Eleio was a skilled kahuna also; his family were kahuna, he was well instructed in their arts. He knew the chants that heal. Also, he could see spirit-people. He could make a person's spirit go back into the dead body, so long as the rotting had not started. These things about Eleio were known in all the land. The spirit-people knew them also.

When Eleio was going to Hana by the north side of this land a spirit-woman used to run after him. Three times this wailua pursued Eleio; she wanted him to return her to her body. She frightened him, that spirit-person, but his sister Pohaku helped him. Pohaku turned round and lifted up her skirt, showed her bottom to the spirit-woman, made her run away for shame. Afterwards Eleio went to Hana by the south side of the land.

A Hawaiian woman

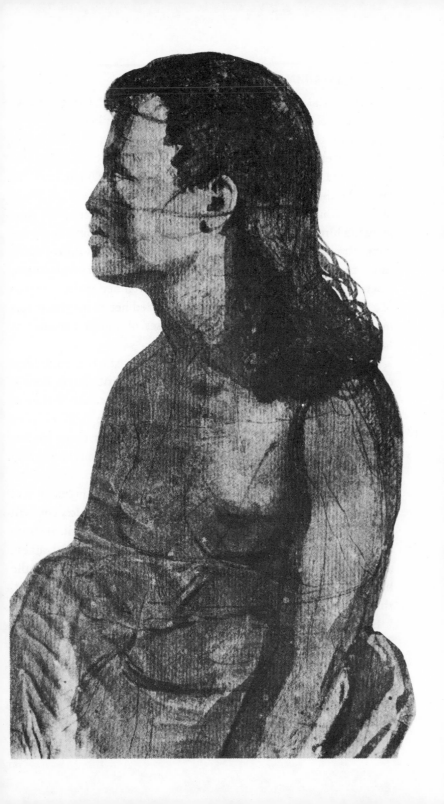

One day Kakaalaneo sent Eleio to Hana for the kava that grows in that place. The people said: 'Eleio will be back before the meal is ready for the chief.' Eleio left, ran swiftly, ran direct.

Soon after leaving Olowalu, as he was climbing up Aalaloloa, he saw ahead of him a beautiful woman. This woman went as fast as he did. Eleio hastened, but the woman kept always ahead of him; whatever he did she kept her distance. His pride was gnawing him. She led him over the rocks and mountains, down the cliffs, through the streams and through the bush, until they-two came to the cave of Hanamanuloa at Kahikinui, beyond Kaupo. Then he caught her; that person let him catch her at the entrance of a puoa which stood in that place. He seized her as she was entering that tower of bamboo where corpses of chiefly persons are laid to rot.

Eleio snatched her garment at the entrance; she turned to him, cried, 'Let me live. I am not human, I am spirit. Inside here is my house.' Said Eleio, 'I know already that you are a wailua. No human person could run more quickly than I, Eleio.' The wailua said to him, 'Let us-two be friends. Over there in that house which you can see live my parents and my relatives. Go and ask them for a pig, for tapa cloth, some fine mats, and the feather cloak. Tell them you have seen me and say that I told them to give these things to you. The ahu ula for which you will ask them is not yet finished. It is only so-wide, but it will measure two tall men in width when it is finished. There are enough feathers and fibre for the netting there to finish it, these things are in the house. Tell them to finish it for you.' Then the wailua vanished, that woman disappeared.

Eleio went into the puoa and climbed to the platform. The body of the girl was there, the rotting had not yet started. He left that place, ran to the house to which that wailua had pointed. A woman wailing. It was this circumstance that caused delay:

'I here am a stranger, but I had a travelling companion who led me to that puoa, then disappeared.'

The woman stopped her wailing, called to her husband, told him what was said. Eleio asked them, 'Does this house belong to you?' 'It does.' Then Eleio said: 'My message is to you. My travelling companion who was running with me owns a hog the length of a tall man, a pile of fine Paiula tapa-cloth, and a pile of fine mats. She also has a feather cloak which is not yet finished. You are to finish this cloak with the things that are here to finish it, and all these belongings you are to give to me. She has told me to ask you for them.'

Then Eleio described that spirit-person, and the woman and the man knew that their daughter who was dead had adopted this kukini as her brother, by giving him her precious things. In their own thoughts, therefore, they-two looked upon him as their son, and they said that they would kill the pig and make a feast. Said Eleio: 'Wait. Are all these people here your friends?' 'They are our relatives. They are the uncles, aunts and cousins of the wailua who has adopted you.' 'Will they do what you ask them to do?' 'They will.'

Therefore Eleio told the relatives to build a large lanai, to be covered entirely with ferns and ginger, maile and 'ie'ie. All these sweet-scented plants were to be used in that arbour. 'At one end of the lanai you are to build an altar.' All the people came to their work, the men and women and the young. That lanai was soon completed.

Then Eleio told them, 'Cook the pig.' He ordered them also to bring red and white fish, black and white fowls, and bananas both lele and maoli, and to place all these things on the altar. 'All the men and women then must remain in their houses, to assist the prayers. The children, the pigs, the fowls and dogs are all to be kept silent. Take the children inside. Put the animals in dark places. Those men who have to work are to be mindful of the gods.'

Then that kukini sped away, he ran to Hana and pulled up two bushes of the kava of Kaeleku, that plant for which his high chief Kakaalaneo had sent him on his errand. He returned to the place before the pig was cooked. Next kava was made, and when all the preparations for the feast were complete, Eleio went away some distance from the people, he went to be alone. Then the people understood the intention of Eleio, they knew that he was going to perform the kapuku and restore the wailua of that young woman to her body.

Eleio went apart, he made his invocations. All the people were quiet in their houses to assist the prayers. Then Eleio caught the spirit again and took it to the puoa, climbed to the platform of the corpse. He placed that spirit against the insteps of the feet, pressed hard, he spoke his chants. The spirit was going in, returning to its former place; but when it came to the knees it would not go any further, because the rotting in the stomach had begun. The wailua did not want to touch that mess. Eleio spoke his potent chants, he called upon his gods and pushed the spirit up the legs beyond the knees. At the thigh-bones, that spirit stopped, refused. Therefore Eleio worked at his chants; he got the spirit past the stomach to the throat. It stopped again, refused.

Here were the relatives around, the father, mother, uncles and male cousins. They gathered on the platform with Eleio, spoke their prayers as well. After much work Eleio got the spirit past the neck, then the girl gave a sort of crow. This made all persons hopeful. Eleio worked, worked at his chants, he got the spirit down the arms, past the elbows and wrists. It struggled to be put through these places, then it gave in—was back in the body. That girl was alive, sat up.

They took her to the ceremonies of purification, cleaned away the stomach. Then that girl was taken to the lanai where the offerings were laid. These things were presented to the gods, who took what they required of them. Could not be seen, that part of offerings. Then all the people feasted on the food, as guests of the gods.

After the feast the tapa cloths and fine mats; the feather cloak as well—these things were brought out and displayed to Eleio. Said the father: 'Take the woman you have made alive again. Have her for your wife and remain here with us. You will be our son, loved by us as she is.'

Hawaiian pendant of sperm-whale tooth and human hair

But Eleio said, 'No, I will take her into my care, but as for a wife she is worthy of a higher one than I. Give her to me and I will take her to Kakaalaneo.' Said the father: 'She is yours to do with as you wish. You made her live. But know that you have parents here, and that this house is yours.'

Then Eleio told them to finish the cloak. All those who could do feather-work sat down to this task; that wondrous cloak was soon completed, full to its size. When the cloak was finished, they told him that the name of the girl was Kanikaniaula. They-two then set out together for Lahaina, carrying with them the cloak, and the remainder of the kava of Kaeleku for the chief. Their going was slow on this journey, for Kanikaniaula had only the strength of a woman, not of a spirit. Said Eleio, 'I am late returning. There is danger. My chief commands my death.'

They arrived at Launiupoko. Said Eleio: 'You wait here in the bushes while I go on alone. If by sunset I have not returned, then I am dead. You are to return to your people. But if I am not dead, I shall return here soon.'

He came on to Makila, near Lahaina, saw some people heating an umu to cook food. They were the high-chief's servants. When they saw Eleio they began to tie him up and roast him alive, as Kakaalaneo had ordered them. But he put those people off with this word: 'Let me die at the feet of my master.' Thus Eleio successfully passed those servants of Kakaalaneo, passed the oven that was heated for him.

He arrived before his chief. 'How is it that you are not yet killed, as I ordered? How did you get past my servants?'

Said Eleio: 'The slave wished to die at the feet of his chief, if he must die. But sir, this would be a great loss to you, for I have brought with me that which will make your name known to the generations.' Then Eleio took his bundle off his back, unrolled the mats and tapa, showed his chief the cloak of scarlet feathers. It was the first ahu ula seen by the people of this land. All were amazed, the chief was greatly pleased. The kava which Eleio brought was used that evening in the offerings of Kakaalaneo to the gods.

Then Eleio told the rest of it. Said the high-chief, 'Bring this woman.' Kanikaniaula was brought from her hiding place. The chief desired her; took her for wife. Thus the highest chiefs of this land Maui trace their descent from Kakaalaneo and Kanikaniaula, and they wear that sacred cloak on ceremonial occasions.

TONGAN GROUP

Kava plant

THE ORIGIN OF KAVA

THE chief called Loau, down in Tongatapu, had an attendant whose name was Fevanga and whose home was on the island of Eueiki. After being the chief's attendant for a time Fevanga returned to live at Eueiki with his wife Fefafa and their daughter who was leprous. Fevanga often visited Loau, and one day he begged that chief to sail across to Eueiki and visit him.

Now the time when Loau chose to visit Fevanga was a time of great scarcity on Eueiki. The gods in their anger had blown a thousand coconut trees upon their sides and spoiled the taro plots, there was no good food left. All that remained on Fevanga's land was one big kape plant, growing near his house. That bitter kape root was all that Fevanga had to offer to his guest.

When Loau arrived, Fevanga came down to greet his visitors and they answered saying, 'Happy to see you in good health in this land.' Then Loau's party pulled up his canoe into the shade. They laid it near Fevanga's house with its outrigger against the kape. And Fevanga and Fefafa began to prepare their oven, whispering how they might dig up the kape without being impolite to Loau. For Loau also was seated near that plant, and they wished very much to get it without disturbing him. Therefore they asked Loau to go inside their small house, and he did so since they said it would be cooler there. To please them that chief went inside.

Then Fevanga and Fefafa dug up the kape and made it ready for the oven. But there was no fowl or pig to be a relish with it, therefore Fevanga with a club killed his leprous daughter Kavaonau, and they made good food for Loau.

And the food was cooked and they brought it from the oven and put it before the chief, and he thanked them for their kindness, but he asked them, 'Why have you destroyed your child?'

Then Loau told them to take that food away. He told them that they must bury her head in one place and her body in another, and he said, 'You must watch them carefully.' After this they made their farewells and Loau returned in his canoe to Tongatapu.

For five nights Fevanga and Fefafa kept visiting the grave of their daughter, and after five nights there was growing from her head a kava plant, and from her guts there grew a sugar cane. That kava grew large, and the cane grew also.

One day when they were almost fully grown Fevanga saw a rat gnawing at the kava plant. That rat became silly, and could not move. Then it gnawed the sugar cane, and it recovered and ran about. This thing it did repeatedly; this is how the people of Tongatapu here learned that sugar cane is to be eaten when kava is drunk.

Then the plants grew large, they were fully ripe, and Fevanga and Fefafa dug them up and brought them here to Loau. And Loau laughed, and he cried out:

'Chewing kava, a leprous child of Fevanga and Fefafa in Eueiki! Bring some coconut-husk to strain it, bring a bowl to hold it, bring a person to make the kava, bring someone for the bowl to be turned toward!'

Therefore this was done, the kava was split up and chewed by persons sitting on that side of the bowl where common persons sit; and the kava was strained and served to those of rank and all was done correctly.

This is the origin of kava. The shoots of the plant when they grow become grey and scaly because of that daughter who was leprous.

THE ORIGIN OF THE MAGELLAN CLOUDS

OVER at Vaini there live certain people who are descended from a great chief of the ancient time named Maafu tukui aulahi. This tale which I will speak is about that chief of Tongatapu and two sons of his.

Maafu made his morning toilet at the spring named Tufa-takale, and his custom was to wipe himself with a piece of coco-nut-husk, he took a new piece every day. Beside that pool there were some fetaanu trees, and in those trees there lived a very large pili, female lizard. When Maafu had finished he threw his piece of pulu on to a flat stone beside the pool, and as soon as he was gone that lizard always swallowed it. This made her pregnant.

After a certain time had passed the pili gave birth, she had two sons. One of them ran about when he was born, therefore she named him Maafu lele; the other boy lay quietly, therefore she named him Maafu toka. Those boys grew up in the care of that lizard of Tufatakale, but one day they said to her, 'We wish to know our father. Tell us who he is and we will go to him.'

'That is difficult for me,' old lizard answered, 'for I am ugly and your father is a great chief of Tongatapu.'

But they-two pressed her to reveal their father's name, therefore she rubbed them with scented oil and picked the lice from their hair, she put fragrant wreaths of perfumed flowers around their necks, and she said to them:

'You will go along the road until you come to a large kava circle in a chief's house. There will be two kinds of people there, you must observe them carefully. Some of those persons will be in a circle which includes the kava bowl; the rest are in a group outside, behind the bowl. Those are the toua, they are not allowed

'*You will come to a large kava circle in a chief's house*'

inside the ring. Do not go to them. Watch carefully the man in the circle who is opposite the kava bowl, observe how the people act towards that man. Go to him then; he is your father. But be proper in your conduct. Be correct.'

Those boys took leave then of their lizard-mother and they followed her directions. On their coming to the kava-circle they-two soon recognised their father by the respect that was being paid to him. They kept their distance therefore until the kava-drinking was concluded. Then they-two respectfully approached, and the people in the party asked each other who the handsome visitors might be, they wondered if a canoe had arrived from Ha'apai or Vavau.

Those boys went before Maafu and sat down with their legs crossed, waiting quietly for him to notice them. After a while he said, 'Young men, we do not know who you are or where you have come from. Please inform us.'

'Sir,' they-two replied, 'you are our father.'

Now Maafu did not contradict them; he did not even ask them who their mother was, lest she should wish to come and live with him as well.

After this occasion those boys lived with Maafu and they began to be men; but they were mischievous. They also ran fast and were good at throwing the sika dart. In their games one day they broke the leg of one of Maafu's nephews. Also they were cheeky, they made a game of throwing their sika as close as they could to Maafu's person, while pretending to be aiming somewhere else. At last, Maafu became tired of them.

He called them both one morning and asked them to fetch him some drinking water from the distant spring called Atavahea. 'You must dip out the water for me in the middle of the day, when it is sweetest.' But Maafu did not tell them that a very large duck lived there and that persons who went to fetch water at noon were never seen again, the toloa ate them.

They-two set off. They travelled all the morning in order to reach the spring at the proper time. Then Maafu lele waded in with the gourds, while Maafu toka waited on the bank. Just as Maafu lele was sinking the gourds to fill them the whole sky became dark, a rushing sound like wind was heard across the land.

Maafu lele looked up, he saw that giant duck and hid beneath the water just in time. Then he threw up his fist with very great force, it broke the wing of that toloa; then he caught the bird, and turned its neck. 'We will give this bird to our father as a gift.' They-two then filled their gourds with water from the middle of the spring, with sweetest water they filled them for their father; then they returned to Vaini.

Their father was not pleased to see them or to have the bird, but he hid his feelings politely and he thanked them for the water and the gift.

Soon afterwards Maafu sent those sons to the spring called Muihatafa, and he said that the gourds must be filled with water from the very bottom of the pool. He did not tell them that at Muihatafa there was a very great parrot-fish which ate up persons who tried to take its water away.

Maafu toka said, 'Let *me* fetch the water this time,' and he dived beneath. Now as soon as Maafu toka began letting the bubbles out of the gourds he saw the humu coming at him with its open mouth to eat him. Therefore he thrust the gourds down the throat of that humu, this killed it, and he brought it up and said, 'Here is a good fish for our father.'

Then they-two returned to Vaini with the water and the fish. And when Maafu saw them he said, 'Now am I finished with you-two. You have broken my nephew's leg, you have been a danger to me on several occasions, you live on mischief. I will give you each a piece of land on the other side of Tongatapu. Do not come and injure me or there will be vengeance.'

They-two replied, 'O Maafu, do not trouble yourself to give us lands. If you wish us indeed to go away we will do so, we will go beyond the reach of mischief. Only give us our duck and our fish and we will take them with us to the heavens. Should you wish to see us at any time you will look upward on a dark night. Should we wish to see you we will look down from there.'

Then Maafu toka and Maafu lele went to the sky, as all men know. They are those two bright patches near the Milky Way by which men steer on voyages at sea. Those clusters of stars called Toloa and Humu are with them also in the pools of the sky, the duck and the parrot-fish.

TOKELAU MOETONGA

TOKELAU MOETONGA was an exceedingly handsome young man because of the manner of his birth and because he was the son of two women, yes, of both of them. Tokelau was a man with woman's beauty.

Those two mothers were Samoan women. They were sailing from Samoa when their canoe went down, and by very strong swimming they reached the islands of Kelefesia and Tonumea, here in the Ha'apai group. They-two lived on those islands for some time, no men were there. After a certain period they believed that they were pregnant and they did not know how it could be so, therefore they turned their bottoms to the wind, to find out. Yes, it was so. Afterwards one of them gave birth to a son and they named him Tokelau moetonga, 'North-wind-sleeping-with-south-wind'.

That son grew well, and when he had become a man he went to Tongatapu. It was the time of the marriage of the Tu'i Tonga to Fatafehi, great was the feasting then. When the ceremonies and the feasting were concluded the Tu'i Tonga said to his men friends, 'We will all go hunting flying-foxes.' So the men went off with spears and nets and the bride remained at home with the chief women.

Now this was the time when Tokelau came from his mothers' island, wearing his beautiful turban of white Samoan tapa. And because of the feasting, all of the people were asleep, except for Fatafehi; that bride without a husband was awake.

Tokelau moetonga went to Fatafehi in her house. Because of his great beauty she admired that man; they slept together. Afterwards Tokelau gave Fatafehi his headgear as a token, Fatafehi in return gave that stranger her girdle of red sinnet.

Now when Tokelau took off his turban the scent of it reached the Tu'i Tonga and his friends in that place where the flying-foxes are. 'We will go back now,' that high chief said, 'as I think some chiefs have arrived.'

Tokelau moetonga was not there, he had departed; but the girl was lying well contented on her sleeping-mat, therefore the Tu'i Tonga killed her instantly, they took her body out.

It was to Kelefesia to his mothers that Tokelau had gone. On the afternoon of that day he said to them, 'I will return now to Tongatapu, for some dreadful thing has happened there.' He returned at once, and when he reached the Tu'i Tonga's enclosure the funeral lights were burning for the wife, therefore Tokelau went and mourned for her.

The Tu'i Tonga asked his attendants, 'Who is that person mourning?' They replied, 'It is a man.' 'Then order him to stop and bring him here.' This was done.

'Was it you who had my wife?' the king asked Tokelau.

Tokelau moetonga raised his eyebrows, saying yes.

'What is your name?'

'I am Tokelau moetonga.'

Then the Tu'i Tonga wept and said, 'Fatafehi did rightly. I, too, am nearly dead with my liking for you. I have done great wrong in killing Fatafehi. Come with me and we will mourn together over our wife.'

So they-two mourned together throughout that night and when the sun came up the funeral was held, they-two were there together.

It was because of his great beauty that Tokelau moetonga was spared from utu by the Tu'i Tonga.

The Tu'i Tonga remained in Tongatapu. Tokelau moetonga returned to his mothers, he lived quietly for some time in Kelefesia.

LOUSE AND FLEA GO FISHING

A tale, ah me:

Louse and flea
Built a boat,
Sailed the sea,
Hooked a fish,
Pulled with joy,
Hauled it up.
—a matakelekele!
Turned about,
Sailed away,
Landed here,
—Haapepe!
Turned about,
Sailed again,
Landed there,
—Haatafu!

Otago, a young Tongan

TU'I TOFUA

TU'I TOFUA was the son of Vakafuhu. His mother was Langitaetaea, but she was only one of the many young women whom Vakafuhu had living behind the fences of his dwelling.

When Tu'i Tofua grew he was given the first-born sons of all the wives for his companions, and they all used to play sika outside the enclosure of Vakafuhu. They made their sika of clean-peeled sticks and threw them in turns along the ground, they glanced them off a mound and each one tried to make the longest throw.

One day while Vakafuhu was sleeping off a kava-drinking those boys were playing their game outside, and Tu'i Tofua threw his sika. Then indeed the enormous strength of Tu'i Tofua made that sika fly over the fences into his father's place. It landed where the women were and they all began to giggle, those girls, and shriek and laugh. They did this because they wanted that handsome youth to come among them, they desired him. More than his father they desired him.

They fell with joy upon the sika of their master's son, and snapped it. When he came inside to get it back they called out things that made him embarrassed. 'Haven't you got another long thing there, Tu'i?' those women said. 'This one's broken.' And they put their hands across their faces and they laughed.

All this chatter woke up Vakafuhu from his sleep. That old man called crossly from his house, 'Can't you keep that game outside? You have got your own place. Do you have to come in here and disturb me when I am trying to sleep?'

These words of Vakafuhu's hurt the feelings of Tu'i Tofua, he was deeply offended by his father's angry words. Therefore he decided to go on a voyage, and never to return.

Tu'i Tofua built a canoe, it was a tongiaki. That tongiaki was the first one that was ever made, and its name was Siivao. When it was finished Tu'i Tofua embarked with all his men, and they all sailed away toward the north, those first-born sons. They passed the island of Kao, it is north of Tofua, then Tu'i Tofua said to his men:

'All of you now will jump into the sea—unless there be one among you who desires to live on land.'

All those men knew Tu'i's meaning; they knew that when they jumped they would be turned into sharks. They replied that they were willing to enter the sea in order to show that Tofua can produce men. But one among them did not wish to be a shark, his name was Faia. He was a Samoan!

Faia said, 'Who wants to grow up like a shark and be snared in a noose by fishermen, and bashed with an oar, and cut up in pieces and shared out with the people while they clap their hands and scream and laugh? Who wants that?'

'Very well then,' said Tu'i Tofua to that Samoan. 'You need not come with us. But cut off one of your fingers and throw that in the sea, it will become a porpoise.' And Faia did so, and his finger was the first porpoise.

Then Tu'i Tofua said to Faia, 'Go back to our relatives and tell them to cut tapa for gifts, and pick sweet flowers and make garlands. Tell them to bring these things to Siuatama beach on the day after tomorrow. Then will we hold a festival.'

That Samoan departed, he returned to Tofua a human being, and he gave Tu'i Tofua's message to all the relatives.

Then indeed Tu'i Tofua and his men leapt into the sea, and they all became sharks. Tu'i Tofua became a tenifa, the shark that eats men. The rest became ordinary sharks.

Here in Tofua all the relatives prepared their gifts of tapa and wove many scented garlands which they laid in baskets. On the day that followed they all went to Siuatama with their gifts. As they waited there they saw that the sea was a different colour because of the coming of Tu'i Tofua and his fish-gods. When all the

'Tu'i Tofua built a canoe, it was a tongiaki.'

sharks were close inshore the parents and relations ran toward them to present their gifts.

But when Vakafuhu and Langitaetaea his wife came to the water's edge Tu'i Tofua felt annoyance and he fled, he swam off swiftly. He did not wish to meet his father any more. And Vakafuhu bowed his head.

After the people had presented their gifts, their fragrant wreaths and lengths of tapa cloth, then the sharks turned about and went their way.

Since that time in this land Tu'i Tofua has been a god and the shark is tapu and not to be eaten, because of what occurred when Vakafuhu was angry with his son.

A Tongan double canoe in its shed

THE CONSEQUENCE

> Listen, you of enlightened minds,
> While I tell you a tale of the shore.
> Two sisters who lived together Hava and Ila,
> They were wives of Naa ana moana.
> They lived together then they quarrelled.
> What a sad thing is jealousy—
> > *Ala!*

HERE in Tongatapu long ago a chief named Naa ana moana had two wives who were sisters, Hava and Ila. They-two came from across the sea at Nukunukumotu, and Ila was the favourite wife.

Those wives went fishing for Naa's food, they always tried to please him with their catch. When there was a raui on fishing in the lagoon, they went out on the reef for crabs. But the time came for the raui to be lifted, therefore they tied up leaves for torches and went nightfishing in the lagoon once more. But they went off separately, those two.

Hava went along the shore past the mangroves and Ila went on the shallow part of the lagoon. With their spears and torches they looked for good food.

Beyond the mangroves, Hava came to a cave in the land, and in that cave she found a hole that was covered with a stone.

> Came and opened it,
> She thought it was a crab-hole.
> Looking in she saw the fish with
> > pouting mouths.
> Brought her basket,

> Opened it out,
> Chose the biggest fish,
> Lifted up her load,
> Wishing to have something to take to her
>   husband.

Indeed Hava lifted the stone from that hole and found that it was filled with mullet: all the mullet of the world were in that hole. Therefore she fetched her basket and picked out the biggest fish and took them to Naa. When she had gone the hole was teeming with mullet again.

Now Ila her sister brought home only crabs that night, and when she saw the many mullet which Naa was scaling and cutting she was jealous, for Naa was pleased with Hava.

Those wives again went fishing on another night, and Ila thought there was something Hava knew. They-two went down to the mangroves and they fished there for a while. Then Ila set off for her lagoon-place again, and seeing her go, Hava left her torch burning on a mangrove tree and went on to her cave.

Ila also deceived her sister. She too left her torch burning in a mangrove tree, and in the dark she followed Hava.

And Hava, thinking that she was alone, went in and lifted up the stone and filled her basket to the brim with fish. Then she returned to her husband.

Ila went in also and lifted the stone, she filled her basket with fish to take to Naa. But she was angry with Hava, angry because of her secret. Therefore she threw away the stone and called to the fish:

'You come out and you go!'

And all those mullet came, they streamed in thousands from the hole and leapt into the sea. They were the first mullet in the world.

When Hava reached their home at midnight she was cold. She therefore put on clothes while Naa cleaned the fish. But while he was doing this Hava heard a great rushing sound like thunder and she cried, 'The fish! The mullet! They have all been let out by Ila!'

Straight off she rushed, she dashed out in the night to prevent her mullet from escaping.

She looked for rocks to block their way, that woman. And with her hands indeed she pulled in the islands Kanatea and Nuku to close the cave. When they would not do so she pulled Houmaniu close. Then the teeming fishes turned in their flight and like a wind they rushed to the other shore, which caused the small bay which is there today.

Then Hava seeing them escaping pulled with all her strength at Toa as well, but the fishes sped back to Folaha, and dented that shore also with their rushing force.

Still Hava persevered, she pulled the ends of the land, Haaloausi and Houmatoloa. She also tugged at Mataaho, the island where the giant ironwood tree is growing; but that tree would not move.

> Was nearly dragged along the toa tree;
> But the fish turned,
> Which made the inlet at Lifuka,
> And the inlet at Faihavata,
> And the beach at Fatufala—
> > *Ala!*
>
> Pulled out Haaloausi,
> Turned the fish to the other side,
> Which caused the inlet at Umusi
> Near to the rock called Tuungasili,
> Afterwards known as Tui—
> > *Ala!*

When daylight came and the flowing of the fish had not been stopped Hava grew intensely angry, she cried out to her own land across the sea, to Nukunukumotu, for all her people to come and catch the fish.

All Nukunukumotu stood and waited for the fish, but they escaped at Fota, Nukunukumotu could not stop them, those mullet utterly escaped.

Then indeed Hava turned herself into a coral rock. And the mullet escaped and increased, and mullet thenceforward were everywhere.

After this Hava was a coral rock for ever, but her husband joined her. From his love for her, Naa also became a stone. And Ila said what is the use of living and became a stone as well.

They are standing together in the lagoon-entrance of Tanuma-popo, Hava on the one side and Ila on the other, and Naa ana moana in between them. This is true.

The house of a chief's wives on Tongatapu

LEPUHA AND THE WIDOW OF UTUMALAMA

LEPUHA and his attendant were travelling by canoe from Vavau to Tongatapu where a husband was to be chosen for a woman of high rank.

As they passed the islet called Utumalama they heard people wailing, therefore they paddled to the shore and landed, to know the cause of that weeping. It was dark when they reached the house of mourning, and looking in they saw the body of a man for whom the weeping was. All the mourners were asleep but one. The wife was wailing, she was weeping there by light of candlenuts, and Lepuha recognized that woman. He therefore broke a stick, and when she heard the noise she looked toward the door. Then Lepuha opened his hand and held it in the light, so that the woman should see the jellyfish which was tattooed on his palm, and would know him. As soon as she saw the jellyfish that woman ceased her wailing, she came outside and spoke with Lepuha. Then they-two spent the night together on the beach.

Before the dawn that woman awoke, and returning to her house she took a mat from her husband's body and gave it to Lepuha for a token.

Then Lepuha and his attendant put to sea and continued their journey to Tongatapu. As the sun was rising from the sea they sang:

> Woman falsely weeping in Utumalama,
> Stirred by the wind from the north . . .

They-two reached Tonga at Talafoou, and came along the shore to Nukuleka, where they left their canoe among the mangroves. Then they went on to the festival at Mua.

SAMOAN GIFT, TONGAN PAYMENT

IN a time long-ago, Tonga had coconuts but Samoa had none. Samoa had fowls but Tonga had none.

A god of Samoa asked a god of Tonga for a coconut, and the god of Tonga answered, 'Yes, for a fowl'.

Then those gods prepared a trick, each man.

Instead of a fowl the Samoa god brought an owl for a gift; and that Tonga god opened his nut and scooped its flesh out, he brought an empty husk.

Then they-two exchanged their gifts. As the Samoan went away he said, 'Alua, mo moa lulu'— 'Farewell, with owl-fowl''.

The god of Tonga answered him, 'Alua, mo niuniu pulu'— 'Farewell, with cut nut'.

SAMOA

FITI AU MUA, WHO WAS BORN IN THE SEA

V EU and Veu were the couple who held land from the chief Tufu le Mata'afa, here in Fiti uta. Veu was pregnant, and had a longing for some kape which was growing in their garden. It was a good one, and ready for digging, but it was marked to go as first-fruit to the chief for using land of his. He was having a canoe built at the time, and he wanted it for workmen's payment. Still Veu had her longings for the kape, and she got it and ate it.

Some person of Mata'afa's family told him that the kape was eaten. Then that chief was very angry, and he drove out Veu and Veu, drove them off his land. They went off in his anger.

They took a swimming-board and swam together out to sea to find some other land. After a time they came to the place called Fanga fetau na'i on the island of Niue.

The chiefess of that place was Sinasina le Fe'e—she had no husband and was chief. It happened that two of her people were in the water fishing for an offering to go as cold-food with her kava. These two were Saumani ali'i and his wife Saumani tamaitai. They were fishing together with a hand-net.

Now Veu who was pregnant gave birth to her baby on the back of a wave, but she could not take the child up—it floated on the sea. Thus that boy was carried into Saumani's net. That man looked down. Something human was there. He poured it out again. The sea returned it to his net. He said, 'A man is caught.' Said his wife, 'Then what are you looking for? Take that thing as an offering, take it as cold-food for the kava of our chiefess.' Saumani took it to the land, to the house of their chiefess.

Veu and Veu went ashore and saw the child. They said to the chiefess who had no husband: 'Do not waste the boy that has been

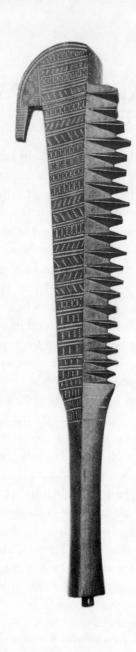

'Fiti cut two clubs for himself out of toa wood'

born. Do not eat him. Let us take care of him as your son. Let us rear him as fondly as a pet and call him your son, Fiti au mua.'

This was done; and an old woman was found who acted as a mother to Fiti au mua. Her own son's name was Lau foli; he was a true Niuean; he was a warrior, that foster-mother's son.

Fiti au mua grew up in the care of this woman. He went about with other boys, but they cast things up at him. 'You are a Samoan boy whose parents were driven out in anger.'

Fiti asked his parents if it were true and they replied that Mata'afa drove them away in anger. 'You were born on a wave in the sea.'

Then Fiti was angry, and prepared to fight. He cut out two clubs for himself of toa wood, one for each hand, and he practised swinging them. He came into the house swinging two clubs, and while he was practising he hit his foster-mother on the head. She died.

Said Veu his mother, 'What is the reason you have killed your mother?' He replied, 'If only Fiti's clubs should revive at home, we would have prosperity.'

Then Fiti went with his parents to visit their homeland, and a battle was fought at once. That was the first fight. Mata'afa's people drove them back and forth, they were driven east and driven west. Fiti was chased and pushed down. The club in his left hand fell, but the club in his right hand remained.

Then Fiti dived into the reef passage at Aumuli, and he swam beneath the sea. He came up first at Fiji. He fought at once with them. Fiji was overcome. Then Fiti swam to Tonga; fought with Tonga, overcame. He returned here to his own land in Samoa, he went inland at A'ana. He crossed over to Savai'i; fought a fight at Pu'a pu'a; continued to fight at Matautu, where Le Fanonga helped against him. Then Fiti was killed and the wars were ended.

THE DOLPHINS AT FAGASA

THE travelling-party of the chief Li'ava'a came from the east and arrived at Fagasa.

It was the custom of this chief to drink kava only when he was at sea, therefore he said to his daughter Sina, 'Go and fetch some water to make the kava.' And to his people he said, 'Make ready our canoe.'

Sina went, she went with her gourds to fetch the water; and after a time Li'ava'a ordered his canoe to sea. They sailed far out, they were far from Samoa, and Li'ava'a called to his daughter, 'Chew kava now to make my drink.' But Sina did not hear him, for she was left behind at Fagasa.

Sina, when she saw that Li'ava'a's canoe was gone without her, broke her gourds. This is the reason for the fresh-water spring on the reef at Fagasa. Then she waited there.

Li'ava'a called again, 'Sina, chew the kava for my drink.' There was no answer, therefore they searched the canoe, and said, 'O chief, your daughter has been left behind in that place we called at.'

Li'ava'a stood up and said to the men who were paddling, 'If Sina has been left behind, then go in the form of fishes to that place.' So they went to the food baskets and took some nonu and bananas for the journey, and they dived into the sea and swam, and came to Fagasa.

Those men were all turned into dolphins; and the dolphins swam to Fagasa, as they do here every year.

Sina stood on the shore with her white fan to welcome them. With her fan she beckoned them to land. They all jumped on to the beach, and the people came and hauled them up like boats, they took them on the land.

The dolphins when they were carried wept, and coughed like men. When they saw the people seizing spears and clubs to kill them, they wept in vain.

When the dolphins were opened up for eating, the nonu and the bananas of Li'ava'a were found inside them.

THE STORY OF THE RAT AND THE FLYING-FOX

THE rat and the peka were friends, but the rat was longing for the peka's thin black wings.

This chief, the rat, sat still and thought, he thought of a trick to get the peka's wings; for the peka flew about in the treetops while the rat crept along the ground.

The rat looked out for a tree with fruit which the peka liked, and one day he noticed that the peka was always eating gatae berries so he climbed that tree to where the bat was eating fruit. The peka flew away, it flew to an ifi tree; so the rat came down and climbed that tree. The peka took fright, but the rat called out: 'Do not run away, for this is my tree. Wait for me, O peka! Let us talk together.' The peka therefore waited in the ifi tree.

Said the rat: 'Sir, peka, how is it that you eat from my tree without the right? I eat this fruit.'

Said the peka: 'Rat, I beg your pardon, you are right.'

Then said the rat: 'But my desire is for a good thing. Therefore I am not angry with you. On the contrary, I wish to conclude a friendship with you. I do not wish to chase you away, peka, but wish you to come here and eat on my tree.'

Then said the peka: 'Chief, it is good. Let us conclude a friendship.'

The rat said then: 'Sir, peka, are you afraid when you fly so high? For when I look this way it seems to me very high.'

The peka answered: 'Sir, rat, I am not afraid.'

Rat: 'Is that true?'

Peka: 'Sir, it is true. I have no fear.'

Then said the rat: 'Peka, have pity on me. Give me your wings

Peka, the flying-fox

so that I may learn, and see whether you are true in your friendship to me.'

Said the peka: 'All right. I shall do this, so that you may learn: so that you may see how wonderful it is where I always go.'

The peka spoke again: 'But sir, when you go, do not go far away.'

The rat replied: 'Oh no, I shall only fly to that tree over there. Then I shall return your wings. In the meantime you must eat of my tree till you are satisfied.'

Then the peka took its wings and fastened them on to the back of the rat, and the rat said, 'Sir, please allow me to hand over *my* things, which only hinder me, for you to keep.' Then it handed the peka its tail and four feet, and the peka took them all and put them on.

The peka spoke again: 'Sir, come back quickly, that I may not be delayed.' The rat replied: 'I will come quickly. You remain here and eat until you are satisfied.'

Then the rat flew away, while the peka ate steadily and watched the rat, which went away and did not return.

Then the peka wept: 'Aue! Aue! Aue! Rat has cheated me! He has gone with my wings!'

This is the story of the peka that lost its wings and now lives on the ground, a rat; while the rat has wings and flies, a bat. Hence our proverb of the orators—when one chief cheats another chief, the rest then say, 'But did you not know of the friendship of the peka and the rat?'

WHY THE SEA-SLUG HAS TWO MOUTHS

THERE was war between the fishes and the birds. The day had been named on which this war would start, and at low tide that morning the fishes' war-party went to the reef. So did the birds. Their chosen battle ground was on that place. The birds and fishes fought, and all the fish were thrown into the sea. Cried the sea-slug, 'Bravo, birds, bravo.'

Then the fishes climbed up again and began to throw the birds upon the land. Cried the sea-slug when the fish were winning, 'Bravo, fishes! O my friends, bravo.'

Thus neither of those war-parties knew which side the slug was on; and thus we say, 'The sea-slug has two mouths—one at either end.'

So it is also with men. When a chief makes a speech both ways we say, 'He has two mouths, like a sea-slug.' For the cowardly men are known.

ATOLLS AND OUTLIERS

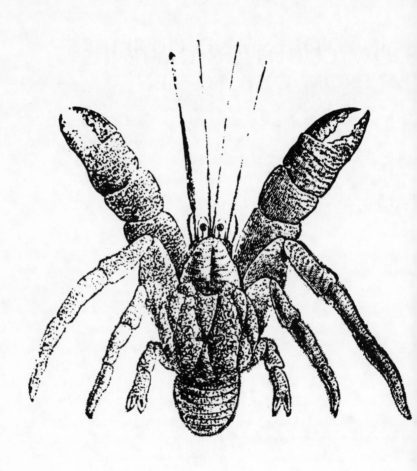

Coconut crab

HOW COUNTING CAME TO BE FROM ONE TO TEN

HERE in Fakaofo old Sina had a daughter called Sina, and ten sons. The names of these sons were Ten to One, that is to say Ulu, Iva, Valu, Fitu, Ono, Lima, Fa, Tolu, Lua and Tasi.

When young Sina was a small girl she was taken away to Fiti by a bad person. Her mother grieved long for Sina, therefore one day the ten sons said that they would build canoes and go in search of her. Each son went into the bush to fell his tree, and as Ulu went along he came across two persons fighting. Their names were Sinota and Te Gata (that is 'Sea-snake'), and just as Ulu came along Sea-snake had got Sinota by the throat. Cried Sinota, 'Help me, Ulu!' But Sea-snake said angrily to Ulu, 'Do not interfere, you owl,' and Ulu was frightened and went away.

Soon the next brother, Iva, came that way, and Sinota asked him for his help, but Iva also was afraid of Sea-snake. Then came Valu; he also ran away. Each brother came in turn, and was afraid of Sea-snake, until Tasi the last arrived.

Sinota was nearly dead, and Tasi only just heard his cry. He did not wait for Sea-snake's words, he jumped and cut off his head. The fight was finished.

When Sinota had thanked Tasi for saving his life he helped him build his canoe. He showed him where the best tree stood, then he called to all the insects to help him cut it out. He got the spiders to make its sail.

All of Tasi's brothers had already made their canoes, and by the time Tasi's was finished they had set sail and were nearly out of sight. He sailed after them, came to Lua's canoe, and said a word which Sinota had taught him. This word made Lua's canoe stop sailing, Tasi passed it. He came to the canoes of all his brothers, said his word, passed them. He passed them all, the canoes of his elder brothers. Thus Tasi arrived first at his sister's house in Fiti. 'I and my brothers have come to take you home to see our mother who is old and sick.'

Sina became very frightened. She was wife to that bad person who had seized her from her home. This bad person was a terrible cannibal, his name Saipuniana. Said Sina: 'This man will not let me leave. He will kill you. He watches me.'

Said Tasi: 'I know a trick. In the middle of the night you will tell the husband you are very hot and want to go outside to get cool. If he suspects you, tie a piece of cord to your waist and leave the end with him.'

Sina did this. Then she tied the cord to a maile tree and ran away with Tasi to his canoe. Saipuniana waited. He pulled the string and called to Sina. He heard the noise of the tree where she was sitting and went to sleep again. Later he pulled again, pulled hard, and the branch came off. Bad was his heart with anger when that person knew he had been tricked. When daylight came he saw a canoe far off and sailing from the land.

Saipuniana called on the Mist to come and help him. With the help of the Mist that person could walk on the sea. He walked after that canoe. When Tasi saw Saipuniana coming up he said his word that called the rain; a heavy squall of rain came down to make Saipuniana cold. Therefore when Saipuniana caught up with them he was so cold that he could only crawl into the bottom of the canoe. There Tasi rolled him in a sleeping mat.

While Saipuniana was resting, Tasi sewed up the mat. Then he tied his anchor stone to it. Saipuniana was waking up. Said Tasi, 'Let me move you. The canoe is leaking just there. You must not get wet.' So he lifted him; but he did not put him down in the canoe again, he tossed him overboard. Thus it was finished with Saipuniana.

All these matters made Tasi's journey slow, and so his brothers passed him on the way, all reached Fakaofo before him. Their mother was waiting for them on the reef, she asked each brother if Sina was in his canoe. When all those brothers had come in, from Ulu to Lua, old Sina was going to drown herself from grief, but she waited for one more canoe—that of Tasi the last.

Then she found her daughter safe with Tasi. Old Sina ordered a very great feast of rejoicing for the coming home of young Sina and she said to Tasi: 'Now I know which is the first of all my sons. In future *you* will be the one we say first and the others will come after you.'

So counting was turned around, and we count: tasi, lua, tolu, fa, lima, ono, fitu, valu, iva, sefulu.

THE BASKET OF SOULS

NONU was a handsome young man here in Fakaofo who was always out surfing. He would take a piece of old canoe and ride in on the combers, riding, riding, always riding. He lived seaward, with his mother Kai.

Lagoonward, not far from Kai's house, there lived an old woman Kui who had three daughters: their names were Tauluga, Taulalo, and Sina. These daughters liked that handsome Nonu.

One day Tauluga came across the land to Nonu's house, but he was out on the surf. His mother came to the reef and called him: 'Someone has come to see you.' 'Who is it that has come?' When Nonu heard Tauluga's name he called out, 'Send her away, I don't like her.'

On another day Taulalo came to see if Nonu was home, but he was always out surf-riding with his friends. His mother called him in, but when he heard Taulalo's name he answered, 'Send her away, I don't like her.'

On another day came Sina the youngest, and Kai called out to Nonu from the reef, 'Here is Sina.' He rode in on the next wave, came to the house to meet her.

Sina was only a young girl, she was not yet ready. She came to live with Nonu and Kai and she treated Nonu as a father. She grew up. One day Nonu touched her, asked her, 'Am I like a father or a husband to you?' Then they-two went off on an inland path, they went into the bush together; then they married and a great feast was held, with dancing also. Many leis were made, there were necklaces of flowers for everyone. All the relations came to the feast, Sina's sisters came, Tauluga and Taulalo were there.

They-two sent a message to Nonu: 'We would like some of the

leis.' But Nonu disliked those sisters, he answered, 'All the neck-laces belong to Sina.'

Those sisters became enraged. After they had spoken together they stole Nonu's soul and ran away with it.

Nonu looked dead. Everyone thought he was dead. Not Sina. She said he was only asleep and had him carried to his house, wrapped him up there in mats: 'No one is to touch him. No one disturb him while I am away.'

Then she ran after her sisters to their mother's house, but they had left, had gone away to the family's coconut trees: 'They are gone with a boy to climb for nuts.'

'Please call them back for me, O Kui.'

Kui did so. She pretended to be ill, and called out to her daugh-ters, 'I am nearly dead.' When they heard this Tauluga and Taulalo hurried back to their mother who was ill, but when they saw it was only Sina who had come they were enraged, and turned away. Their mother said, 'You-two must wait and hear what Sina wants.' 'I want my husband's soul which you-two took away.' Then Kui told those girls to give it back.

There was a basket of souls hanging in the rafters, so Tauluga reached up and took one out, threw it across to Sina. Said Sina, 'That is not Nonu's—I can see his, moving in the bottom of the basket.' Taulalo therefore took one out, but Sina would not catch it. 'Not my husband's.' In the end they gave her Nonu's soul. She wrapped it up and took it home.

On her way home the soul asked Sina, 'Why is the path so muddy?' Said Sina, 'There has been some heavy rain.' Farther on the soul said, 'I can smell a maile tree.' Said Sina, 'Yes, someone has been making a skirt from its leaves.' After this the soul smelt blood but Sina said, 'We are passing a place where they have been cutting up a turtle.'

Sina got back to her home and found that no one had interfered with Nonu's body, it was still wrapped up. She untied the mats, took Nonu's big toe, and began putting his soul back. She pressed it through his toe, up through his legs until it reached his head: Nonu lived again.

Nonu and Sina lived quietly together. The tale is finished.

THE EITU WHO WENT
AS A MAN'S WIFE

RIUTA and her husband Tuikoro were living quietly together. One day they took their fish-traps and paddled out to a coral patch in the lagoon to catch some fish. They put their traps in the water, waited, lifted one, and emptied the fish into their canoe. Said the husband, 'You can scale them. But when you wash your hands, do it on the outrigger-side, do not wash them on the open side.' Then he dived down to the other traps to see if there were any fish in them. While he was below Riuta disobeyed him. She washed her hands on the open side.

A calm patch came on the water. Out of this calm patch an eitu-woman floated up, climbed on board, came to Riuta, threw her to the stern and took her place.

Then Tuikoro came up again, shook the water from his eyes, came with his trap to the canoe. He saw *two* women! Both the same. Their faces both the same.

Said the eitu, 'I here am Riuta. That one there is an eitu who came up from below.'

Riuta said, 'Do not believe her. I, here, am Riuta. I am sitting here because she threw me here, then took my place.'

Then Tuikoro went to Riuta his wife in anger, pushed her overboard. Thought she was an eitu.

Riuta was pregnant, and she floated. She floated away and landed on the islet Pumatahati in the south.

Then her husband and the eitu paddled off, they went to live on his land at Torongahai in the north. They dwelt there quietly together.

Riuta at Pumatahati gave birth, she had twin boys, she called them Manu tuia and Manu toa. Those boys grew up.

One day they asked their mother to hew them a canoe. Riuta felled a tree, she hewed a canoe for them. When it was finished she plaited a sail, she made a mast, a bailing scoop, paddles, booms, and rigging. When all was done that mother said to her sons: 'You-two do your fishing here in the lagoon at Pumatahati. Do not go up north. Up there, an eitu lives.'

Those boys ignored their mother's word. They sailed up north, went fishing there. When they reached Torongahai the eitu was on the lagoon-shore, beating coconut husks for fibre to make string. The boys sailed up, they let their sail down, chanted this:

> We two, we two, Manu tuia and Manu toa,
> We are just fishing on our reef,
> We have left our mother Riuta behind;
> Our father is Tuikoro.

That eitu who was beating fibre heard the chanting, heard the boys. She ran to her man: 'E, Tuikoro, Tuikoro! Two boys on the lagoon are saying a chant that has your name in it.'

'Go back and hear the words, return and tell me.'

The eitu went back, she got the chant, told Tuikoro what it said.

'Then go and call them, call them here.'

The eitu did as she was told, the two boys came. They said their words again, and Tuikoro thought within himself: 'These two are sons of mine. That woman whom I pushed overboard was truly Riuta.'

Then he said to the eitu, 'You go inside the house while I speak to these two.' The eitu went.

Then Tuikoro closed the door. The eitu complained, 'The door of the house is shut. How can I get out?' But Tuikoro answered, 'It is shut indeed, it will be opened though.' Then quickly Tuikoro fetched a burning stick, he ran around the house and set it all on fire, the flames leapt up, the whole house burned. The eitu cried inside. She died, that eitu, died in Tuikoro's flames. Those boys were glad.

Then all three went off in their canoe, the canoe Riuta made. They sailed to the south, toward Pumatahati. Said Tuikoro to his sons, 'When we are close to your mother's land, let down the sail and put me in it. Put the fish-trap also in the sail. You-two can then go ashore to your mother and ask her to come and carry your sail because it is wet. We will make this surprise to your mother. Do not be long.'

The two boys landed, hurried to their house, to Riuta's house. 'E Riuta! Come and carry our sail which is wet! It is too heavy for us! Come quickly!'

Then Riuta scolded them. 'You two are bad, you are disobedient boys. I told you that you must not sail up north.'

She went to the lagoon, took up the sail which she had made. The sail was heavy, was not wet. Then Riuta knew that Tuikoro was in the sail—Tuikoro who had pushed her overboard, had not believed her.

She carried that bundle inland, threw it hard upon the stones. Tuikoro groaned, died.

That is all. Just a tale that people tell. It is concluded.

THE LOBSTER AND
THE FLOUNDER

LOBSTER said to Flounder: 'Let us-two hide from each other, see who is best at that.' Flounder agreed to play this game.

Lobster went to a hole in the coral, hid his body; but his feelers stuck out, he could not hide them. Flounder knew where he was, found him.

Said Flounder: 'Now it is my turn.' He stirred up a cloud of mud and scooted into it. Then he returned to Lobster's side, so quietly that Lobster did not know he was there.

'Here I am sir, Lobster!'

Lobster was so angry at being beaten that he stamped on the fish and smashed him flat. Cried Flounder: 'Now I've got one eye in the mud!' Therefore Lobster gouged it out for him and roughly stuck it back on top.

This is the reason why men tread on the Flounder, but can always see the Lobster's feelers outside his hole.

THE WOMEN AND THE BATS*

IN former time land this the land of females only; not any males. Dwell the female, bear the female; dwell another female, bear the female. The children [were] of the bats, females only. Not a male may come. Make husbands only from the bats. Do, do thus.

Came the man, came from Motulava; his name, 'Swift Whistling'. Came, went then to live with the females, house with the females. Look then at his anchor is standing in enclosure from seawards with his stone coconut. Married to the female in Fareautaka. Thereupon [she] make her children from the male. Go there the bats to females; by him slain bats and take them to roast in the fire to eat for himself. By him eaten then in land this. Goes then the male to his land, abides, goes then to Motulava, are dwelling his children in land this. That the story of the bats it.

* From a literal translation.

NEW ZEALAND AND
THE CHATHAMS

A very old carving from New Zealand

MATAORA AND NIWAREKA

We Maori people tell how Mataora in this world married a woman from below, and after visiting her parents' land brought back the art of tattooing to the World of Light; as also the pattern-cloak called Rangi haupapa. But afterwards, none but spirits could return from that place.

MATAORA learned the art of tattooing in the world below and brought it back with him to this world, Te Ao tu roa.

One day when he was lying asleep in the sun a party of turehu came by and they stopped to gaze at him. These young women were not of this world and they had never before seen such a handsome young chief. The turehu are a strange small people with pale skin and fair hair which is very long. Their country is in Rarohenga, below this world. They are turehu when they visit Te Ao tu roa; in Rarohenga they are spirits. Those turehu gathered round Mataora admiring his good looks, and their presence woke him up. He was so surprised that he asked them, 'Are you females?' and they answered, 'Are you male?' He therefore showed them. Then he asked them, 'Come to my place,' and they did so. But they would not go inside Mataora's house, neither would they eat any of the food he offered them. It was cooked food, they had never seen it. They said that it was rotten, and they would not touch it. So Mataora had to get raw things for them.

After they had eaten Mataora wished to entertain his guests. He therefore brought out his maipi and did some showing off with it. He pranced and leapt about, he pulled faces and stuck out his tongue until it covered his chin, and he tossed that maipi in the air as if it were no heavier than a flaxstick. Afterwards they tried to lift the maipi themselves, and they marvelled at Mataora's strength.

In return the turehu gave Mataora an exhibition of their dancing. They formed up in two rows, and one of them came to the front to lead them, and Mataora heard them say her name, it was Niwareka. They performed an item that was unlike any dance Mataora had seen. They held each other's hands in pairs and danced and sang, and then two of them joined their hands and held them high while all the others trooped through underneath. Those turehu had so much hair that it hung to their waists and covered them. The skirts they wore were made of seaweed.

Now Niwareka was the daughter of Uetonga, who was descended from Hine nui te Po, the goddess of night, and her husband Ruaumoko, god of earthquake. Niwareka was beautiful; Mataora wanted her. When the time came for the turehu to leave his house he persuaded Niwareka to remain there and be his wife. They lived quietly together and were content, even though Mataora was a man of this world and ate cooked food, and Niwareka belonged to the world below. But one day something happened which made Mataora jealous, and he hit his wife.

Niwareka was so upset that she could hardly speak. In her country the husbands did not strike the wives, and Niwareka was so frightened when Mataora struck her that she left that house and returned to her people.

Mataora regretted what he had done. He grieved for Niwareka, and he missed her greatly. At length he decided to go and look for her. He went first to Tahuaroa, it is in the very distant land called Irihia, where the immense mountain called Hikurangi stands with his head in the heavens. The people there had no news of Niwareka, so he went on to Poutererangi, the entrance to Rarohenga, which is guarded by Te Kuwatawata. He asked that person, 'Have you seen a young woman pass this way?' 'What is the token?' asked Te Kuwatawata. 'She has fair hair,' said Mataora. 'She passed here, weeping as she went,' Te Kuwatawata answered; and Mataora was heartened by this news, that Niwareka was weeping yet.

Te Kuwatawata allowed Mataora to pass the entrance to the world below, carrying with him his supply of the food of this world, and as he continued on he met Tiwaiwaka the fantail, who flitted about in front of his face and was pleasant to him. 'What are the people doing, below here?' Mataora asked this bird. 'They are busy with the kumara crops,' said Tiwaiwaka. 'Some are building houses, some are fishing. Some are flying kites, and some are at work tattooing.' Mataora then asked Tiwaiwaka if he had seen Niwareka. 'She passed by here with swollen eyes and hanging lips,' Tiwaiwaka answered, and Mataora went on his way with a hopeful heart.

He continued travelling until he reached the house of Uetonga, whose name all men know: he was the tattoo expert of the world below, and the origin and source of all the tattoo designs in this world.

Uetonga was at work tattooing the face of a chief. This chief was lying on the ground with his hands clenched and his toes twitching while the father of Niwareka worked at his face with a bone of many sharpened points, and Mataora was greatly surprised to see that blood was flowing from the cheeks of that chief. Mataora had his own moko, it was done here in the world above, but it was painted on with ochre and blue clay. Mataora had not seen such moko as Uetonga was making, and he said to him, 'You are doing that in the wrong way, O old one. We do not do it thus.'

'Quite so,' replied Uetonga, 'you do not do it thus. But yours is the way that is wrong. What you do above there is tuhi, it is only fit for wood. You see,' he said, putting forth his hand to Mataora's cheek, 'it will rub off.' And Uetonga smeared Mataora's make-up with his fingers and spoiled its appearance. And all the people sitting round them laughed, and Uetonga with them.

'Oh, the upper world, its adornments are only painted on, like rafter patterns,' Uetonga said. 'Listen, you from the world above,

Tattoo designs on a Maori chief

the kinds of adornment are these: there is taniko weaving for the handsomest of cloaks; there is wood carving for houses and weapons, and for great canoes; and there is moko such as this. These things remain, these things go in. But that on your face does not go in, it is only tuhi. It can be rubbed away.'

So Mataora reflected, and then he said to Uetonga: 'Sir, you are right. You must now make my moko properly. Make it as you have made that man's.'

And so they sent away the chief whose face was bleeding, and Uetonga's helpers washed Mataora's face-paint off and made him ready. Then Uetonga took his chisel of bone, he dipped its points into his mixture of kauri soot and shark oil, and he set to work, he began the moko on Mataora's chin and his lower lip. Mataora clenched his hands with the pain, and his legs writhed; but he was determined that he would not let them see how much it hurt him. His lips swelled up around his mouth, and when Mataora grew thirsty from the pain he was unable to drink. Therefore they brought him water in a gourd and poured it through a funnel into his mouth, it was a finely carved wooden funnel, the first original of all those that our tattooing artists use.

The pain of that work it made Mataora nearly faint. To strengthen him therefore some women of the place sat near him and sang this song that soothes the pain of moko:

> We are sitting eating together,
> We are watching the designs
> On the eyebrows and nose of Mataora.
> They are crooked as a lizard's leg.
>
> Be tattooed with the chisel of Uetonga, Mataora!
> Be not impatient to go to the girl
> Who brings you sweet raupo shoots.
>
> On the face of the man who pays his utu
> Let the designs be handsome.

On the man who is mean when paying
Make them crooked, leave them open.

Let our songs lull the pain
And make you brave, Mataora.

E hiki Tangaroa!
E hiki Tangaroa!

Then to show those people that he could endure that pain,
Mataora sang them a song of his own, a song confused:

Niwareka!
Niwareka, great delight!
Who has caused me
To come to darkness,
To utter darkness!
Speak of the pain
Of the beloved one
Who is at Ahuahu,
And at Rangatira,
And at Nuku moana ariki.
Yes, the bloom of red
Which has swiftly passed
Along the road to Taranaki:
Yes, at Taranaki
Is the loved one,
To whom your nimble feet
Sped swiftly.

Tell it to the west,
Tell it to the south,
Also to the north.
Look at the stars above,
Glance at the glimmering moon.
I am as the tattooed tree.
Say who is thy beloved,

And let the fragrant breath
Of mokimoki fern
Give forth its sweetness
And foster those desires,
That in the midst of waving fronds
I may a listener be.

Now another of Uetonga's daughters heard her sister's name in the song of this man from the world above, and she ran off to Taranaki, where Niwareka was at work on a cloak with taniko border which she was weaving.

'O Niwareka,' said this woman to her sister, 'there is a good-looking man being tattooed by our father, and he sings a song that has your name in it. He is all in a muddle.'

So Niwareka and all the people present got up and went to Uetonga's house to see this man. When they arrived his face was so swollen that he could not see out of his eyes. 'That man looks like Mataora, and his cloak is like one of mine,' said Niwareka. She sat down beside the man and whispered to him, 'Are you Mataora?' He nodded for answer, and stretched out his hands to her, and Niwareka greeted her husband with weeping. Then she gave him water to drink, and pounded some food and gave it to him through that funnel.

When his face was healed Mataora was exceedingly handsome, he was admired by all those people; and in due time he said to Niwareka, 'Let us return to my land now.' But Niwareka did not wish to go with him. She said: 'I must speak to my relations. The ways of Te Ao tu roa are bad ways, the husbands hit the wives in that land. Both worlds have heard of our trouble, Mataora. This world has heard of it as well as Te Ao tu roa.' Afterwards she spoke of the matter to her relations, and Uetonga came to Mataora.

'Perhaps you are thinking of returning to the place from which you came,' said that old one. 'If that is so, let Niwareka stay here. Is it the custom in your world for the men to beat the wives?'

Then Mataora felt ashamed, he hung his head.

Next Niwareka's brother came to Mataora and he said: 'Why do you not stay here, Mata? You are welcome in this land, as you have seen. You must have noticed that the troubles of the world above cause all of its people in the end to come to this land.' After this, Uetonga spoke again to Mataora.

'O Mata,' he said, 'do not let us hear of your repeating what you did in the world above. This world and yours are divided by a great difference. We here live peacefully.'

Then Mataora knew from these words of Uetonga's that the people had decided to let the woman go with him. He made his preparations to depart, and his father-in-law spoke to him again. 'Do not hit Niwa a second time,' that old man said.

'No, Uetonga,' said Mataora, 'the moko I am wearing now will not rub off.'

Mataora and Niwareka set off together for this world above. As a gift on parting Uetonga gave Mataora the cloak called Rangi haupapa, it is the original from which all the taniko cloaks in this world have been copied. Mataora rolled it in his raincloak and laid it across his back in his pack straps.

On this journey those two met Tiwaiwaka, who was still flitting about in the place where Mataora formerly met him, flicking his tail and snapping his beak. Tiwaiwaka detained them until the season of Tatau uruora, that is late spring. Then he sent them on their way together with Ruru the owl, Pekapeka the bat, and also Kiwi, to be their guides. Mataora was afraid these people of the night realm would be killed by the light in Te Ao tu roa, but Tiwaiwaka told him he must always keep them hidden in dark places. It is for this reason that the owl, the bat and the kiwi go out only at night. They are birds that come from the world below.

When Mataora and his woman reached Poutererangi the guardian of that place asked them what they were taking away from Rarohenga to the world above.

'Only these birds and the art of moko, which was taught to me by Uetonga,' Mataora answered.

'What is in that bundle on your back?' Te Kuwatawata asked.

'Only some old clothes,' Mataora replied.

'Oh, Mataora!' said Te Kuwatawata in anger. 'Never again, after this falsehood, shall people of the upper world pass out from this entrance! Henceforward they shall go downward only. None but spirits shall be allowed to go above from here.'

'Yet why is this?' asked Mataora of that man.

'You have the Rangi haupapa with you in that bundle,' Te Kuwatawata replied. 'Why did you not say so?'

And Mataora was ashamed of his forgetfulness. This is why living men have never returned by that road since the time of Mataora and Niwareka. It is the road from which no traveller returns, because Mataora did not declare the Rangi haupapa.

After Mataora had returned to this world the art of moko was known among our people. It was learned by Mataora from Uetonga, and by his descendants it was carried from Havaiki to Tonga nui, to Ra'iatea, to Hui te Rangiora, and to this land also.

The designs that were made on Mataora's face by the chisel of Uetonga were the tiwhana, those lines that sweep over the eyebrows to the temples; the rerepehi, those lines which sweep from the nose around the mouth to the chin; and also the two spirals on the side of the nose of a man, they are called ngu and pongiangia. We call this work moko because of the lizard whose twitching tail is seen in all its curving lines.

TE KANAWA AND THE VISITORS BY FIRELIGHT

THE patupaiarehe are a very numerous people, they have fair hair and skins of light colour, and their faces are papatea, they are not tattooed. They build their forts on the tops of hills, and they had all the best positions when our people came to this land.

The patupaiarehe hold very long council meetings and are loud speakers; they talk a great deal, they chatter all the time, and also sing very loudly. Our ancestors often saw them sitting down in the cultivations, they completely filled them up; but they never did any damage to the ground, the food still grew there. The only harm which they did was to press people to death inside their sleeping-houses, if they had broken a tapu. If the charcoal for the fires inside the sleeping-houses had been taken from a cooking fire, then the patupaiarehe would come in the night and press all the people to death. Even though the window and the door were quite closed up, they came in to punish them, and all the people lay as if they were dead, the gods alone could revive them. Our people were frightened of the patupaiarehe in former times, and took care not to offend them.

One night Te Kanawa, a chief from the Waikato, met a troop of these people on the top of Pukemore, it is a high hill in that district which belonged to them. He was out to hunt kiwi with his dogs, and the clouds came over the moon, the night became so dark that he could not find his way down. Therefore he and his party made a fire to keep them warm and they all lay down. They found a pukatea tree and made their fire beneath it, and they lay in the comfortable hollows between the roots. They laid their cloaks in those places, and the fire was at their feet. And their dogs found places of their own.

Now as Te Kanawa and his friends were dropping off to sleep they all heard the loud voices of many people who were coming toward them through the forest. When Te Kanawa looked up he saw nothing but the shadows of the fire, and so he knew those clamorous people must be patupaiarehe. He was therefore very frightened, and so were all his party, all except the dogs. They continued sleeping. Since there was nowhere to hide, those persons all lay shivering with fright and saying karakia to their gods to send those forest folk away.

Hei tiki, a Maori pendant in nephrite

Those voices grew louder and they came nearer, and Te Kanawa's party drew their cloaks over their heads and wrapped their arms together and shook all over. They hoped that they would not be noticed, in among the roots. Only Te Kanawa kept his head out, for he was their chief; and soon those little people crowded round to look at him, all the women and the men and the children wished to see that handsome man. When a log fell in and the fire blazed up, they rushed away and hid. But when it burned low they all crept out again. They sang a song that ended thus:

> Have you come climbing
> Over the mountain,
> The mountain Tirangi,
> To visit the handsome

Chief of Ngapuhi
Whom we have done with?

Since the patupaiarehe were growing very bold, Te Kanawa was wondering how to make them go away, and he thought of his precious greenstone ornaments. He thought that they might depart if he gave them those. He therefore took his greenstone tiki from his neck, and also the greenstone pendant that hung from his ear, and he held them out. But the patupaiarehe did not rush to snatch these things. They only crowded round to look at them and chatter, trampling all over the cloaks of Te Kanawa's friends, and also walking on the dogs, which shivered in their dreams. They were so delighted with the pretty things that Te Kanawa also took off his shark's tooth ornament from his other ear. Yet they would by no means take them from his hand, and Te Kanawa was indeed frightened lest they touch him soon. He therefore found a stick and stuck it in the ground, and he hung his ornaments upon it for those patupaiarehe. He wished that they would take them and depart.

When the patupaiarehe had finished their song their leader took the shadow of the greenstone pendant, and the shadows also of the tiki and the shark's tooth, and he handed these to his people, and they were very pleased with these, the shadows of Te Kanawa's ornaments. They passed them around from one to another, with little exclamations of their pleasure until every one of them, the men, the women and the children, all had seen them. Then suddenly that whole troop disappeared; nothing more was seen of those people. Also, the fire went out, and Te Kanawa slept.

Those patupaiarehe left behind them Te Kanawa's greenstone and his shark's tooth ornaments; they did not steal them from him. But they took the shadows with them to their village, to show to all the old people. In the morning, just as soon as it was light, Te Kanawa put his ornaments back upon his person, and with his friends he went quickly down that mountain, he hurried away from that place.

KAHUKURA AND THE NET-MAKERS

KAHUKURA was going up along the coast to visit some relations of his in the far north of this land, and he passed a
certain spot where some people had evidently been cleaning a
very large catch of mackerel. This was in that time when our
people caught their fish with hooks and lines. The innards of a
thousand fish were lying on that beach in heaps, with footmarks
beside them; and from these signs Kahukura knew that immense
numbers of tawatawa had been caught by very few people, for
the footmarks were not many. He at first supposed that they must
have been people of the district, and he was amazed at this. But
then he observed that those footprints had been made in the
night, they were night-time footprints. 'This is no ordinary people
who have been fishing here,' said Kahukura. 'Those footprints
are the marks of patupaiarehe. Only patupaiarehe could catch so
many fish with their lines. If men had been here there would be
marks of their canoe, and other signs of men.'

Kahukura decided to come to that spot by night. Instead of
going on to Rangiawhia he therefore returned to a house where
he had spent the previous night, and he told the people there
what he had seen. He asked them to return with him to the beach
after it was dark, but they said they were afraid.

That night he returned alone, Kahukura went to that spot where
the mackerel had been cleaned, and he hid. After a very long time
he heard the voices of many people out on the water. They were
calling to one another, 'The net here! The net here!' and other
things which he could not understand. And while he watched them
in the darkness they ran out something from their canoe which
he could not clearly see. Then they dragged this rope toward the

beach. As they put the rope out in the dark they sang their song: 'Drop the net in the sea at Rangiawhia, haul it at Mamaku.' Those patupaiarehe were cheerful people, they were in good spirits.

Now Kahukura was ehu—he was a fair-skinned man, like the patupaiarehe; and as they were hauling their net up on the beach he got amongst them and pulled at the rope to help. Since his skin was so pale they did not notice him. They got their net ashore without its becoming snagged upon those rocks called Tawatawauia, and this they did many times throughout the night with Kahukura helping them, until there were a thousand fish upon the sand. The name of those rocks means 'Disentangling of mackerel', and Kahukura was astonished that these people did not catch their net upon the sharp points of Tawatawauia.

Before the first light of dawn was felt by those people they had caught all the fish they needed. Then Kahukura noticed that they did not do as men do and divide the catch into separate loads for each. They all took lengths of flax and chose the fish they wanted for themselves, threading them on the flax by the gills and making a loop of it with a slip-knot. 'Hurry up now,' the leader of those people kept shouting to them. 'Hurry and finish before the sun comes up.' If the sun should touch the bodies of the patupaiarehe, then they die.

So Kahukura therefore strung his fish as the patupaiarehe did, but he took only a short length of flax; and he also made his slip-knot with its thick, stiff end—he made it insecure. Therefore every time he filled his loop with fish it came undone, and he had to start again. He made this happen so many times that one of the patupaiarehe kindly put his own fish down to help him. But still his knot gave way. Thus did Kahukura delay those fairies in their work till daylight showed.

As soon as there was light enough to see, the patupaiarehe realized that Kahukura was a man. Then they all became terrified and shivered and shouted, and they fled without a thought for all their fish, or for their net. Kahukura also saw now that their canoes

A New Zealand Maori chief in his dogskin cloak

were not canoes at all but merely flaxsticks.

In this way Kahukura made the patupaiarehe leave their net behind. And by taking some fishing line and copying the stitch, he discovered how a fishing net was made. It was not known by men before.

Kahukura took their net away and used it as a pattern, and he taught his children how to do the same. In this way the art of net-making was learned on the coast near Rangiawhia, and it was passed down to our people from ancient times, so that many fish are caught instead of one or two.

LIZARD-HUSBAND, SCALY SKIN

AT Orawaro near Pakerau there lived a taniwha whose name was Taraka piripiri. He had the shape of a lizard and a scaly skin. He was of such a size that his belly would hold a man with his cloak and all his spears. The taniwha of the sea were kindly demons, but not this person. One day he swallowed two children of a chief at a single meal and their greenstone ornaments with them, their family heirlooms.

Upon a certain occasion a woman who did not know about this taniwha passed close to his hole, and he crawled out and seized her, and he made her his wife. He tied her with a rope and made her eat with him and share his sleeping-mat. Being much afraid of so horrible a husband, this woman one day said to him, 'I have a terrible thirst, husband, I must go to the water.' He would not untie her, but he let out enough rope for her to reach the stream. To show him that she would soon be back she left her skirt behind, and she slithered down that bank. When she reached the water she tied the rope to a tree and ran for her life, she went to her people's village.

When Taraka considered that his wife had had enough to drink he hauled up the rope with his tail, and found her very obstinate indeed, and also very strong. Then he discovered how she had deceived him, and was angry.

When the woman reached the village they gave her clothing. She told her people that after living with the taniwha as his wife she believed the only way to kill him was by means of a poapoa, live bait. Her relations therefore armed themselves with wooden spades, which they sharpened, and all went together to Taraka's house. They went behind it, all but one, who went where the

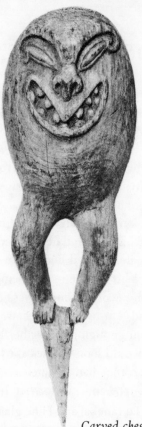

Carved chest to hold a chief's bones

taniwha would see him. This person was their poapoa.

When Taraka piripiri saw this person he crawled from his hole, blinking, and the man began to walk away. He pretended not to notice Taraka. When Taraka had come right out of his hole and the tip of his tail could be seen twitching on the ground, those others rushed upon him with their spades, the whole fifty of them. They cut him up and scraped out his innards, and they found there all the greenstone ornaments of the children and other people he had eaten. They also found that woman's skirt inside the cave.

HINE AND TU

RANGI URU was the wife of Whakaue kaipapa, from whom we name the Whakaue tribe. First she had three sons who were Whakaue's children: their names were Tawake, Ngarara, and Tutea. Then she had a son whose father was Tu Wharetoa (the ancestor of the Tu Wharetoa tribe) and this son was named Tu tanekai. Afterwards Rangi uru had two more children of Whakaue's, and all this family lived here on Mokoia in the middle of lake Rotorua. Whakaue behaved toward Tu tanekai as if he were his own son.

Word came to all these sons of Rangi uru that there was a young woman of high rank and great beauty living across the lake at Owhata, on the shore facing this island. This young woman could not be approached. Her father was the high chief Umukaria and she was kept apart by her parents to be given to a chief whom they would choose. Those sons of Rangi uru all desired her.

Soon all the sons saw Hine moa at the assemblies of the Rotorua people. When the peoples were gathered they saw her in the meeting-house. Then Tu tanekai and Hine glanced at one another; and Hine looked down.

Tu and his friend Tiki used to play on their flutes by night on a platform which they had built on the slopes of Kaiweka, here on Mokoia. Tu's instrument was the putorino, Tiki's the koauau. When they climbed the hill in the evening and played there, the sound went over the water to Owhata, where it was heard by Hine. And Hine who had seen that handsome person in the meeting-house said, 'That is Tu's flute.'

There was a very great assembly of all the peoples. The tribes came from far, and remained at Rotorua. Tu saw Hine many times

and felt desire. Hine looked down. Tu was thinking, 'If I press her hand, will she press mine? But I may not please her.' Hine was thinking, 'If I send one of my friends to tell him of my desire he may not be pleased with me.'

After they-two had met each other many times and glanced often, Tu sent a messenger to tell Hine. Said Hine then, 'Eh hu! Then we both do.'

Afterwards the tribes returned to their homes, and all of Whakaue's people got into their canoes and returned here to Mokoia. Said the elder brothers of Tu, 'Which of us by signs has known the love of Hine moa?' One said, 'It is I.' Another said, 'But I have.' They also asked Tu, those sons of Whakaue. He replied, 'I have pressed Hine's hand and she pressed mine.' This made those elder brothers angry and they jeered at Tu. 'Do you think she would take any notice of you?' Therefore Tu told Whakaue of this matter, and he said, 'She will come to me. She will come to the sound of my flute in the night.'

Always Tu and Tiki played their music in the night.

'Tu's flute was the putorino . . .'

But Hine's people dragged up all their canoes, dragged them where Hine could not haul them back.

Therefore Hine sat and thought. She listened to the putorino of Tu and she thought, 'Then I will swim across.' Then Hine took some large dry gourds and string, and made two floats, a float for each side of her. She went out to the rock called Iri iri kapua; and into the water at Wairerewai, there she threw her clothes off. Supported by her gourds she swam to the sunken tree-stump Hinewhata. There she rested, at Hine's Platform. Then she swam on again. In the darkness her only guide was the putorino of Tu.

'Tiki's flute was the koauau'

By that she swam on to Mokoia and came out of the water by the hot spring Waikimihia.

Hine got into the pool to warm herself, she was cold. A servant of Tu tanekai came with a gourd for drinking-water from the lake. Hine made a deep voice like a man's: 'Who is that water for?' 'It is for Tu.' 'Give it to me, then.' And she broke the gourd on a rock. That servant returned to Tu tanekai. 'Your gourd is broken.' 'Who broke it?' 'The man in the hot pool.' 'Go back then and fetch me water.'

The servant went, drew water again, and Hine in a man's voice asked him for the gourd. 'I am thirsty.' Then she dropped it and it broke. These matters occurred again between these persons.

At length the servant told Tu tanekai, 'Your gourds are all broken.' 'By whom?' 'By the man in the bath.' 'Who is he?' 'I cannot tell. He is a stranger.'

So Tu took up his weapon and went to the pool, crying, 'Who broke my gourds?' And Hine, knowing his voice, hid under the overhanging rocks of the hot spring. Tu searched. He groped in the darkness about that pool. At last he felt a leg, and was angry. 'Who is this?' 'It is I—Hine.'

'It is *you*! Then let us go to my house.' Then Hine went with Tu to his house and they-two spent the night upon his mat.

In the morning all the people came out and lit their cooking fires and they ate. But Tu remained within. Tu was not up. Said Whakaue, 'This is not like Tu. Go and wake him.'

The man who was sent slid back the door. He saw four feet! This man ran back to Whakaue: 'I saw four feet in Tu's house.' He was sent again. 'Go and find out who it is with Tu.' That person did so, and he cried out to the village, 'Here is Hine moa! Here is Hine in Tu's house.'

Then the elder brothers of Tu were jealous and amazed at what was seen. And Hine remained with Tu. She is the ancestor of many persons of this place.

Afterwards Tu said to Whakaue, 'I am ill with grief for my friend

Tiki. Every night we played our flutes together. Now we do not do that.'

'What is your meaning?'

'I am referring to my young sister Tupa. Let her be given as a woman for my friend, for Tiki.' Whakaue consented, and this was done.

It is the end of this story of Hine and Tu.

MANAII AND THE SPEARS

MANAII was a chief in Havaiki. His children were born there, and there in that land he grew old and bent.

Hard trouble rose between the tribes, therefore Manaii ordered the making of spears. He said to his sons: 'Go into the bush and cut down an akepiri tree. When you have felled it split it into eighty pieces. Make those pieces into spears.'

Therefore the sons of Manaii felled the akepiri tree and split it into eighty pieces, and of them each one had a piece; and they adzed those pieces into eighty spears.

But the heart-wood of that tree remained; they could not adze the crooked heart-wood, it was twisted in the grain. They returned to their home and said to Manaii, 'We cannot chip the heart to make it straight; the wood is crooked in the grain.'

'Go again to chip the heart of your tree to finish it properly.' But those sons of Manaii could not chip the heart to make it straight.

'How many spears then have you?'

'We have eighty.'

Said Manaii, 'That is enough, that every one of you may have a spear.' After this the sons of Manaii threw away the heart-wood of the tree.

Then Niwa the wife of Manaii spoke to the youngest of her sons, her last-born child, to Kahukaka: 'Go you and adze the heart of the tree of your elder brothers. Go at early dawn lest they should see you.' Then Niwa showed her youngest son the way to adze that wood, she gave him the pattern secretly, and said, 'Go you and chip it quickly, come back soon. Then your elder brothers will not know.'

Kahukaka went, he found the timber of his elder brothers lying

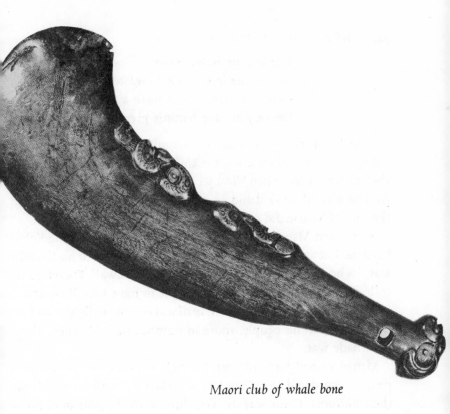

Maori club of whale bone

and he quickly chipped that wood, he followed carefully the teaching of his mother; he chipped the heart into a well-made spear, most smoothly worked. He left it and returned.

Afterwards those elder brothers came to the place and saw the work. They were amazed, the adzing was so skilled; it was more beautiful than theirs, and they asked one another, 'Who has chipped this heart-wood which we could not?'

They took the spear to their home, and showed it to Manaii, and all the people gazed at it and asked who worked this wood so well. But that was not discovered. For Niwa concealed the sacred knowledge of her youngest son.

Then the people went about asking, 'Who has done this?'

One night Manaii heard Niwa make a saying about her youngest son. She said this word:

You are my Kahukaka nui,
Got by me in the kakahi wastes.
Hence you have come forth a man,
Hence you have become great.

Thus Niwa spoke about her son Kahukakanui.

Now Kahukakanui was not the child of Manaii but was begun in the kakahi wastes, when Niwa went there secretly with Porotehiti. And he was full of skill and knowledge, this son of Porotehiti. But the sons of Manaii did not know the adzing of heart-wood.

Now when Manaii heard the word of his wife concerning Kahukaka, he knew that Niwa had done a wrong thing, and his thought was, 'Who has done this wrong thing with Niwa?' Therefore he collected seven-score men, and he went to fight with Porotehiti.

When Porotehiti heard that Manaii was coming to fight with him he gathered all his people, more in number than Manaii's. They-two made war.

Manaii rushed forward with his eighty spears, and Porotehiti's people turned and ran. Then Manaii spiked them all in the holes in their bottoms. Great was the slaughter made by Manaii of Porotehiti's people.

And Porotehiti himself was wounded in the eye by Manaii's spear. For that reason he made the chant which healed his eye, the whai konehi; it is the chant our people use when anyone is wounded in the eye, by a spear or by a splinter.

In this fighting between Manaii and Porotehiti in Havaiki, many were lost on both sides. Through this was the cause of man-eating.

It was through Manaii also that war grew with the people of Havaiki, and Manaii's evil clung to them until they sailed away to this land, to Rekohu.

UGLY-UGLY! FRIZZLED-HEADS, FRIZZLED-HEADS!

OLD Muru whenua with her people and her grandchildren dwelt in their homes. One day word was brought to them about two beautiful girls, Rau kata uri and Rau kata mea. These girls were not of a different people, they were of their own race. But when the grandsons of Muru whenua went to those girls to get them to be their lovers the girls would not look at them. They said: 'Who do these two ugly frizzled-heads think they have come to visit? Go away, you two! Go home! We don't want to look at things like you. Ugly-ugly! Frizzled-heads, frizzled-heads! Frizzled to your bellies!'

And the sons went away from those jeering girls and told the tale to their grandmother. 'We have been called bad names by our girl-friends,' said Ngongoro kino and Ngongoro i takupu. 'They called us "ugly-ugly"; they called us "frizzled-heads". They said our hair is like our other hair.'

Then Muru whenua said to them: 'Go you two to your ancestor, the feather-box of Muru whenua.' Those grandsons therefore went to the well-carved feather box, the kawa in which the old one kept her treasures. They slid back the sacred lid, and crept inside and slept, as they were bidden. After a while their grandmother sang this chant:

> Broad flat face,
> Broad round face,
> Open then the kawa of Muru whenua.
> Now you stand free from all ill taints,
> All beautiful you are.

Forth goes my son,
Gotten from beyond the Earth.
Grow, increase with the winds of your birth.

Then the singing of Muru whenua for her grandchildren ceased, and when the children were let forth their heads were smooth, the hair of their heads was long and wavy, and their faces had become small and neat.

When those two young ladies heard that their lovers had become beautiful—O! they-two came to their lovers, to the two indeed whom they had formerly despised.

Maori feather-box (inverted) with its lid

But when Rau kata uri and Rau kata mea came to their lovers—
Pu!—Ngongoro kino and Ngongoro i takupu jumped up and
dashed away, shouting at them from a distance, 'We will have
nothing to do with you-two. You are nasties! You are stinkers! Go
away! Go home! You-two despised us-two.'

Those two young women went, threw themselves over a cliff,
died.

'FROM DARKNESS TO LIGHT'

RAO'S DIRGE FOR HERSELF

The lament improvised by Rao on knowing that her husband desires to eat her shaven head.

Root:

Alas, how close our thoughts have been!
　O, weep, O, weep for me.
Farewell, we part for ever soon,
　O, weep for me.
How we have talked together, we alone!
Have you no pity, no relenting?
My time grows short, my end is near.
　O, weep, now weep for me.
　Aue, aue—karireira e!

First offshoot:

O, weep for me!
The sun goes down behind our lands.
Have you no pity, none for me?
There stands our well used cooking-place—
　He is splitting up the firewood:
　Aue! It is to cook this flesh of mine!
O, weep, O, weep for me.
Farewell we-two, we-two farewell!

Second offshoot:

O, weep for me!
How happily we used to lie
In all the pleasurings of love—
Two heads like one!

I my father's favourite girl
And you the helpful son-in-law,
Through all the famine times.
   O, weep, O, weep for me.
   Farewell we-two, we-two farewell!

Third offshoot:

   O, weep for me!
I am but a big fresh fish
Just caught—
A fine cavalla, right for grilling on our fire.
And husband you—you are as fair
As breadfruit-cloth bleached in the sun.
   O, weep, O, weep for me.
   Farewell, farewell—we-two farewell.

Fourth offshoot:

   O, weep for me!
My husband, look—
Leave the men's house and these ideas,
Come back to me!
   O, weep, yes, weep for me.
   Aue, aue—karireira e!

THE COMING OF TUTE

THE pe'e manuiri or 'visitor's song' which follows is the libretto of a musical play commemorating Captain Cook's short call at Mangaia on March 29, 1777, and it allows us to observe the 'discovery' of a Pacific island from the native viewpoint. It is the only known native composition which does this. Complete with its references in the native text to 'Beretane', 'Tute' himself, and Mai, the *Resolution*'s Tahitian interpreter (the famous 'Omai' of the *Journals*), it is a genuine piece of Polynesian oral literature, and a spirited example of a form of entertainment that was also known elsewhere, and very well known to Cook himself. We even know its author's name: it was composed about 1780 by Tioi (a Mangaian warrior who later lost his life in battle) as one of the items in a night-long entertainment known as a kapa. It was collected on the island nearly eighty years afterwards by the missionary W. Wyatt Gill. The present account gives what is needed for an understanding of the text. There is some further information in the Notes.

Cook spent only a few hours off Mangaia, and did not land. The reef at Avarua was treacherous, as it mostly is, and in any case some hundreds of natives made the beach a fence of spears. However, some men swam out to the ship's boat while Cook was looking for a landing-place, and later a young chief named Mourua paddled to the *Resolution* and was persuaded to go on board—to be given a knife and other things, to have his portrait drawn by the expedition's artist (see next page), and to stumble over one of the goats. He took back word that 'Tute' was the chief of the vast canoe and Beretane was his land. He would have learned these facts through Mai—whose name was got wrong by Cook and later by all of

*Mourua, the only Mangaian brave enough
to go on board the 'Resolution' in 1777*

London society, but not by Mourua. ('o Mai' is two words in effect, and was the answer to the question, 'What is your name?' The 'o' is a particle indicating the nominative case.) Mourua regarded the ship as belonging to Cook and Mai. For artistic reasons, perhaps, the piece makes no reference to the second ship in the expedition, the *Adventure*.

Gill does not tell us whether he saw this piece performed. As explained in the Notes, he may have preferred it to be thought by his brethren in London that he had only been told about it. At any rate his excellent commentary (four times as long as the text, and packed with detail still remembered after three generations) enables us to imagine the magnificent night-time entertainment of which it formed about one-twentieth part—a torchlight affair from dark to dawn involving ten-score dancers, six poets, hundreds of flambeau-holders, and a year's preparation by the island's dancing-masters, caterers, and beauty experts.

This long preparation was necessary, Gill explains, 'first, for the making of the songs and the rehearsal of the performers; secondly, for the growth of taro, etc., etc., requisite for the grand feasting, which is a necessary sequel to any assembly in the mind of a Polynesian; and, thirdly, for the very important purpose of blanching the complexions and fattening the persons of those who were to take part on the occasion. The point of honour was to be the fairest and fattest of any present.'

This particular kapa took place a few years after Cook's visit. Constant warfare in the meantime had prevented such costly entertainments, but at last a victorious chief named Poito was in a position to mount a suitable display. Writes Gill: 'A level spot was selected for the festival and carefully weeded. From one end to the other, a spacious canopy of plaited green coconut leaves protected the many hundreds present from the heavy dews of night—as such entertainments never took place by day.'

Mangaian kapa dances were either for men or for women—never both together—and Poito's was for men, 'the entire remain-

ing population being present as spectators and flambeaux-holders.'
Twenty items were needed for one kapa, and they were often
encored. The show began at sunset, was interrupted for an enormous feast at midnight, and continued until the day-star appeared,
when the final item was produced. 'Six artists,' says Gill, 'were
usually employed to compose the songs, and arrange the whole
proceedings.'

The words of this 'visitor's song' were slowly chanted (not sung,
in our sense of the word) in a 'pleasing though monotonous tone';
sometimes, says Gill, by the master-of-ceremonies alone from a
raised platform, sometimes by all the cast. The chanted opening
section here called 'Introduction' (which alludes to a previous
foreign visitor named Tamaeu) had neither drums nor dancers.
These only entered—with immense effect, as Gill's footnote
suggests—after the 'First Call', when the dancing began.

Three types of drum were used: the kaara, a very large slit-drum
of hollowed miro wood suspended on cords from a tree, 'prettily
carved all over' and capable of deafening loudness when correctly
struck (the name means 'wakener'); the pa'u, a tall cylindrical
drum with a tympanum made of shark's skin, which was played
on with the finger-tips; and the riro, being two lengths of dry
hibiscus wood lightly struck with sticks of ironwood—a sort of
two-note xylophone. The cross-rhythms in Polynesian drumming
are tremendously exciting. The kaara that was used in this performance still existed in Gill's time on Mangaia (1851–73)—'and is
used by the police in drumming their prisoners to court.'

Tamaeu, the visitor alluded to in the opening lines, crossed to
Mangaia from the small island of Manuae (150 miles away) a year
or two before Cook's visit. Normally, says Gill, the Mangaians
regarded all strangers as mortal foes, to be opposed and slain if
possible: 'The only exceptions recorded by tradition are those
referred to in this song. Tamaeu and his friends escaped because
they carried a priceless treasure of red parakeet feathers for adorn-
ing the gods.'

by Tioi of Mangaia
(about 1780)

VISITOR'S SONG

INTRODUCTION

Chorus: Great Tangaroa and Tu assist
           In the caulking of Tamaeu's canoe.
             O, the noise! The workmen's noise!

Solo: Caulk the seams! Caulk the seams!   (1)
Chorus: Ngu! Ngu!
Solo: Here's plenty of fibre!
           Good coconut fibre!
Chorus: Ngu! Ngu!
Chorus: Then grant, O god and ruler of the winds,
           Good sailing weather.
           Calm the reef! Make safe the entrance!
           Send your servants—
           Obedient winds!

Chorus in *'This way! This way!*
falsetto: *'No, no, that way! Over there!'*   (2)

Solo: O that vessel! Mighty vessel!
           Off the Avarua reef.   (3)
           Get out the paddles!
           Man canoes!

---

(1) The soloist held a stone chisel and a wooden mallet with which he vigorously showed his workmen what to do; and they struck chisels into softwood logs which lay the whole length of the dancing ground. The scene was encored.

(2) Re-enacting the confusion observed by swimming natives among the officers in the ship's boat—who were undoubtedly being plied with false directions in the hope of luring them on to the reef. The *falsetto* throughout, says Gill, 'is an absurd mimicry of the language of the visitors'.

(3) Avarua was the name of the reef-passage where Cook's officers might have landed.

Cook and his officers watch a human sacrifice in Tahiti

Chorus (using falsetto):	They say they're Britons— *'We're from Britain.'* Yes they're Britons, they are Britons, Beretane is their land. —And here is Mai. They talk through Mai: *'O Mai! O Mai!'*
Chorus:	We come in hundreds, (4) Warriors! Hundreds! With our spears put up to fight We lusty people of Mangaia Will destroy this boastful ship: Kua ta Mangaia, Kua ta te pa'i!

THE FIRST CALL (for the drums and the dancing to begin)

Solo: Tangaroa has sent a ship,
                It has come bursting through the sky—   (5)

Solo: And here's a stranger—call him Mai!

Chorus: It is Cook who's come to visit—
                Call him Tute—bringing Mai.

Solo: Who has come, then?

Chorus: —What a boatload!
                Gabbling boatload! Hear them jabber:

                'Ouaraurau, raurau, raurau,
                'Ouaraurau, raurauae.'   (6)

Solo: No good counting them, that boatload,
                They are foreigners—and Mai!

Solo: Blow then, softly—softly, softly!

Chorus: Blow ye softly, holes-in-sky.   (7)
                Send your gentle winds to waft them,
                Calm the seas and waft them nigh.

Solo: Where, then, are they?

Chorus: Yonder! Yonder!

Solo: Yes, they are there! Aere mai!   (8)

Chorus: Aere mai, you Beretane!
                Come on Britons, Aere mai!

---

(4) 'Here a mimic attack was made with real spears upon imaginary invaders.' (Gill's note.)

(5) Hitherto, as Gill explains, no drum had been beaten nor any dancing performed. Hence 'the call' now is for dancing and music, beginning at the words 'come bursting through' and pausing a while on the mention of 'Beretane' (at the end of the section). After a moment's rest the master of ceremonies gave the 'second call' in a soft and plaintive voice, and when he pronounced the word 'bursting' for a second time, 'the whole two hundred performers were on their feet once more, chanting and performing the remarkable evolutions which they term a Kapa, or dance.'

The sky, to the Mangaians, was a vault of solid material. It was through this that the visitors had burst.

(6) 'Ouaraurauae', in the native text, is Mangaian for the 'jabber-jabber' of the Beretane people.

(7) There were holes in the sky through which the gods amused themselves by blowing the various winds.

(8) 'Aere mai!'—'Welcome', or 'Greetings'; (cf. New Zealand Maori 'Haere mai'.)

THE SECOND CALL *(for the dancing to lead off)*

Solo:	Tangaroa has sent a ship,
	It has come bursting through the sky—
Solo:	And here's a stranger—call him Mai!
Chorus:	It is Cook who's come to visit—
	Call him Tute—bringing Mai.
Solo:	Who has come, then?
Chorus:	—What a boatload!
	Hear them jabber—'Jabber-jabber-jabber!'
	'Ouaraurau, Ouaraurau,
	'Ouaraurau, raurauae!'
Solo:	No good counting them, that boatload,
	They are foreigners—so's Mai!
Solo:	Lord of the winds—
Chorus:	— send down some seabird
	On their shoulders; hold them nigh!
	(Here the rhythm changes for a comic display of Bere-
	tane paddling—wrong way round)
Solo:	Splash go the oars!
Chorus:	—Splash, Splash!
Solo:	Splash go the oars!
Chorus:	They are white-faced!
	Beretane!
	They are white-faced Beretane!

CONCLUSION

Chorus:	People talking very strangely
	Have arrived from far away.
Solo:	Far away? and talking strangely?
	Of what sort then, what are they?
Chorus:	They are god-like, something god-like. (9)
	Beretane—far away!

---

(9) The whiteness of the Beretanes' skin betokened divinity in Polynesia, since the gods are naturally the forebears of the aristocracy (see the Introduction, and Gill's reference on p. 355). Hence, in part, the tragic misunderstanding that led to Cook's death in Hawaii two years later.

Chorus: A mighty chief is off our reef,
Cook's ship and Mai's is here today!
Solo: Of what sort, what sort are they?
Chorus: A god-like people! White-faced people!
White-faced people—o murenga!
White-faced! White-faced!
God-like! God-like!
Thing unheard-of, till this day.

CANOE-LAUNCHING SONG

On the day that Captain Cook discovered Atiu a shore party spent some hours among friendly natives, but was so late returning that the ship's guns were fired, to create alarm. This chant, collected nearly a century later, recalls the guns.

Solo:	O I'm bound for Great Tahiti
	O you gods, O Tu, O Tangaroa!
	We're all provisioned—she'll be right!
Chorus:	You there, haul there—haul away!
Solo:	The food's on board—we're off! Let's go!
Chorus:	Haul there, haul! Now haul away!
Solo:	They make a noise, these pupui!
	—What are these 'puffers'—what?
	They scare a man, these pupui!
	—Who do they frighten—who?
	They cry out, 'Tute's ships are here!'
	Now you haulers—haul away!
Chorus:	You there, haul there—haul away!
Solo:	*—Who are they shouting at, these guns?*
	They're shouting at the sons of Tu,
	At Tu's descendants do they roar.
	They frighten even World-below!
	Look out, there!—the rollers slip!
	She's keeling over!
	Right the ship!
Chorus:	The ship, you haulers—right the ship!
Solo:	She floats, she's right, our handsome ship!
	Now dip your paddles in the tide,
	And let her feel that wind! That's it!
Chorus:	Aea e pa'i e!
	Aea e pa'i e!

BY WHOSE COMMAND?

*Rongomatane, ariki nui of Atiu, forbids his people to attack
the first ship seen since Cook's visit. It brings the first
missionary, John Williams.*

> By whose command shall an attack be made
> On a race of Gods from World-below?
> Shall a race of weaklings
> Dare to molest so wise a people?
> Look at that vessel—
> Gaze at her masts:
> At her multitudinous, innumerable ropes.

by Tiwai Paraone, New Zealand (c. 1880)
Translated by Hare Hongi

CHANT TO IO

Io dwelt within the breathing-space of immensity,
The universe was in darkness, with water everywhere.
There was no glimmer of dawn, no clearness, no light.
And he began by saying these words,
   That he might cease remaining inactive:
'Darkness, become a light-possessing darkness.'
And at once a light appeared.
He then repeated these self-same words in this manner,
   That he might cease remaining inactive:
'Light, become a darkness-possessing light.'
And again an intense darkness supervened.
Then a third time He spake, saying:
   'Let there be one darkness above.
   'Let there be one darkness below,
   'Let there be a darkness unto Tupua,
   'Let there be a darkness unto Tawhito,
   'A dominion of light,
   'A bright light.'
And now a great light prevailed.
Io then looked to the waters which compassed him about,
   and spake a fourth time, saying:
   'Ye waters of Tai kama, be ye separate.
   'Heaven, be formed.'
Then the sky became suspended.
   'Bring forth thou Te Tupua horo nuku.'
And at once the moving earth lay stretched abroad.

NOTES ON THE TEXT
AND ILLUSTRATIONS

In the following pages every item in the text and every illustration is provided with a note, however short, which attempts to give any necessary background and answer any queries the reader may have. At the same time it shows with the help of the numbered references (page 397) what sources have been used.

The notes on the stories and poems are in roman type, headed by the titles and ending with the source-references in square brackets. Those on the pictures are in italics. The story notes may readily be located by using the page folio guides in the inner margin of the headline and by the paging of the picture notes.

As far as possible the illustrations have been chosen so as to belong to the same moment as the narration of the stories and poems—the somewhat elastic 'moment of contact'. By keeping to a minimum any intruding hints of European vision or influence (such as the muskets on page 259), I have tried to present a view of the Polynesian environment and culture as it might have been seen by the first Europeans in the Pacific, excepting the Spaniards. With regard to the *text*, the collecting period runs from 1769 (Cook at Tahiti) to 1947 (Emory and Elbert at Kapingamarangi). The engravings and drawings all come from the period 1769–1876. With regard to the artifacts, the span is harder to establish. The most modern item in the book is the Marquesan tattoo design which Mrs. Willowdean Handy copied from the body of an old woman in 1920, but the oldest is probably the 'Kaitaia lintel' (page 318) which was found preserved in a New Zealand swamp, and is of undetermined age.

NOTES

INTRODUCTION

Creation Original Cause

As explained where it is given in the Introduction, this piece can be regarded as the first example of Polynesian mythology ever collected by a European. It was evidently related to either Captain Cook or his companion Sir Joseph Banks in Tahiti in 1769,—probably by Tu, the chief who later became known as King Pomare I—and versions of it are given by both Cook and Banks. That of Banks (2:380) is a description with commentary, but Cook's transcription (35) is more direct and includes more names. It is to be found among some fragments of Cook's handwriting preserved by the British Museum in a bound volume entitled 'Cook's Second Voyage, Fragments' (Add. Ms. 27,889, folios 73 and 74; see also item 35 in my References). Dr. J. C. Beaglehole, who has edited the journals of both explorers, believes it was probably Banks who collected the piece, even though Cook's version is fuller. The ascription of the Cook fragment to the second voyage, he says, is certainly incorrect.

What makes the piece of prime importance now is that it departs radically from the classic pattern of the Polynesian Creation myth—which, though locally varied, is of very general distribution, and is found conserved in remote areas.

In that version the Sky-father and Earth-mother beget numerous sons— the departmental gods—one of whom has the task of pushing the parents apart to admit light to the World of Being. Soon there is a 'first man', and eventually a 'first woman'. Tangaroa is usually one of the departmental gods. But Cook was told—as was J. M. Orsmond forty-nine years later—that Ta'aroa was the original creator of all things. According to Carrington, who first published this part of the fragment in 1939, Cook was also told the story of Maui separating Rangi and Papa. (These are the primal parents; but Maui was not their son.) Evidently, then, some 'revisionists' had been at work in Tahiti.

It was Sir Peter Buck who first suggested (7:88) what must have happened to the myth, although at the time he must have been unaware of this Cook fragment. 'After the pattern [of marriage of Sky and Earth] had been carried to distant lands,' Buck wrote, 'the priests of Opoa elevated Ta'aroa above his brothers and made him Creator of all things. . . . I cannot help thinking that the highest-ranking chief and his priestly advisers belonged to a lineage tracing descent from Ta'aroa, and hence their selection of this particular god for promotion.'

When Buck wrote this he was referring to the version collected by Orsmond in 1822. We can assume, I think, that if he had known of the Cook fragment he would have mentioned it, or shown some knowledge of the reference to Maui. But he did of course know that Tu (or Pomare I) had acquired unusual power in Tahiti shortly before Cook's arrival, which he was helped to consolidate by his becoming the friend of Cook. Tu, in fact, was the chief who fitted Buck's hypothesis.

In 1956 the Danish scholar Torben Monberg, without referring in any way to Buck's intuitive guess, examined the matter in the light of the Cook fragments and other information and produced convincing evidence (42) that Buck was right. Both Cook and Banks, says Monberg, heard of Ta'aroa as an original Creator (though Banks also spoke of Te Tumu and Te Papa as a primal pair). After discussing the historical background to Tu's position when Cook arrived, Monberg shows pretty conclusively that Tu's divine ancestor Ta'aroa was indeed exalted for political reasons, to provide sanction for the new order.

But older myths die hard—and while Banks was told of Te Tumu and Te Papa, Cook was told of Maui separating sky and earth—a deviation, certainly, from the 'classic' pattern, but Maui is known as a sky-lifter in certain other islands.

Since Carrington's exact transcription of Cook's holograph is on record in JPS, I have felt entitled to render the native names in the form I believe they would take in modern Tahitian, and I have made corrections in square brackets for what I think were three verbal slips. Where I have supplied he, Cook has and. Where I have conjectured man, Cook has Ti'i the first was the son. . . . Where I have supplied on, Cook has one. The orthography of both Cook's account and that of Banks gives reason for believing that the name of Ti'i, which would be spoken 'o Ti'i', was confused by both of them with the word 'oti', which does mean 'finished'.

This version of the two stories provides an interesting comparison with Orsmond's account of Tangaroa collected in the same place some fifty years later (see 'Tangaroa Maker of all Things') and with other versions of the story of Tiki. It makes nonsense of the old belief that the texts of Polynesian myths were sacred and immutable. They were obviously extremely plastic—as common sense suggests they would be in the total absence of writing. In this version of the Polynesian Garden of Eden we have a woman blamed for some of what went on—as in our own. Things are different in the versions collected in other islands. [Carrington, 35; Banks, 2(1): 369 and 379–380]

p. 3 The tamanu flower (Calophyllum inophyllum) is from a drawing by Sydney Parkinson, the artist on Cook's first voyage. (By courtesy of the Trustees of the British Museum.)

p. 6 The two Tahitian birds were painted by Lt. George Tobin, R.N., who was there with Captain Bligh in 1792. The parakeet called vini supplied the Tahitians with their precious kura, or red feathers. The other bird is called by Tobin 'omawmow'. (From 166, by courtesy of the Mitchell Library, Sydney.)

p. 8 The plump Tahitian fish is another of the water-colours of George Tobin, who rendered its name as 'Oeeree'. (From 166, by courtesy of the Mitchell Library, Sydney.)

p. 10 These Tongan artifacts were collected on Cook's second voyage and engraved in London. (From 148, by courtesy of the Turnbull Library, Wellington.)

p. 12 Tattooed Marquesan chief. This lithograph after L. le Breton, Dumont-d'Urville's artist on the Astrolabe, shows designs that were in fashion about 1840, with a good specimen of the Marquesans' handsomely murderous club, and a conch-shell trumpet. The first Polynesians ever spoken to by Europeans (that is, by Mendaña and Quiros in 1595) were men like this, and the Spaniards shot about two hundred of them, apparently for sport. Three hundred years later Paul Gauguin lived for a time among their descendants, with a happier result. (From 152, by courtesy of the Turnbull Library, Wellington.)

p. 15 This red-tailed tropic bird (Phaethon rubricauda) is from George Raper's Birds of Australia and South Seas: Original Drawings, 1788–90, in the Turnbull Library, Wellington, but apparently it was painted by someone else. It has not previously been

published.
(From 158, by courtesy of the Turnbull Library, Wellington.)

p. 18 The Marquesan fan with a carved bone handle is in the Bishop Museum, Honolulu.
(By courtesy of the Bishop Museum.)

p. 25 The Marquesan bowl is made from a gourd and braided with sinnet.
(By courtesy of the Museum of Primitive Art, New York.)

p. 35 The Marquesan flute, of cane with inscribed design, is in the Bishop Museum, Honolulu.
(By courtesy of the Bishop Museum.)

THE OFFSPRING OF THE SKY AND EARTH

Chatham Islands

Here we have the classic pattern of the Polynesian Creation myth in its simplest form. Its occurrence in a remote corner—the cool and windy Chatham Islands, six hundred miles east of the South Island of New Zealand—suggests the conservation, by migrants long isolated from outside influence, of an ancient 'original'—though no more ancient than the Maori departure from Central Polynesia, which is believed to have been one of the last to occur. The New Zealand account (Grey, 72) is similar.

This version was collected around 1869 by the Chatham Islands sheep-farmer Alexander Shand from Hirawanu Tapu, a true Moriori (indigenous Chatham Islander). He, however, had grown up as a slave of invading Taranaki Maoris who had commandeered a whaler and 'conquered' the islands in 1835. He only spoke Maori. In consequence he could not put the stories down in the Moriori dialect; nor could he or anyone explain certain words in the first chant. In order to complete it I have ventured to translate 'memea' as 'thought' (its Rarotongan meaning), leaving 'kahi' unattempted.

The Chathams are not only exposed and cool: they were entirely without the breadfruit, coconut or aute ('tapa cloth' tree) of tropical Polynesia, and also lacked the taro and sweet potato, which the Maoris were able to grow in New Zealand. The hog, dog and fowl were absent. (There were, however, colonies of seals, which were carefully conserved.) There were no big trees for building canoes, nor any building-stone. Today the main island, the former 'Rekohu', has a green coastal belt of pasture, but the interior is peaty moorland, with some scrub and a little bush, the vestige of old karaka forests.

The Moriori, an offshoot of the early colonizers of New Zealand, had apparently been isolated for about six hundred years before the European contact and the far more disastrous Maori invasion. Their skin was said to be a little darker than that of the Maori. Those who owned good land had sealskin cloaks to wear in winter—the rest wore cloaks of flax. On November 30, 1791, Lt. W. R. Broughton of the brig *Chatham*, the islands' discoverer, saw a chief wearing a sealskin cloak—only three weeks off midsummer's day!

None of this sounds quite like a 'South Sea Island', and the spare existence of the Moriori is reflected in their stories, several of which stand out in this book from all the rest by virtue of their terse, hard objectivity, and of other characteristics possibly given them by their narrator. They are, nevertheless, the 'same' stories as were told much nearer the Equator. There are several explicit references to the local climate—even one in this Creation myth. December's 'summer' weather in the Chathams is hesitant and unstable, a fact that is expressed here in a pleasing image. [Shand, *JPS* 3:121–123, 1894]

p. 46 This Maori fish-hook, made of wood and tipped with bone, was of a large type used for catching sharks.
(By courtesy of the Dominion Museum, Wellington.)

p. 49 'Stick figure'. Various figures resembling this were found incised in the bark of kopi trees in the Chatham Islands over fifty years ago.
(After H. D. Skinner, 90, by courtesy of the Bishop Museum, Honolulu.)

TANGAROA MAKER OF ALL THINGS

Tahiti

This is a version of Tahiti's revised or 'Pomarist' account of the Creation, as related to Orsmond in 1822 and later. Except that 'the egg came first', it sets up Tangaroa as a Supreme Creator. Since this is anomalous in Polynesia (see preceding notes) and since the piece was collected a full twenty-five years after the first London Missionaries landed on Tahiti, one might suspect Christian influence; but the Cook fragment of 1769 rules out that possibility.

Another account collected from different priests pleased Orsmond (or Miss Henry; the authorship of her footnotes is unclear) by 'suggesting the Scriptures'. It speaks of 'Great Ta'aroa who ended sins and evil', 'whose curse was death', etc., and is given precedence in Miss Henry's book. But this version has a purely Polynesian ring, and is fully compatible with the Cook fragment.

As a latter-day Creation myth, this composition is proof of the continuing vitality of Tahitian religious thought. It was recited to Orsmond in 1822 by Pao raro and Ra'i tupu, priests of Porapora, and in 1833 by Tamera and Anani of Tahiti. I have adapted the translation given by Miss Henry, in which Tangaroa is, naturally, spelt in the Tahitian manner. The 'Tu' referred to near the end is the god, not Cook's Tu. His anomalous presence is of course a survival from the older myth. [Henry, 39: 339–340]

p. 52 'Tangaroa creating other gods.' This wooden figure, 44⅝ inches high, comes from Tubuai, in the Austral group. It has a hollow back with a removable lid, containing some other progeny like those on the front, but loose.

(By courtesy of the Trustees of the British Museum.)

p. 53 The breadfruit was drawn by Sydney Parkinson, the artist on Cook's first voyage. (From 148, by courtesy of the Turnbull Library, Wellington.)

CREATION

New Zealand

Actually the opening sections of a genealogical chant, freely translated by the Reverend Richard Taylor, who collected it in the North Island of New Zealand around 1850. I have transcribed Taylor's beautiful rendering virtually without alteration as far as the 'Third Period'. The remainder has been slightly rearranged. The chant traces the descent, from the Nothingness, of all things and all men, and would eventually reach the speaker's immediate ancestors. [Taylor, 83: 14–15]

HAVAIKI THE LAND

Tahiti

In effect a continuation of the earlier account of Tangaroa as Creator. Recited to Orsmond in 1822 by four priests of Porapora (including Pao raro and Ra'i tupu), and in 1835 by Tamera and Anani of Tahiti. This rendering abbreviates Orsmond's translation, in which the repetitive sections are much longer. [Henry, 39: 340–344]

p. 60 The banyan tree was drawn in Nuku Hiva by Dumont-d'Urville's artist, L. le Breton, about 1840.
(From 152, by courtesy of the Turnbull Library, Wellington.)

WHEN THE SKY LAY ON THE EARTH

New Zealand

Another section of the New Zealand account of the Creation as given by Richard Taylor from genealogical chants. It describes the state of Earth's surface when Sky-father lay upon her and only shrubs and creeping plants could flourish in the gloom. The first progeny of the primal parents were brought forth in this confined space, but after catching a glimpse of light through their father's armpits they decided to force their parents apart. Eventually the forest-god Tane, by his great exertion, succeeded in propping up the sky, but jealousies then arose between the brothers, which the elements reflect today. Compare with 'The Offspring of the Sky and Earth' above, and see also Grey, 72: 1–11, or my *Maori Myths*. [Taylor, 83: 18]

THE CONFLICT OF THE GODS

Tuamotu

Adapted from a rather free narration described by Miss Henry as being 'obtained from Taroi nui, a Tuamotuan chief, by the aid of Mrs. Walker'—that is, in 1893. Collected rather late, in other words (at any rate for Tahiti), but in-included here because it completes the Creation cycle—the usual 'conflict' not being mentioned in the opening Chatham Islands example. 'Atea' has the meaning of 'light' as well as 'vast expanse'. Faka-hotu means 'cause to form', and Tane's name can also mean 'husband'. [Henry, 39: 349–352]

p. 65 The Marquesan bone figure—4¾ inches high—is from the Museum of Primitive Art, New York.
(By courtesy of the Museum of Primitive Art.)

TIKI THE FIRST MAN

Tuamotu: Mangareva: Marquesas

Tiki, like Adam, was the first man—but as in Adam's case, there were usually other persons then existing. His name and characteristics were very widely known. He was probably pan-Polynesian, like Maui, and we first hear of him from Captain Cook (see Introduction, and Note above), but it is understandable that all the missionary collectors should have dismissed him with the fewest possible words, passing over such deplorable scandals from the Polynesian Eden as these. We must have him nevertheless, and for want of any suitable extended account I have pieced this tale together (the joins are clearly shown) from three non-missionary sources.

The opening and the beach episode are from Anaa, in the Tuamotu; the second (incest) section is from Mangareva; and the final retribution scenes are from Nuku Hiva (Marquesas).

The London Missionary John Williams, who put the first native evangelists ashore on Rarotonga in 1823, describes with a perfectly straight face overhearing one of his sailors, Faaori, answer questions from the Rarotongans about the First Man, who he said was Adam: 'The people affirmed that it was Tiki. Faaori then asked them who was the first woman? They answered, Tiki's wife. He inquired of them where she had come from? To this question they could give no answer. He then told them the first woman's name was Eve, and that she was a rib taken out of the first man that Jehovah made. . . . This was all new to them, and they listened with intense interest to his statements—many exclaiming "Perhaps this is the truth"' (34: 27). [Stimson, 50: 4; Buck, 92: 307; Handy, 94: 123]

p. 70 The eel is the Mangaian 'Vaaroa', or 'long-mouthed' sea eel (Muraena), which comes in sizes up to eight feet long and as thick as a man's leg. Wyatt Gill (55, whence this engraving comes) relates some grisly encounters between men and this lurker in the crevices of coral reefs.

HINA AND THE EEL

Mangaia

Though this is possibly the most ancient and most remote in origin of all Polynesian myths, referring as it does to that one who in *our* Genesis was 'more subtle than any other wild creature that the Lord God had made', its meaning has usually been disguised in printed versions on grounds of delicacy—Tuna being said to have 'struck Hina with his tail', or 'bitten her', or something of that kind.

Since snakes are unknown in the Pacific Islands, our very old friend the phallic serpent must needs assume the form of a monster eel (tuna) in stories that require his ritual killing to originate the principal food-plant of the region. In the present book we also meet Te Tuna in a Tuamotu section of the Maui cycle (p. *107*), while a reference to him in an Easter Island Creation chant proves a pre-migration date for that piece (see next note). But this is stating antiquity at its least. Tuna's origins are much more remote than anything that can be described as Polynesian. He is Joseph Campbell's 'great Serpent of the Earliest Planters' (8: 384–391). Campbell has shown us there that the myth must be related to that critical point in the palaeolithic at which 'the idea occurred to some of the women grubbing for edible plants to concentrate their food plants in gardens'. It is certain, he says, 'that the functions of planting and of this myth are related and that the myth flourishes among gardeners. . . . We may guess the date [of its origins] to have been somewhere in the neighbourhood of 7500 B.C.' Elsewhere in the same work Campbell discusses three other Polynesian occurrences of the serpent-and-maid mythologem—from the Tuamotu, Tonga and Hawaii. Dixon (14: 56) has incorrectly stated that the myth is 'absent from Hawaii'.

This Mangaian version collected by Gill was localized to a certain pool below the inner cliffs of the 'makatea', the high rim of raised coral that encircles the island (a former atoll) and entraps the waters of its taro swamps. Gill says that he himself saw a *seven-foot eel* at that spot in 1855! The eating of eels, he adds, was tapu to women. In the Mangaian dialect 'Hina' is 'Ina', but I have supplied the 'H'. For a general note on the ubiquitous Hina see the Glossary. [Gill, 56: 77]

A CHANT OF CREATION

Easter Island

Such oral literature as survived the calamitous destruction of the Easter Island culture in the nineteenth century was nearly all 'local history', concerned with Hotu matua's migration, the origin of the island's tribes, etc. One fragment of ancient mythology which did come through was this creation chant, which I have adapted from Métraux's reconstruction of the garbled version given by Paymaster Thomson of the U.S.S. *Mohican*, who obtained it from Ure vaeiko in 1866. It proves its own antiquity: neither coconuts nor eels were known on Easter Island (which has no streams of any kind) and the word for coconut, 'niu', was used for the fruit of the miro tree. Yet the eighth line of the chant preserves a memory of both, in an allusion to the extremely ancient myth about the eel and the coconut (see preceding note). Tiki and his wife the Woman of Earth are also mentioned toward the end, and the cryptic last three lines again refer to eels, according to Métraux. A chant of almost identical pattern is recorded by Buck from Mangareva. Both doubtless had a common source in the Marquesas, whence the Easter Islanders evidently migrated in about the fourth century [Métraux, 99: 320–322].

p. 77 *The Easter Island headdress, made of rushes covered with painted tapa cloth, is in the Peabody Museum of Harvard University. (By courtesy of the Peabody Museum.)*

by J. F. Miller.
(By courtesy of the Trustees of the British Museum.)

TURTLE, FOWL AND PIG

Porapora

Recited to J. M. Orsmond in 1825 by Mo'o, of Porapora, and here retold from Orsmond's version. 'Havaiki' in this case possibly refers to the island now called Ra'iatea (for which it was the ancient name), rather than to the general 'place of origin' of Polynesian myth. [Henry, 39: 380]

p. 79 *The house with fowls and pigs was drawn in Tonga by William Hodges, artist on Cook's second voyage, and later engraved in England.*
(From 148, by courtesy of the Turnbull Library, Wellington.)

THE WOMAN IN THE MOON

Tahiti

The Polynesian 'woman in the moon' is usually there as punishment for some such earthly wrong as allowing the rain to spoil some mats, or—in the New Zealand story of Rona (83: 95)—violent swearing. In this little fragment cited by Emory we can briefly hear what must often have been an extremely annoying though necessary noise in any village of tropical Polynesia—the clatter of the women beating tapa cloth with mallet and wooden block. It comes from an account of the Creation written down by a Tahitian named Mare in 1849 and first published in L. Gaussin's *Le Tour du Monde*, 1860. [Emory, *JPS* 47: 45–63, 1938]

p. 80 *The tapa beater—a wooden mallet used for beating the bark of the paper-mulberry tree into tapa, the universal Polynesian cloth—was drawn for Sir Joseph Banks*

ATARAGA AT THE POOL

Tuamotu

How the demigod Maui was begotten. A good example of the lewd and garrulous style of story-telling obtained by Stimson in the Tuamotu, but not a typical account of Maui's origin. For a more 'classical' version, see Grey (72: 12–44), or my own *Maori Myths*, where Maui's *mother* is Taranga and he is named Maui tikitiki a Taranga because she bore him as a premature foetus and threw him into the sea wrapped in her top-knot (tikitiki), an ornament which only men possessed among the Maori. 'Ataraga' and 'Taranga' are therefore in effect the same person.

The opening scene at the pool is from the island of Anaa and the remainder of the story, from the entry of Huahega on, was given by Fariua a Makitua, of Fagatau. A key to the song of the dancing girls:

Te kiri vi!	= the tight-stretched skin (the hymen)
Te momotu	= take by force
Tu i mimi . . .	= stands the clitoris . . .
He vahine . . .	= 'here is a woman; below is the cleft portal, opened by the fingertips'
He tiriga pa . . .	= 'it is Tu-of-the-long blade who has-thrown her down'
Ka horo ra	= 'the blade plies in and out'
Toropi, toropa	= 'a sudden flow escapes'
Kokokokina!	= 'slappety-slappety-slap'.

The 'eel-with-a-slit-skin' refers to the Polynesian practice of super-incision.

[Stimson, 50 and 49]

p. 82 Fly-whisk handle. This excellent specimen of the Society Islands' finest sculpture comes from Huahine. The object was probably both ceremonial and functional, having a 'horse's tail' of sinnet fibres hanging from it which would suitably emphasize the gestures of a chief while also keeping off the flies to some extent. Both Tahaki and Rata would probably have made good use of such a whisk.
(By courtesy of the Museum of Primitive Art, New York.)

p. 85 Utu flower and leaves (Barringtonia speciosa). This is the tree whose grated nut yields a paralysing fish poison, formerly much used in Central Polynesian lagoons; after a drawing by J. F. Miller.
(From 148, by courtesy of the Turnbull Library, Wellington.)

p. 88 This tiare (Gardenia taitensis), the loveliest of Polynesia's perfumed flowers, was drawn by Sydney Parkinson in 1769.
(By courtesy of the Trustees of the British Museum.)

MAUI-OF-A-THOUSAND-TRICKS

Manihiki

Maui tikitiki a Taranga, as he is called in New Zealand (see preceding note), is Polynesia's best-known mythical character. As culture-hero, fire-bringer and trickster who improved the universe for man, he seems to have been known in all the major groups—deserving his description by W. D. Westervelt as one of the strongest links in the mythological chain of evidence binding the scattered inhabitants of the Pacific into one nation. Eastern Melanesia, as well, has stories of Maui Kijikiji, and even in Europe his name is known, at least to those who study the psychology of myth. The first European to write about him was Captain Cook, who in Tahiti in 1769 was shown a basketwork figure that was taller than a man, and told that it represented Maui. The figure was covered with white and black feathers and had three knobs on its head which Joseph

Banks was told were 'little men' (2 [1]: 302). This description makes the object resemble the Rarotonga and Ra'ivavae wooden figures of gods bringing forth their 'sons'. Cook's interpreter Tupia told him some stories of Maui, but unfortunately for us Cook thought them 'too absurd' to note down.

The now famous New Zealand version of the Maui cycle was published by Grey in 1855, and its discussion in Europe began in the following year, with Schirren's *Die Wandersagen der Neuseelander und der Mauimythos.* Since then Maui has been discussed by Bastian, Tylor, Frobenius, Roheim, Rank and numerous others. He has been compared at various times to Hercules, Joshua, Loki, Brer Rabbit, the inventor of daylight saving, Manabozho and Prometheus, and there is an interesting section on him in Suzanne Langer's *Philosophy in a New Key.* The authoritative work is Luomala (24).

It is obvious that any collection of Polynesian mythology must reserve an important place for Maui, but in fact he is rather difficult to include, since no account of him exists which holds for Polynesia generally, and most accounts have gaps. The only one that is complete (in the sense that it starts with his birth and ends with his death and includes all his principal adventures) is that of Grey (72: 12–44), which is, however, unique in its character as well as its completeness. New Zealand's Maui, because of his 'universality' and even more because of his last sexual encounter with death, is the one who has interested Western scholars; but he is not the one the other islands know. The more 'typical' Maui of tropical Polynesia is in no way a tragic figure.

My own retelling of the Maori version is already published in my *Maori Myths,* so for this book I have devised (as two stories) a composite version, bringing together material obtained at periods sixty years apart in two parts of Polynesia. Wyatt Gill's entirely reliable version of 1870 (from which I have drawn 'Maui-of-a-Thousand-Tricks') comes from the glorious 'blue-lagoon' atoll of

Manihiki in the northern Cook Islands (where, as it happens, I myself have seen part of the legend acted by school-children); and Stimson's Tuamotu version (from which I have taken 'Maui and Tuna') was obtained from Fariua of Fagatau about 1930. My prefacing the tales with Fariua's amusing account of Maui's begetting is an indulgence, excused in the preceding note.

Such a montage raises problems with regard to names. Having prefigured a Maui of the Tuamotu who is begotten of Huahega by one Atara(n)ga, we then have to accept a Maui of Manihiki who has different parents, and a sister named Hina; and finally to switch back to the Tuamotu where his mother once more is Huahega and his wife is Hina. I know this is confusing, but had I drawn on versions from Samoa, Hawaii or the Marquesas, the problems would have been greater still.

It should be realized that unlike Tahaki, Rata and Tinirau, Maui is a proletarian, not a chiefly hero—if hero he is at all. Certain chiefly or priestly informants, indeed, have brushed aside his story as 'ovenside tales'. (Sacred stories would never be associated with a cooking-fire.) I believe he should be thought of as small and rather ugly, and though obviously more than a mortal he is much less than a god. Mrs. Chadwick, noting that he rarely fights, remarks that 'his sense of honour is very low'; and Miss Luomala, observing that only one deity was destined to overcome him, calls him 'not absolutely good, not absolutely bad, loved but not worshipped. Earthbound, but a heavenburster. Comic yet tragic. Petty and heroic . . . he represents man-kind.'

An episode usually associated with Tahaki is used by the narrator in this composite Maui cycle (a frequent occur-rence in Polynesian story-telling). The encounter with the old blind woman whose sight will be restored by striking the eyes will be found in its more usual place in the story of Tahaki (p. 128). I myself am responsible for adding the beautiful image of Hina's hair as the 'ropes of Maui' extending from the setting sun. This comes from Gill's Mangaian version. [Gill, 56: 51-71 and 62-63; JPS 24: 144-148]

p. 93 Horned fish. Lt. Tobin heard the Tahitian name of this graceful fish as 'ai oomee'—probably umi.
(From 166, by courtesy of the Mitchell Library, Sydney.)

p. 95 Fruit and foliage of the nono (Morinda citrifolia) drawn by Sydney Parkinson, 1769.
(By courtesy of the Trustees of the British Museum.)

p. 102 The octopus lure and fish-hooks were brought back from Polynesia by Sir Joseph Banks on Cook's first voyage, and drawn by J. F. Miller. Nos. 2 and 3 are of shell, No. 4 is of wood and bone.
(By courtesy of the Trustees of the British Museum.)

MAUI AND TUNA

Tuamotu

Obtained by Stimson from Fariua, of Fagatau (see the two preceding notes). This lewd encounter of Maui with the monster eel has a politer counterpart in New Zealand, and the planting of Tuna's head is of course the central motif of 'Hina and the Eel' (see earlier note). A fuller version of the text and some of the chants is readily accessible in Joseph Campbell's *Primitive Mythology* (8: 191-197). Tane means husband, and Tu means erect. All the personal names, according to Stimson, have erotic double meanings. [Stimson, 49: 28-35]

p. 106 A 'fisherman's god' from Rarotonga. A similar figure and so described, but emas-culated, is in the London Missionary Society collection in the British Museum. This intact specimen is 14½ inches high.
(By courtesy of the Staatliches Museum für Völkerkunde, Munich.)

(*By courtesy of the Dominion Museum, Wellington.*)

HINE AND TINIRAU

Chatham Islands

We really feel the Chathams climate in this chilly tale, the only Polynesian story to my knowledge in which fog is experienced. It is the Moriori version (written down for Shand by Hirawanu Tapu) of one of the most widespread of all Polynesian stories apart from those of the ·'major heroes'—Hine's seduction of the extremely handsome chief called Tinirau, who had two wives already, and his subsequent unkind neglect of her. My *Maori Myths* gives a rendering of the New Zealand version (in which Hine's brother comes to her rescue in the shape of a pigeon). More than one variant is known in Tonga, while a good deal is heard of 'Sina and Tigilau' in Samoa, and, in fact, the reader of Polynesian myth and legend must be prepared to meet the pretty Hine almost anywhere—especially in the water—and recognize her name however it is spelt.

In the cryptic speeches near the beginning of this Moriori tale, Kahukura is proclaiming Tu moana a future leader (because he caught his pute), and this makes Horopapa jealous and assertive. In the South Island Maori version in my other book the lovers are found under a cloak by two owls, who report seeing only 'two heads and four feet'—a joke that seems to have an echo here.

The Living-Waters-of-Tane is a myth-motif of wide distribution in Polynesia, in some way connected with the moon and the origins of life, and perhaps with pregnancy. It is sometimes asserted that Hine 'is' the moon, eternally returning from those waters whence she rises. Her name here (Hine te iwaiwa) appears to refer to nine moons. [Shand, *JPS* 5: 131–133, 1896]

p. 114 This neck pendant, shaped like a seagull's head and inlaid with an eye of paua shell, is typical of the harsh, cold art of the Chatham Islands.

TAHAKI OF THE GOLDEN SKIN

Tahiti

'Tahaki the perfect chief,' as Miss Luomala aptly calls him, was the epitome of a Polynesian aristocrat, 'a chief's chief'; whose form was handsome to perfection and whose skin was like kura, the sacred colour—'Everyone admired him, especially the women.'

Like Maui, Tahaki was known all over Polynesia—but not for rebelling against the accepted order. On the contrary, Tahaki's excellence lay in what he could achieve while doing everything correctly —like a chief. 'He is in direct contrast to the grotesque little social misfit Maui,' says Miss Luomala in her *Voices on the Wind*, '—an integrated personality.' Tahaki makes his mistakes, and does have enemies. But Maui, once dead (remarks Miss Luomala), stays dead; Tahaki is revived. In the end, he fades from the earth, but he continues in the other world.

Tahaki's name, unlike Maui's, changes in sound from one area to another, and hence in our orthography as well. In the Tuamotu he is Tahaki; in New Zealand, Tawhaki; in Hawaii, Kaha'i; and in Tahiti he is properly Tafa'i. For the reasons explained at the front of the book, 'Tahaki' is adopted here.

Three main themes are usually found in the story of Tahaki: the jealous cousins who try to kill him; the estranged lover or wife; and the lost father, who must be rescued from the World Below. Having already given a rendering of the New Zealand version (which contains all those themes), I have chosen here to assemble a composite account, of which the divisions are clearly shown, but which involves a repetition of the delousing episode.

The story I have called 'Tahaki of the Golden Skin' is basically a reconstruction from Orsmond's prose summary of the legend as given to him by Tamera in 1855, but *omitting* a later section added by Miss Henry, and *adding*, as an interpolation, an earlier fragment obtained by Orsmond. This is the section on 'the cutting of the sinews of the fish' (Tahiti), which occurs at page *126*. It was given to Orsmond in 1824 by three persons: King Pomare II, the chief Mahine and the priest Tamera. All this material comes from Miss Henry's book. In one or two places I have added certain vivid details from a later Tahitian version, published by Leverd in 1912.

The section from Miss Henry's book which I have omitted as probably spurious describes a contest between rivals for the hand of a distant princess. It strongly suggests the influence of European fairy-tales, and I think it must be the section referred to in Miss Henry's words, 'and added to in 1890, with the aid of Mrs. Walker, by Pe'ue of Fautau'a ...' etc. Orsmond himself had died in 1856.

This version, then, up to the encounter with the old blind woman, is based on what I believe to have been the material collected by Orsmond himself, with certain details added from Leverd's version. Some adjustment of personal names has been made to link this part of Tahaki's story with what follows. [Henry, 39: 552–560 and 439–442; Leverd, 41]

p. 119 *Lagoon-fishing at Te Taha, Tahiti. It is certainly a pity that Bligh's companion Lt. Tobin did not have more talent for the human figure, but this water-colour of 1792 gives us a unique portrayal of native fishing at Tahiti. The woman sitting by the canoe wears a woven eye-shade against the glare of the sun. The upturned sterns of these small fishing canoes no doubt prevented their being swamped by following waves when returning across the reef with a catch of fish.*
(From 166, by courtesy of the Mitchell Library, Sydney.)

HOW TAHAKI LOST HIS GOLDEN SKIN

Mangareva: Tuamotu

For the rest of Tahaki's story (see preceding note) I have turned with delight to the glittering Mangareva version obtained by Buck in 1934—when Mangareva was still as 'fresh', from an ethnologist's viewpoint, as Tahiti had been seventy or eighty years before. We are constantly aware of sunlight-on-water in this vivid addition to the legend. Its characterization of Tahaki and Karihi is sharper, and only small adjustments to personal names have been necessary to make this part read on from what precedes it. Karihi is referred to indiscriminately as 'brother' and 'cousin' because he is literally both. Under the Polynesian kinship system no distinction was made. The word was the same in either case.

The section in which Karihi deceives the fishes is my importation from Stimson's Tuamotu version of the legend. [Buck, 92: 319–324; Stimson, 50: 89–91, 95–96]

p. 136 *This pretty little Tahitian fish was named 'Tateehee' on Lt. Tobin's water-colour of 1792.*
(From 166, by courtesy of the Mitchell Library, Sydney.)

THE LEGEND OF RATA

Tuamotu: Tahiti

The story of Rata and his magical canoe must have been known to nearly all of Polynesia in the time of the great canoes, though it is oddly absent from Tonga, and was not much in vogue in Samoa. On islands where the actual story is lacking some allusion in a chant may be found as proof; or the central episode will prove its popularity by appearing in a different tale (see the building of Tasi's canoe in the Tokelau story on page *305*). Rata, then, though not quite as famous as Maui, was at least as well known as his own grandfather, Tahaki.

Miss Henry's *Ancient Tahiti* gives two long versions of the tale—one from Tahiti collected by Orsmond in 1825, and one from the Tuamotu, obtained by Mrs. Walker in 1893 from the scholar Taroi nui. The differences make them incompatible, and for this book it was a case of one or the other. For the sake of its drama and imagery I have chosen the Tuamotu version, but I could not resist the Boar Chase and its associated speeches in Orsmond's Tahiti version. I have, therefore, after making some adjustment to the names of characters, inset the Boar Chase in a reconstruction of the Tuamotu tale. This has had the unintended effect of giving a strong but strictly un-Polynesian element of dramatic necessity to Rata's quest for a canoe that can be built without human friends—a 'Western' intrusion which I hope will be excused, along with my conflating Rata's mother (Tahiti version) and grandmother (Tuamotu) as one maternal figure, Kui kura. Some details of Tahitian life and rituals have also been imported from other parts of Miss Henry's book, and here and there I have borrowed details from two later Tuamotu versions—Leverd, 1910, and Stimson, 1937. For easier reading I have supplied in certain names the consonants which in Tahitian are represented by the glottal stop. The villain of the tale, Matuku tangotango, has been given his New Zealand name.

An accessible recent book which can be recommended for its vivid portrayal of the life that formed the background to this legend is Roderick Cameron's *The Golden Haze*. The great canoes, the extravagant apparel, and the famous 'Scarlet Girdle' itself are there described. [Henry, 39: 495–512 and 476–495; Stimson, 50: 117–146; Leverd, 44]

p. 141 Kotuku, the Tahitian reef-heron (Demiegretta sacra), a water-colour by George Tobin, 1792.
(From 166, by courtesy of the Mitchell Library, Sydney.)

p. 143 Tahitian canoes, by George Tobin. Few pictures exist that show the detail of Tahitian canoes under sail; this is one of the best of them.
(From 166, by courtesy of the Mitchell Library, Sydney.)

p. 152 This fine Tahitian adze was carried off to England by Banks, and drawn by J. F. Miller. No doubt the sacred adze Te pa hurunui, which faithfully served Tahaki and his grandson Rata in the ancient time, had the same handsome lines and skilful lashing.
(By courtesy of the Trustees of the British Museum.)

p. 158 Tahitian war canoe. One of the great fleet that Cook saw at Tahiti on his second voyage, from the original wash drawing by William Hodges. The three priests are wearing the feather gorget shown in the picture on page 184.
(From 165, by courtesy of the Mitchell Library, Sydney.)

p. 165 This chief's stool from Atiu, in the Cook Islands, could scarcely have been Puna's stool (in the legend of Rata), but it might well have belonged to Rongomatane, the Atiuan chief who uttered the 'impromptu poetic words' given on page 363.
(By courtesy of the Museum of Primitive Art, New York.)

p. 167 A sea crab, or 'tupa tai'. All land crabs were edible, some sea crabs were poisonous. This happens to be the poisonous angatea, or white-shelled crab, of Mangaia.
(From an engraving in Gill, 55.)

APUKURA'S MOURNING FOR HER SON

Chatham Islands

Apakura (as she is spelt elsewhere) was Polynesia's 'famous mourner', well known for her wails in Samoa (Schultz, 121) in Mangareva far to the east, and of course in New Zealand, whence this Moriori version ultimately derives. The New Zealand version of 1840 may be found in Grey (72: 77–83).

The chants and poems embedded in Polynesian tales are often very ancient, and Shand says that the old men who related this story to Hirawanu Tapu could not explain the meaning of some of the words in Apukura's wail (not given here). The poem, says Shand, is 'archaic, interjectory, and highly elliptical'. It is, in any case, mostly names; so I have broken one of the rules of this book and imported from far across the Pacific the beautiful chant which occurs at the same point in the Mangareva version of the tale, as given by Buck (92: 330).

Shand says that the Ngunguwao, or 'people of the forest', represented a 'different race' to the Moriori, and the story expressly says that when Apukura found her brother in that land they only recognized each other (after long separation, presumably) because 'their skins were alike'. In other stories also there are hints of an active 'racial feeling' in the Chathams, which perhaps we should attribute to the Maori conquest of the group in 1835. The Moriori do seem to have had a slightly darker skin than the Maori, and among themselves (as among the South Island Maori also) there were both straight-haired and frizzy types—as we can see in the story, 'Ugly-ugly! Frizzled-heads!' (p. 345). The result, after conquest, is a complex picture of mutual prejudice, with both sides guilty of attitudes that would hardly win approval at the United Nations today. Here is a description of the Moriori given to Elsdon Best (87: 436) by the Maori elder Te Whatahoro:

'They were a very dark-skinned folk of repulsive appearance, tall, spare, and spindle-shanked, with up-turned nostrils; in some cases the nostrils seemed to be all the nose. They had flat faces and overhanging eyebrows. They were big-boned people, and they had curious eyes, like those of a lizard. An idle folk and chilly, who felt the cold much, and slept anyhow; they were of a treacherous disposition. They did not preserve their traditions as we do.'

Te Whatahoro had never been to the Chathams. With great care and ample evidence Skinner (90) has shown that there was no foundation whatsoever for this interesting case of 'coloured' colour-prejudice. The Moriori were short and bulky, with prominent noses, a brown Polynesian skin, and hair that sometimes was not straight. In fact they resembled most the Ngati mamoe—a Maori tribe!

The Moriori exist no more. The Maori invasion finished them. The last accredited survivor, Tommy Solomon, died in the 1920's. (See also Buck 69: 14.)

Apukura's grisly tale of justified revenge is given by Shand in prose that transmits Hirawanu Tapu's obviously vigorous style of story-telling, including his interjections. (I suspect that other informants told their stories just as effectively, but not all collectors knew, as Shand did, how to retain their verve.) The extensive use of the passive mood is a characteristic of Polynesian narration.

The references to Tu whakararo's head as food (and left-over food at that) constitute the vilest insult known in Polynesia, the ultimate provocation, only to be avenged by the eating of Maurea's eyes while she is still, presumably, alive, if not exactly able to watch. [JPS 4: 161–166, 1895]

p. 172 Hand-club, in the form of a bird, of the Moriori people, Chatham Islands. It is carved from the bone of a whale.
(By courtesy of the Dominion Museum, Wellington.)

p. 174 The embalmed body of the Tahitian chief Ti'i was drawn by John Webber, artist on Cook's third voyage.
(From an engraving in 148, vol. III, by courtesy of the Turnbull Library, Wellington.)

p. 177 Tattooed chief, Te Pou, of Rarotonga. Published in John Williams' Missionary Enterprises in 1837, this Baxter print was made from a painting by John Williams, Junior.
(By courtesy of the Turnbull Library, Wellington.)

p. 180 Handle of a ceremonial paddle. Paddles for everyday use were presumably smoother and more comfortable than this, a good example of the intricate carving style of the Austral Islands.
(From the Oldman collection; by courtesy of the Dominion Museum, Wellington.)

p. 184 Known as a taame, this gorget or neck ornament was worn by Tahitian priests on ceremonial occasions (as in the picture facing page 158). It is made of finely woven sinnet on a light cane frame. The plaques are of pearl shell, surrounded by black feathers. Three rows of drilled shark's teeth are fixed to hoops of the frame, and the tufted edge is of dog's hair.
(From 148, by courtesy of the Turnbull Library, Wellington.)

ANOINTING OF A NEW-BORN CHILD

Tahiti

After the baby had been washed, the paia, or officiating expert, took the white core of a young banana stem, and with it rolled scented coconut oil over the baby's skin, saying this chant. The 'cord' in the last stanza is the umbilical cord. [Henry, 39: 182]

BAPTISMAL CHANT FOR A CHIEF'S FIRST CHILD

Tahiti

Adapted from Miss Henry's translation of the original collected by Orsmond. All the family weapons were stacked up like a crate in the middle of the marae as a show of wealth, and in the hollow centre of the pile a large kape leaf formed a basin for the sacred water. The child was brought by the parents and elder relatives and handed to a priest, who washed it with the water while saying this chant. There followed a symbolic mixing of the relatives' blood (from punctured foreheads) on a miro leaf. [Henry, 39: 184]

CHANT FOR A NEW TOOTH

Mangaia

Rats' teeth, says Gill in recording this little jingle, were the hardest thing Mangaians knew. In Tonga also the milk tooth was thrown on to the roof, with these words recorded by Collocott (129: 108): 'White with spots/Give me your bad tooth,/But take your good tooth for yourself.' Johannes Andersen (*JPS* 54: 222) says that as a child in Denmark he was taught to bury the loose tooth in the garden, saying 'Rat, rat,/ Here you have a bone tooth/Now give me a gold one.' Professor J. Prytz Johansen, of Copenhagen, confirms this, but adds, 'only it is never the rat, but the mouse, who is apostrophized. The custom is known from Central and North Europe (including England).' [Gill, 58: 222, 1885]

LAMENT ON LOSING A KITE

Aitutaki

In adapting this charming poem from the version given by Buck in his *Material Culture of the Cook Islands*, I have presented it as a scene from boyhood, but it may have been nothing of the sort. On the neighbouring island of Mangaia, kite-flying was the pastime of elderly men, and the kites were huge things, far too big for a small boy to hold in a brisk wind like the South-east Trades. All the kites there had individual names and there were contests to see who could fly his kite the highest, and if possible make it disappear into a cloud. Many hours must have been spent in rubbing sinnet on the thighs to make the twine. A story recorded by Gill (57:18f.) tells of a beautiful pair of twin kites called 'The Sorrowful Ones' which were being flown by a chief on Atiu in a north wind when the string broke. The wind being toward Mangaia, the chief's son, Akatere, manned a canoe and sailed for that island (120 miles), where 'The Sorrowful Ones' were found. Mrs. Chadwick (11) has made a valuable study of Polynesian kite-flying, relating it to Asian origins. [Buck, 52: 334]

p. 189 Kites from Aitutaki have not survived to illustrate the lament for a lost kite, but this eight-foot specimen from New Zealand is preserved in the Auckland War Memorial Museum.
(By courtesy of the Auckland War Memorial Museum.)

CONFIRMATION OF A WARRIOR

New Zealand

In addition to the rite of baptism, says Taylor, the Maoris had a second rite for male children, 'resembling confirmation'. The infant was already dedicated to Tu, the god of war, 'but he did not presume to fight, until he had received a second sprinkling. On this occasion the priest again used a branch of karamu.' The water was sprinkled from a leafy bough dipped in the stream. The translation is Taylor's, unaltered. [Taylor, 83: 76–77]

TWO LOVE SONGS
CHANT TO DUMP A SURFER

Easter Island

Only four love songs were remembered by the natives of Easter Island when Métraux was there in 1934, and here are two of them, with one other fragment also from Métraux. Evidently surf-riding was a local sport, though the beaches are poor. [Métraux, 99: 117, 356]

A BOASTING CHANT IN WAR

Tahiti

Collected by Orsmond. [Henry, 39: 305]

CHANT ON THE DYING OF AN ONLY CHILD

Chatham Islands

This hiri was recited while holding the head of the dying person (not *necessarily* a child) in the hollow of one arm, and gesturing with the other to the skies. Obtained by Shand about 1870 from Makora, of Rangiaurii. [Shand, *JPS* 6: 164, 1897]

p. 195 Tahitian mourning robes. The costume itself, or what remains of its splendour, is in the British Museum, but this is part of an engraving based on a drawing made in Tahiti by William Hodges on Cook's second voyage, about 1775.
(Detail from a plate in 148, by courtesy of the Turnbull Library, Wellington.)

TONGA'S LAMENT FOR HIS DAUGHTER

Mangareva

One of several chants relating to the same legendary personage, given to Buck in 1934 by Karara, a female pou kapa or 'song expert' of Mangareva. In order to avoid an importunate young woman who had an ugly face and frizzy hair and had been dreaming about him, Tonga spent most of his time fishing, outside the reef. His daughter, Tepeiru raranga kura ('Princess who plaits precious things'), went with him. On one of their excursions Tepeiru became ill and died, and Tonga buried her at sea; at which point in the story comes this chant, which I have adapted from Buck's rendering. [Buck, 92: 356]

A WIDOW'S FUNERAL CHANT

Easter Island

A glimpse of the pride a Polynesian wife

could take in a husband who was a good provider. [Métraux, 99: 117]

ONOKURA LAMENTS HIS OLD AGE

Mangareva

This compassionate and moving glimpse of old age—a rarity in Polynesian tale or verse—was collected by Buck in 1934. He gives the native text and a translation which I have slightly adapted. 'To go inland' with a girl was an expression well understood throughout Polynesia. It represented what the missionaries sometimes called 'the evil', and on Rarotonga at one time it was an offence punishable by having to work at road-making. [Buck, 92: 390]

p. 198 The wooden gorget (neck ornament) is from Easter Island, and is known as a rei miro (a lei of miro wood). Perhaps there is something Spanish about the faces, but the tight, thin lips recall the island's stone statues. (By courtesy of the Museum of Primitive Art, New York.)

KAE AND THE WHALE

Hiva Oa, Marquesas

The widely distributed story of Kae and the whale is usually associated with the legend of Tinirau (see, for example, Grey, 72: 69–76, or my *Maori Myths*), but in this lively Marquesan variant Tinirau is forgotten, and the business with the whale is subordinated to another widespread theme which might be called the 'land without men' motif—where all births are caesarean, and in a manner of speaking virgin, and no explanation is offered as to what occurs when the male children grow up.

The tale was narrated to Handy in 1921 by Haapuane of Atuona—that very 'Sorcerer of Hiva Oa' whom Paul Gauguin had painted in a glorious scarlet robe in 1902—so it shows us what riches Gauguin managed to overlook in his curious attempts to become acquainted with the antique gods of Polynesia. (See also note on 'Tahia the Fragrant Girl'.)

The partners in obstetrical practice, Pohihia and Pohahaa, are sometimes referred to as experts (tuhuna) and sometimes as gods (atua), so I have followed the text on that point. The naming of paired characters on the pattern of our own Tweedledum and Tweedledee is common in Polynesian story-telling. For another version of the 'land without men' motif, see the Tikopia fragment, 'The Women and the Bats' (p. 315). [Handy, 94: 56–63]

p. 202 Marquesan canoe ornament, carved in wood. This figure was fixed on the prow and faced the paddlers, like a coxswain in reverse. (By courtesy of the Bishop Museum, Honolulu.)

TAHIA THE FRAGRANT GIRL

Hiva Oa, Marquesas

This flower-decked, perfumed tale collected by Handy in 1921 is another example of the lively art of Haapuane, of Hiva Oa—the 'sorcerer' whom Gauguin had painted as a young man in his twenties. Nothing could be more genuinely 'Gauguin country'. It is the past, and the native vision, that the painter sought to know. Yet Gauguin missed it; he bought a Government handbook in Tahiti and borrowed a Moerenhout—but failed to get his sorcerer talking!

The story is unusual in containing almost nothing that can be recognized as a stock theme of Polynesian story-telling. It is in every way strongly local—perhaps was even the personal creation of its energetic narrator. The pun on 'vahana', which means both 'half' and 'mate' in the Marquesan dialect, is in the native text. The use of 'better half' is therefore authorized.

Mrs. Handy's book, *Forever the Land of Men*, contains an excellent description of Haapuane and the sessions her husband held with him. [Handy, 94: 26ff.]

p. 212 'Patini, a chiefess of Nuku Hiva', as drawn by 'le Breton et Marescot' about 1840, may suggest for us the beauty of Tahia the Fragrant Girl, and also the style of the tattoo designs which were shown off by their owners on the Second Night of the Moon (p. 215). To see what changes had occurred in Marquesan women's fashions over the next forty years or so, compare Patini's designs with those in the next picture, from the buttocks of a chiefess of Nuku Hiva who was probably tattooed around 1880.
(From 152, by courtesy of the Turnbull Library, Wellington.)

p. 217 Tattoo design. Mrs. Willowdean C. Handy, after some difficulty, was permitted to copy this girdle design from the person of an aged chiefess of Nuku Hiva in 1920—see note on previous picture.
(From 95, by courtesy of the Bishop Museum, Honolulu.)

p. 223 Marquesan headdress known as a paekaha, made of tridacna and turtle shells on a head-band of sinnet. Some authorities have preferred to show this crown the other way up, but to do so puts all the faces upside-down (which is surely unthinkable), and also deprives the sinnet links between the plaques of their obvious function—to prevent the plaques from falling outwards.
(By courtesy of the Museum of Primitive Art, New York.)

p. 226 Design from a paekaha, or Marquesan headdress. Mrs. Willowdean C. Handy says that this design, from one of the turtle-shell segments of the crown in the previous picture, depicts the ceremonial placing of a child on its uncle's head and shoulders—as at the end of 'Tahia the Fragrant Girl'.
(Reprinted by permission of Dodd, Mead & Company, Inc. from Forever the Land of Men by Willowdean C. Handy. Copyright © 1965 by Willowdean C. Handy.)

KUIKUEVE

Mangareva

One of a number of short tales collected on the island by Buck in 1934, this glimpse

of family tenderness is a Mangarevan variant of the 'Orpheus' legend found in several parts of Polynesia. Compare, for example, 'Mataora and Niwareka' (p. 319). [Buck, 92: 334f.]

p. 229 Carved figure. Not much survives of Mangarevan sculpture or artifacts, but this standing figure (38¾ inches high) indicates that the island possessed its own distinctive style.
(By courtesy of the Museum of Primitive Art, New York.)

A MOTHER SHAMES HER SON

Mangareva

When the Mangarevan chief Tupou was decisively defeated by a rival, he was granted the right to leave the islands with a remnant of his people. For some reason he went out to sea on seven rafts of the sort used for fishing and inter-island travel; but one of his sub-chiefs, Mapukutaora, who had a sea-going double canoe, remained behind with his mother and followers. He delayed so long that his mother feared he might forfeit his honour by not embarking —hence this chant, ostensibly a lament for her exiled ariki, but actually intended for the ears of her son, who then sailed away into the unknown, his honour upheld. Métraux (100) gives a slightly different version which overlooks the important difference between raft and canoe, making all the craft canoes. I have drawn on both versions. [Buck, 7: 221 and Métraux, 100:35]

HOW HOTU MATUA FOUND THIS LAND

Easter Island

No collection of Polynesian oral literature could be called complete without a specimen of one of its principal modes— the migration-and-settlement sequence of legends which explains, in effect, 'How we came here and how the tribes split up the land.' Such legends commonly divide the local literatures in which they are found into two parts, which are thought of as quite distinct. The Morioris of the Chatham Islands called the whole of their pre-migration myths Ko Matangi ao—'The Wind Clouds'; and all that came afterwards Hokorongo tiring'*—'The Hearing of the Ears'. New Zealand and Hawaii had this clear division in their literature too, for obvious reasons, and so did Rarotonga. The Marquesans, however, produced no migration stories for collectors—a fact in harmony with the role of dispersal-point now assigned to those islands—and Tahiti lacks the mode. Tonga had no tradition of migration (131: 12); and Samoan chiefs assured Buck, somewhat stiffly, that *they* originated in Samoa. The dissident Mangaians, too, were firmly of the opinion that their island rose from the World Below with their an-cestors already on it (7: 115). But Easter Island, like Hawaii and New Zealand, took much pride in its tale of 'how we came'. In fact, as explained in the note on 'Chant of Creation', above, very little of Easter Island's oral literature *except* this local history survived the calamities of the nineteenth century, when the island's culture was destroyed.

It seems clear now that Easter Island was occupied by at least the fourth century from the Marquesas, and that the vigorous development of stone masonry and carving arose quite natur-ally from Polynesian causes without any Inca assistance, reaching its high point some time before the first Europeans saw the amazing statues in the eighteenth century. Genealogies would put the migration at about the twelfth century A.D., as they do in New Zealand; but recent archaeological discoveries (as in New Zealand) have pushed that date back by several centuries (see page 4).

Hotu matua, then—'Hotu the parent'—is a Marquesan, and 'Marae renga' is in that group. His period could be anywhere between the fourth and twelfth centuries,

but I think it unlikely that his story was fifteen centuries old when it was collected.

I have drawn on the account of Hotu matua given by Métraux, because he has synthesized all the preceding material and made careful use of what he was told by his informant Juan Tepano. However, I have also drawn a phrase here and there from Mrs. Routledge; and I have proffered an interpretation of Hotu's cryptic words about the 'tide' on his arrival. Métraux found them puzzling, but it seems to me that they could well have referred to the island's waving grasses, ·which the men on shore had just mentioned. If read in this way they are immediately filled with meaning. The grasses would certainly have been an ominous sign to any Mar-quesan hoping for suitable land to grow coconuts and breadfruit, neither of which survive on Easter Island. The account of Tu'u ko ihu's birth ceremonies provided sanction for the customs of the land. [Métraux, 99: 58–65]

p. 232 Stone figure, Easter Island. This eight-foot figure from Orongo village was trans-ported to England in the nineteenth century, and stood until recently in the portico of the British Museum, London.
(By courtesy of the Trustees of the British Museum.)

THE FIGHT WITH OROI

Just as in the New Zealand migration legend of Tama te kapua (72: 109f.), so in this story a disgruntled rival comes to the new land, unknown to the chief, but is eventually defeated by him in personal combat. Oroi comes as a stow-away in the priest's canoe, just as Ruaeo went to New Zealand in a canoe that left the homeland at the same time as Tama's. The resemblances are rather fishy, and suggest that the Easter Island story (first published by Thomson in 1866) may have a 'source' in Grey's book (1855).

The reference to rongorongo—the 'script' of the famous wooden tablets—raises the vexed question whether some

---

* Certain final vowels were dropped in the Moriori dialect. The word is actually 'tiringa'.

form of writing was in fact known to Polynesians. It is not inconceivable that a form of script was in use among some of their early forebears which was later lost (or successfully kept secret by the elders concerned), and of which a trace has survived in the Easter Island tablets. But this would not disturb the general position: that Polynesia's myths and legends were handed down without the use of writing. The researches of Dr. Thomas Barthel into the rongorongo inscriptions are discussed by Métraux (100) and Suggs (32).

The Humboldt current keeps Easter Island rather cool by Polynesian standards, and this story is unique, I believe, in containing what would seem to be a reference to sunbathing. Hotu's calling out to the akuaku in Marae renga, at the end of the story, is from Mrs. Routledge's account. [Métraux, 99: 65–69]

p. 239 Ceremonial paddle, Easter Island. This sacred staff, with its 'face' and perhaps its 'long ears', is said to have been used against evils that might visit the island's kumara crops. It is nearly 34 inches long.
(By courtesy of the Museum of Primitive Art, New York.)

THE STORY OF THE WOODEN IMAGES

Métraux says that the well-known moai kavakava, the wooden images of Easter Island that show protruding ribs, 'were intended to represent the spirits of dead people'—a conception borne out by traditions and by the statements of natives who still (i.e., in 1934) visualized the spirits of the dead in that form. The ending shows us the Polynesian craftsman holding out for his pay. [Métraux, 99: 260–263]

p. 242 Moai kavakava (male figure). Though Easter Island's ample stone invited carving of the famous statues there were no large timber trees, so the wood carver was restricted to pieces of miro (often crooked) about the thickness of a man's arm. This specimen of the island's 'emaciated' style of sculpture shows the exposed ribs and hollow cheeks which are

said to denote a spirit returned from the dead· It also displays the much discussed 'long-ears' of the Easter Islanders, which were seen by Cook, and were still in fashion a hundred years ago.
(By courtesy of the Auckland War Memorial Museum.)

p. 245 Moai paepae (female figure). Easter Island—as referred to in the 'Story of the Wooden Images', page 244; carved from the stunted miro wood which was all the island offered to the carver, unless good stuff was washed ashore.
(By courtesy of the Auckland War Memorial Museum.)

HOW THE SHORT-EARS . . .

At the eastern end of Easter Island there is a knob-like headland called Poike, once an island, joined on now by a neck of land that is traversed by what looks like a filled-in ditch. This is the trench or 'earth-oven' of the present story. Mrs. Routledge and her party came to the conclusion that it must be a natural feature (101: 281), and Métraux seems to take the same view, seeing it as created by the lava flow that joined up Poike.

The story of the war between the Long-ears and the Short-ears has been much debated, being found useful by those who wish to believe that there were once two 'races' on Easter Island—a Negroid race, perhaps, which wore distended ears, and Polynesians who did not. Stretched ear-lobes are shown in some moai kavakava images (p. 242) and Cook records that many persons were seen to have them in 1774. The practice continued until about 1850.

Luckily we are not concerned here with the 'mystery' (if it is one) of who the Long-ears and the Short-ears were. The problem is fully discussed by Métraux, and quickly dismissed by Suggs. As to the story, Métraux suggests that an old version may have referred to a people living in Poike who bullied the others over moving stones, and finally were burned in an oven; and that the motif of the Long-ears may have been added in recent years when distended lobes were going out of fashion. [Métraux, 99:69–73]

p. 249 Tattooed human figure. Because wood was so scarce, some Easter Island figures are more like stuffed toys than sculpture. This one is made of rushes covered with tapa, and painted in the style of local tattooing.
(By courtesy of the Peabody Museum of Harvard University.)

THE ERUPTION OF PELE'S ANGER

Hawaii

Very few major gods in Polynesia exist without either equivalents or relatives in some other part. Nearly all of them can be related to some postulated 'basic pantheon', which cannot itself now be located or derived. An exception, for obvious natural reasons, is Hawaii's Pele, goddess of the largest active volcano in the world. Pele seems to have been created in Hawaii in her own image. Her story has other Hawaiian characteristics, too: it is immensely long and archipelagic. In the part which describes her arrival from a distant land and her search for a suitable pit, Pele has first to try all the other islands of the Hawaiian chain, starting with Ni'ihau, the farthest away. (This procedure, incidentally, has some geological sanction.) The second part, where she sends her sister Hi'iaka to find and bring her lover Lohiau, is for similar reasons among the longest pieces of Polynesian narrative surviving. Calling at all islands is a stock device of Hawaiian story-telling.

For this book it has been necessary to choose some lesser tale that has the smell of Kilauea's smoke and ash but not the great duration of the journeys. The story of Pele and Kahawali, first told by Ellis in his *Tour of Hawaii*, seems to meet the case. Besides, it lets us view a popular Hawaiian sport, and gives some further insight into the sort of relations that

were regarded as normal between gods and mortals in Polynesia.

Pele was deemed to control the lava flows of Kilauea, and various stories explain local land features in terms of her wrath. Kahawali's last words to his mother—'Aloha ino oe, eia ihonei paha oe e make ai, ke ai mainei Pele'— were proverbial. [Ellis, 107 and Thrum, 116]

p. 252 Carved figure of the god Ku, from Hawaii—where 'k' replaces 't' in modern orthography, so that Ku is the 'Tu' of other regions. This figure came from the heiau, or sacred enclosure, of the chief Kaili, at Kawai-ahae, Hawaii.
(By courtesy of the Trustees of the British Museum.)

p. 254 A scene on the pali, the precipitous volcanic cliffs near Honolulu, drawn by Fisquet, artist aboard the corvette La Bonite on its voyage around the world, 1836–7. (From 161, by courtesy of the Turnbull Library, Wellington.)

LONOPUHA OR THE ORIGIN OF HEALING; AND THE STORY OF MILU

Hawaii

In so far as it ascribes diseases to the visitations of some foreign gods, this story may possibly date from the time of early European contact, while the fact that the evil gods are followed up by a beneficent healer may even indicate a post-missionary date. Thrum, its translator, names no source, and gives it as all one piece, but it seems to me to be two stories told in summary by an informant not addicted to the device of prolongation mentioned in the previous note. It is hard to believe that a professional would have passed up the opportunity to describe in detail what happened on all the other islands; and Milu is obviously an important personage, of much greater weight than is suggested. I have chosen the story partly for the glimpse it gives us of the

glorious Hawaiian sport, now redis-
covered, of surf riding. Miss Beckwith
(102: 117–119) discusses other versions.
[Thrum, 116: 51–57]

*p. 259 Hawaiian chief in his house. A litho-
graph after Louis Choris, artist with the
Russian explorer Otto von Kotzebue in the
brig Rurik, 1815–18.
(From 147, by courtesy of the Turnbull
Library, Wellington.)*

AHU ULA: THE FIRST FEATHER CLOAK

Maui

The gorgeous scarlet cloaks, or anu ula,
that were made for Hawaiian chiefs
from the feathers of the mamo (*Drepanis
pacifica*) were symbols of divine power.
As such, they obviously had to have a
supernatural origin—as did the best
tattooing and cloak-making in New
Zealand. This story, then, is the equivalent of 'Mataora and Niwareka' (p. 319),
though it is not on the Orpheus pattern.
I have used the version collected by Mrs.
E. M. Nakuina and given by Thrum,
but have added some details from Fornander's version. 'Ula' is the same word as
'kura' in other dialects.

Good examples of the cloaks are held
in the Bishop Museum, the British
Museum, and the Canterbury Museum
(New Zealand), and colour photographs
will be found in Bühler, 146, and Guiart,
154. How the feathers were collected
and the cloaks woven is described in
detail in *Ancient Hawaiian Civilization*,
102: 135–139.

The correct method for restoring a
spirit to its corpse is also described in the
Hawaiian story of Hiku and Kawelu
(116: 47). The chewing of kava is part of
its preparation for drinking (see note on
'The Dolphins at Fagasa', below). Eleio
was merely getting it ready while
travelling. [Thrum, 116: 147–155]

*p. 263 Hawaiian woman. Some seventy years
before Paul Gauguin went to Tahiti the
artist Louis Choris had already caught the*

*qualities of Polynesian beauty without making
it appear European. This is from an original
water-colour in the Honolulu Academy of Arts.
(By courtesy of the Bishop Museum, Honolulu.)*

*p. 267 The Hawaiian neck pendant is called
'lei niho paraoa', or 'lei made of sperm-whale
tooth'—'lei' being the word for anything worn
about the neck, whether it be made of perfumed
flowers, or (as in this case) of whale's tooth
and human hair, or, nowadays, crêpe paper.
(By courtesy of the Auckland War Memorial
Museum.)*

THE ORIGIN OF KAVA

Ha'apai

Gifford gives four versions of this tale of a
Polynesian Saint Nicholas. The two I
have drawn upon were told by Mrs.
Rachel Tonga and Malakai Lavulo,
both of Lifuka. The human-into-food-
plant theme is of great antiquity—see
the note, above, on 'Hina and the Eel'.
Kape (*Alocasia macrorrhiza*) is a relative of
taro with an extremely bitter taste, so it
is often the last thing left in the garden.

The kava drink is not alcoholic, and is
therefore not intoxicating in our sense.
It produces an agreeable feeling of
relaxation, but does not have the same
effects as wine or beer. The Polynesians
had no alcohol until after European
contact. [Gifford, 130: 71–75]

*p. 270 The kava plant (Piper methysticum).
This is Sydney Parkinson's drawing (1769) of
a specimen from Ra'iatea.
(By courtesy of the Trustees of the British
Museum.)*

THE ORIGIN OF THE
MAGELLAN CLOUDS

Ha'apai

Not much light on Polynesian knowledge
of the heavens, but an engaging sample
of Tongan story-telling, which is typically
secular, gossipy, and light in tone. Dark

themes are rare, religious matters seldom present. Gifford gives three versions of this story; my rendering is based on that recorded by W. H. Murley, of Lifuka, but also draws on that of Mesake Lomu, of Foa—both islands being in the Ha'apai group.

The kava ceremony was of great importance in Tongan life, and this tale affords a 'native' glimpse of it. Pieces of coconut husk were used by Tongan men as toilet wipers—not for washing, as Murley's polite reconstruction suggests. The women used old tapa cloth; it was a point of contempt among the Tongans that Samoans used a stone! Some use was made of the Magellan Clouds in Polynesian navigation. They are seen in the southern sky as separate blobs of the Milky Way. [Gifford, 130: 103ff.]

p. 274 Kava ceremony, Tongatapu. From a drawing made by John Webber on Cook's third voyage (c. 1777), this engraving shows all the formality of the Tongan drinking ceremony described on the same page.
(From 148, by courtesy of the Turnbull Library, Wellington.)

TOKELAU MOETONGA

Ha'apai

A rare instance of something approaching a homosexual affection in a Polynesian tale. Narrated to Gifford in 1920 by Mary Fifita, of Pangai, Lifuka. [Gifford, 130: 118–119]

LOUSE AND FLEA GO FISHING

Tongatapu

Evidently by some Tongan Edward Lear, but Collocott gives no source. The body-louse was not unknown to the Polynesians, but the flea (according to Gill) was bestowed by Europeans. [Collocott, 129: 59]

TU'I TOFUA

Ha'apai

If a Polynesian story begins with a young man playing the dart-game known as teka, we may be sure that fairly soon a misdirected dart will enter an enclosure, where a woman will get hold of it; certain suggestions will then be made to the owner wishing to retrieve it, and there will follow some sort of troublesome journey to the nether world, or magic transformations with a resurrection theme.

New Zealand has the motif in its story of Hutu and Pare (where Pare seizes Hutu's dart, he rejects her advances, she kills herself, and he has to retrieve her from the World Below). Hawaii has the almost identical tale of Hiku and Kawelu; and from the Marquesas (94: 21–25) we hear a lively variant in the tale of Huuti and a 'wild woman' called Te Mo'o nieve. 'Hutu', 'Hiku' and 'Huuti' are dialectal variants of the single name.

This Tongan story of the consequences of a sika game departs so far from the pattern that its connexion with the others has not been noticed, but it clearly shares a common origin with them—an origin presumably as old as the teka game itself. The two versions I have drawn on were told by Moungatonga, of Fotuhaa, and Ana manu, of Lifuka. The misdirected-dart motif also turns up in one version of the tale 'The Origin of the Magellan Clouds'.

Davison (13) has studied the geographical distribution of the dart game here described, which is also found in North America, Australia and the Gran Chaco; and Firth (140) gives very full details, with photographs, of the game as played in Tikopia. [Gifford, 130: 76–81]

p. 280 The young Tongan, 'Otago', was sketched by William Hodges about 1775, and the original drawing is in the Mitchell Library, Sydney.
(By courtesy of the Mitchell Library.)

p. 283 A tongiaki, or large sailing canoe of Tonga, of the type that Tu'i Tofua built. From the original wash drawing by William Hodges.
(From 165, by courtesy of the Mitchell Library, Sydney, and the New South Wales Government Printer.)

p. 284 A Tongan double canoe in its shed, protected from the sun. The Tongans used their large canoes in frequent voyaging within their own group, and in expeditions to Fiji as well as Samoa. This handsome ship was drawn on Vavau, about 1839, by Dumont-d'Urville's artist, L. le Breton.
(From 152, by courtesy of the Turnbull Library, Wellington.)

THE CONSEQUENCE

Tongatapu

More than any of their Polynesian kin, the Tongans went in for narrative poetry of exuberant variety, with the result that many Tongan myths and tales are available in both prose and verse. They were particularly fond of what Mrs. Chadwick terms 'topographical poems'— long recitals introducing many place-names, with descriptive explanations of natural features. There is reason for believing that some were produced for contest purposes (Chadwick, 9: 406). Since the poems assume the audience's complete familiarity with the subject they are barely intelligible to us without the prose equivalent; yet the verse has charm. In this case I have taken some excerpts from 'Metevae's Chant', as translated by Miss Beatrice Shirley Baker for the 'Makazini a Koliji' in 1875, and linked them with a narrative based on that given to Gifford in 1920 by John Tupou, of Nukualofa. In Polynesia it is quite usual for fish caught in the middle of the night to be cleaned and eaten immediately. 'Wake up! We've got some fresh fish!' [Gifford, 130: 90–96]

p. 288 House of a chief's wives in Tongatapu. The domestic architecture of the Tongans and Samoans was among the best in Polynesia.

They developed a handsome lashing technique for the rafters, where they also stored their finest mats. A kava bowl hangs at the right, and a four-legged wooden 'pillow' stands in the foreground.
(From 150, by courtesy of the Turnbull Library, Wellington.)

LEPUHA AND THE WIDOW

Tongatapu

Lepuha, as Collocott explains, belonged to a class of young men in Tonga whose profession was to attract eligible young ladies. They were 'amorous dandies' who had no real place in Tongan society and were regarded as foreign and bad— probably Samoan. [Collocott, 129: 46]

SAMOAN GIFT, TONGAN PAYMENT

Tongatapu

Another mighty blow in the war of wit between the Tongans and their un-respected neighbours to the north. But according to the Rev. George Turner (124: 132–133) the Samoans told the self-same tale, with roles reversed. [Collocott, 129: 61]

FITI AU MUA

Manu'a

Our basic Polynesian hero-tale once more: birth in unfortunate circumstances, a 'broken home', a career of juvenile delinquency and magic, dreams of glory realised, and eventual vindication before society (compare with Maui, Rata, and others).

As with certain Tongan tales, we have the piece in two forms, prose and verse— a 'tala' and a 'solo'. This one was collected by the Rev. Thomas Powell from a man named Tofo in 1871, and translated by George Pratt and Dr. Fraser.

Pregnant cravings as the cause of a food-theft that leads to a whole series of wrongs, revenges, etc., are a frequent Polynesian theme, as the reader of this book must notice. For a note on kape itself, see under 'The Origin of Kava', above. 'Cold-food' (fono) was eaten with the kava while the main dish was being prepared. Some Eastern Polynesian instances of the episode of the taunting boys ('Who's *your* father?') will be found on pages *142-44* and *207*. Fiti's underwater swim to Fiji was of about 650 miles. [Fraser, *JPS* 9: 125–134, 1900]

p. 294 A Samoan club, such as Fiti au mua might have used when he killed his foster-mother while practising (p. 295). The pattern is inscribed with white pigment, and some of the teeth are broken, though probably not in battle.
(By courtesy of the Museum of Primitive Art, New York.)

THE DOLPHINS AT FAGASA

Savai'i

An interesting Polynesian parallel with the Greek legend (*Homeric Hymn VII*) of Dionysos and the pirates, who were all turned into dolphins for conspiring to abduct the god at sea. Collected by Augustin Krämer sometime before 1900, the story is an explanation of the custom observed at Fagasa: once a year, usually in February but sometimes in November, a 'taupo', or village virgin, stood on the reef in festal attire with a white fan, summoning dolphins, which came ashore in considerable numbers to the slaughter. (Cf. Sir Arthur Grimble's story of porpoise-calling in the Gilbert Islands, discussed in my *Dolphins, The Myth and The Mammal*, 1961.) Krämer says that in his time, if dolphins were caught in large numbers they were kept in a pool to be eaten up gradually.

To prepare kava, the root of the kava plant traditionally was chewed by a female attendant to express its juices. In modern times (more especially for visits of Royalty, Governor-Generals,

etc.) some other method is employed. [Krämer, 119, vol. I, pt 4: 680—682]

THE RAT AND THE FLYING-FOX; and WHY THE SEA-SLUG HAS TWO MOUTHS

Samoa

Moral fables about animal characteristics are not common in Polynesia, but here are two from Samoa which add to our meagre bestiary. The flying-fox, being a fruit-eater, is palatable, and on some islands has become an item of food, in the age of the shotgun. [Krämer, 119, vol. I, pt 4: 688–695]

p. 299 The flying-fox or fruit-eating bat of Polynesia, drawn by one of the artists of Dumont-d'Urville's first Pacific voyage.
(From 151, by courtesy of the Turnbull Library, Wellington.)

FOUR TALES FROM THE ATOLLS

Tokelaus: Kapingamarangi

The reader of these little stories should try to picture a truly different type of island from the rest: a 'fairy ring' of coral merely breaks the ocean's surface, being seldom more than ten feet above sea-level or wider than a few hundred yards from 'seaward' to 'lagoonward', and offering as sustenance mainly coconuts and fish, with breadfruit, some seabirds' eggs and the occasional sacred turtle for the chiefs. The magic of these lovely islands of the blue lagoons is not to be denied. Life on an atoll was thinly poised between the two green realms: of the treetops (to which every small boy had to climb for nuts), and of the brilliant waters of lagoon and ocean— daily familiar both to women and to men. Between these two realms, life and death dwelt side-by-side in the village of perfumed thatch and coral gravel; it was usual, in pre-Christian times, for the bones of departed relatives to be hung in a basket from the roof (as in 'The Basket of Souls'), and indeed the houses today are interspersed with graves, on which the relatives sleep during the period of mourning.

There is thus a sense of mystery on an atoll, even in the high illumination of bright cloud and glittering lagoon, which I think can be sensed in these charming tales. There is also a wonderful simplicity in the people's lives. Since no wealth can be accumulated, undue power is not known. S. H. Elbert in 1947 asked several people on Kapinga-marangi to describe 'the kind of person everybody liked'. The answers illuminate these kindly tales. Hetata, who was 39, described a man whose 'living was good, he did not steal, did not act haughtily, scold, or vandalize. He was modest ("he looks down") and all thought well of him'. Ropetete, who was 18, described one who was kind to everyone, who stays at home welcoming all who come, and greets the people he meets on the road—'all the people of the land would treat him as a brother'. And Iohanis (aged 47) said that such a person was 'modest, good to other people, and not haughty; he does not steal, is not greedy, does not do evil, he loves people—That is all.'

The two Tokelau stories given here were collected with many others by William Burrows, an official who spent six weeks on Fakaofo in 1921. The first is surely a child's counting-lesson, in part; it is also a perfect example of the Poly-nesian storyteller offering the stock ingredients of his art in yet another local rearrangement: a fragment of the Rata myth in the magical canoe-building; and the widely known monster-husband whom we also meet in New Zealand as a taniwha (p. 355), with the same Brer Tarrypin device for eluding him; while the whole tale follows the widespread 'Benjamin motif', the vindication of the youngest son. The place called Fiti is of course Fiji. [Burrows, *JPS* 32: 143–173, 1923]

Kapingamarangi, a lonely outlier of Western Polynesia, is a fascinating paradox of Pacific history, whose story is told in the Introduction.

It is a coral ring six miles across with thirty-four islets along its western rim, and it supports a flourishing population of five or six hundred people who re-ceived the Gospel from a native pastor only in 1919. The collecting of tales which was done there by Emory and Elbert on a Bishop Museum Expedition in 1947 must be regarded, I think, as the 'last' collecting of genuine Polynesian oral literature, unaffected by Western contact.

The people were afraid of ghosts—females to the north of the main village, males to the south—until after the Christian church was established in 1922. All the tales collected by Emory and Elbert end with the words 'Waranga tangata hua'—'Just a tale that people tell'. The story of the female eitu turns up in other parts of Polynesia also. The story of the Lobster and the Flounder is a rare example of the animal tale in Polynesia. [Emory, 138 and Elbert, 137]

p. 304 Coconut crab. The 'robber crab', or Birgus latro as it was known to Wyatt Gill, is the well-known crab of the atolls, where the present author has known it to pull socks, among other things, into its hole in the sandy ground.

(From an engraving in Gill, 55.)

THE WOMEN AND THE BATS

Tikopia

The brevity of this little Tikopian version of the 'land without men' motif enables us to see what a Polynesian tale looks like in almost literal translation. Dr. Firth's text (which, he wishes to emphasize, is 'merely one of a number of alternative ways of attempting to give as close a rendering as possible of the Tikopia conception') was printed word-by-word beneath its original when it appeared in *Oceania*, and was accompanied by a free rendering to make the story clear. But since the parallel tale of Kae and the ladies of Vainoi (with pandanus roots as husbands instead of bats) is available in this book as a key (p. *203*), I have given the literal rendering only, with a few slight changes to remove obscurity. 'Do, do thus' is the narrator's way of indicating the passage of time. His pointing to the 'anchor' and the 'stone coconut' is his claim of veracity. The last word, 'it', is not a misprint. [Firth, 141]

MATAORA AND NIWAREKA

New Zealand

One of the innumerable variants of the world-wide 'Orpheus' myth, adapted to Maori purposes in that it gives a super-natural origin for the arts of tattooing and weaving fine cloaks. Compare with 'Ahu ula', above. According to some accounts Mataora was descended from Maui. Uetonga, at any rate, was apparently an ancient personage. The story hovers in character between myth and folk-tale, and its unusual moral passages on wife-beating, and beauty that is not skin-deep, may be the result of European contact. The dance which resembles The Lancers is also surely an intrusion of European influence. [Best, 68, vol. 2: 546–548]

p. 318 The 'Kaitaia lintel', as this carving is known, was found in a swamp near Kaitaia, in the far north of New Zealand, and is thought to be very old. With a few other pieces, also found in unusual circumstances, it is distinctly different in style from most known Maori carving, but has affinities with certain Central Polynesian styles. It possibly dates from some early migration to New Zealand, and is probably the oldest specimen of Polynesian sculpture shown in this book.
(By courtesy of the Auckland War Memorial Museum.)

p. 322 Tattooed Maori chief. One of the many drawings done by Major H. G. Robley in New Zealand in the 1860's, while the owners of such designs were still alive.
(By courtesy of the Hawke's Bay Museum and Art Gallery, New Zealand.)

TE KANAWA, and KAHUKURA

New Zealand

Two charming Maori fairy tales given to Sir George Grey, the Governor of New Zealand, for his *Polynesian Mythology*, 1855. The narrator of Te Kanawa, and perhaps of Kahukura too, was the warrior-chief Te Wherowhero (see frontispiece). The patupaiarehe, or Maori 'fairies', are always said to have fair hair and fair complexion, as also are the turehu in 'Mataora and Niwareka'.

In 'Te Kanawa' a supernatural explana-tion is given for what was probably carbon-monoxide poisoning, a likely hazard of the winter fug in any Maori house—perhaps especially in the Waikato district, where the air lies still on winter nights. [Grey, 72: 225–227 and 221–224]

p. 329 Maori neck pendant, 'hei tiki'—loosely called a tiki in New Zealand and widely known in degenerate plastic reproductions given to airline passengers, etc. The figure, usually from 2 to 4 inches high, was normally carved in the nephrite known as 'greenstone', and always with the tilted head.
(By courtesy of the Dominion Museum, Wellington.)

p. 333 'A New Zealand Warrior in his proper dress and compleatly armed, according to their manner'. Engraved after Sydney Parkinson for his posthumous Journal.
(From 157, by courtesy of the Turnbull Library, Wellington.)

LIZARD-HUSBAND, SCALY SKIN

New Zealand

A piquant example, adapted from Richard Taylor, of a macabre speciality of the New Zealand Maori, the taniwha story. Sea-taniwha were benevolent creatures, like dolphins, but land-taniwha were horrors, in the shape of a lizard and very large—perhaps related more to New

Zealand's 'living fossil', the tuatara, than to the pretty little lizards most Maoris would have known. In the woman's method of escape, American readers will recognize Brer Tarrypin: 'he dove down inter de water, he did, en tie de bed-cord hard en fas' ter wunner dese yer big clayroots'. [Taylor, 83: 51]

p. 336 Carved bone-chest from New Zealand. The bones of chiefs, being highly tapu, were placed in ornamental containers, of which this is a particularly grisly example. Evidently it was made to be stuck in the ground, perhaps the floor of a cave.
(By courtesy of the Auckland War Memorial Museum.)

HINE AND TU

New Zealand

Averred by Grey's unnamed informant to be the true story of the courtship of a pair of tribal ancestors. Actually nothing but a rearrangement of well-known stock themes from the repertoire—Hina's water-journey, and the 'Benjamin motif'.

Hina's journey across the sea to Tinirau is usually made with some sort of magical assistance—a fish in Mangaia (56: 95), a turtle in the Tokelaus (136: 156), an enchanted girdle or other unspecified marvels in New Zealand (72: 41, 62; 83: 108); and when at last she reaches Tinirau's island the first thing she does is to loll about in his precious pools (83: 108) until a messenger fetches him, in a state of annoyance which is soon corrected

An inland lake of New Zealand affords no plausible magic carrier, so in this story we have gourds being used as buoyancy aids. However, the Rotorua thermal district does afford its magic pools, and Hine finds one on Mokoia, the island in Lake Rotorua. As for Tu—he is our old friend the 'outsider' and youngest of the family (cf. Maui himself, or the other New Zealand hero Hatupatu (72: 143), who shows his brothers what stuff *he* is made of).

The 'romance of the swimmer' is not as common in Polynesia as we might expect it to be. No doubt swimming was too commonplace in the smaller islands to serve a story-teller's purposes—but was less so in the only part of Polynesia that might be described as distant from the sea. Grey gives a similar tale from another lake nearby. The style of both is sentimental and corrupt. [Grey, 72: 183–191; 240–242]

p. 338 Maori flute. This is the putorino, the type of flute Tu tanekai played while his friend Tiki played the koauau (next picture). (By courtesy of the Auckland War Memorial Museum.)

p. 339 Short Maori flute. This is the koauau, the kind that Tiki played while Tu tanekai played the putorino (previous picture). There are three holes on the other side of this finely carved example.
(By courtesy of the Auckland War Memorial Museum.)

MANAII AND THE SPEARS

Chatham Islands

The Moriori version (written down for Shand by Hirawanu Tapu about 1870) of a story about a cuckolded chief, which is also found in New Zealand. In the Maori myths as well, war and man-eating are spoken of as evils that were once unknown. [*JPS* 3: 187–189, 1894]

p. 343 Maori hand-club, patu paraoa. This handsome weapon for in-fighting, made from the bone of a whale, was taken from New Zealand to England by Captain Cook, but has since been returned to its homeland. (By courtesy of the Dominion Museum, Wellington.)

UGLY-UGLY! FRIZZLED-HEADS!

Chatham Islands

A nasty little tale of prejudice amongst the young, and its due avenging. For a further note on racial feeling in the Chatham Islands, see 'Apukura', above. The personal names of all three females in this tale are also found, in totally different connexions, in New Zealand stories given by Grey (72: 24 and 72). [Shand, *JPS* 5: 133–134, 1896]

p. 346 Carved feather-box. The Chatham Islands feather-box in which Muru whenua kept her treasures (p. 345) would have been more stark and less ornate than this example of New Zealand Maori carving, which is of wood inlaid with paua-shell 'eyes', and is 22⅜ inches long.

(By courtesy of the Museum of Primitive Art, New York.)

RAO'S DIRGE

Rarotonga

In 1872, returning in the cool of evening to Avarua, Rarotonga, after a peaceful Sabbath's preaching at Titikaveka, William Gill was shown by his native companions the remains of an abandoned house and told that it was once the home of Tupa, *'the man who ate his own wife'*.

Tupa, though well known as a cannibal, had always lived on good terms with Rao, who was equally well known for her skill in composing songs. Tupa's invalid sister lived with them, and there were no children. One day Rao asked her husband to shave off her matted hair. When he had finished doing it (with a shark's tooth fixed on a reed) Tupa remarked the whiteness of her scalp and said, 'I long to eat thy head.' Rao merely answered, 'Do as thou wilt.' Then, says Gill, 'as with the marvellous stoicism of heathenism she watched the preparations for the horrid banquet, she vented

her feelings in a dirge, which was carefully treasured up by her afflicted sister-in-law, and thus transmitted to Christian times. It is now for the first time written. . . .'

After the family umu had been heated Rao was 'strangled, cut up with a bamboo knife, and cooked by her tiger-hearted husband'. He ate alone. His sister refused to join him.

Gill the Christian adds a gratifying account of how Tupa was dealt with by Rao's brothers on the following day. One of them called to see her, but found only Tupa's sister, who told him with tears what had happened. He fetched his brother, they took their weapons, found Tupa in hiding with the left-over food, and speared him to death. 'In the evening of the same day the brothers baked the body of Tupa in the very oven which had been prepared for the re-cooking of Rao.' (In the absence of refrigerators it was usual to recook good meat that could not be consumed immediately.)

The first stanza, called 'tumu', or root, is actually a refrain, repeated between the others ('offshoots'). Its last line, says Gill, is 'meaningless, like our *Fal, lal, lal*', and on this hint I have ventured to set the poem, as it were, to the music of some sad pavane by John Dowland. But the liberties involved were few. Gill says the lament was well known in the Hervey Islands (i.e., Rarotonga and its neighbours). The father of his informant was well acquainted with all the parties concerned, when young. The episode and the lament may therefore be roughly dated 'circa 1800'. [Gill, 55: 164–168]

THE COMING OF TUTE

Mangaia

Even in its Religious Tract Society setting (*From Darkness to Light in Polynesia*, 1894), Gill's printed translation of this song-and-dance production reads as if Gilbert and Sullivan had turned to the

South Seas for a new locale. It is full of light movement and sprightly pomp, and so I have allowed myself to think of it in Sullivan's rhythms, while strictly following the substance and even some phrases of Gill's rendering. There are no rhymes in the native text.

The piece is far from unique. Cook himself was offered such entertainments at Tahiti, in which frequent references were made to the distinguished visitors (3, vol. 2: 209, 227); while on the atoll Tongareva (Penrhyn Island), some seven hundred miles to the north, the castaway trader E. H. Lamont had the rueful experience in 1853 of seeing his own shipwreck-and-landing re-enacted in a performance just as lively and absurd as this. The piece there had 'several scenes', a platform was built to represent the wreck, Lamont had to lend his own sword for the occasion, and he also 'assisted them a little in rigging the vessel'. The actors themselves 'were so amused that they could scarcely play their parts' and a good-humoured feast followed (144: 318–319).

A play based on the legend of Huku, performed in the village square of Rakahanga for Peter Buck (7: 55f.), was in the same style, and so evidently was an Easter Island pantomime described to Métraux (100: 177). The resemblances suggest a recognized form of entertainment which was obviously common (cf. Chadwick, 9: 381–382). The uapou, or church pageant, so popular in the Cook Islands today, must be the modern descendant of these shows.

The clear-cut 'sonata-form' of this Mangaian example should be noticed: an unaccompanied recitativo introduction (with some lively 'business', to be sure, but not yet any drums or dancing); then into a vigorous allegro which is repeated da capo before a short development section brings as its climax the 'white-faced men' (O murenga oa); and a finale or coda for which the composer has saved up his most important statement.

The original native text took its own liberties for the sake of rhythm, as Gill explains. In it the Beretane are first alluded to as 'Bere', and likewise Tute is shortened to 'Tu' when only that would fit; while the officers' no doubt frequent appeals to 'Omai' seem actually parodied as 'Maio! Maio!'

Unfortunately Gill, to whom we must be grateful for giving us this gem, had also to record the sorry fact that because of certain 'very serious evils' which invariably accompanied this sort of dancing, 'upon the establishment of Christianity it was entirely abolished'. (The chiefs, he explains in a footnote, 'whether married or not', often wore phallic ornaments; and he adds, 'Two of them may be seen in the British Museum'.) [Gill, 59: 251–258]

p. 354 Mourua, of Mangaia, was the bold young chief who dared to go aboard Cook's ship the Resolution, alone, on March 29, 1777 (see p. 353). His portrait was drawn (after he had put the knife that was given him into his 'pocket') by John Webber, and this engraving was made for Vol. III of the Voyages. He was also given an axe and some beads. For the details of Mourua's later life and violent death, see Gill, 59, page 243f. (From 148, by courtesy of the Turnbull Library, Wellington.)

p. 358 A human sacrifice in Tahiti witnessed by Captain Cook and his officers during Cook's third voyage—engraved after a drawing by John Webber, who also attended. (From 148, by courtesy of the Turnbull Library, Wellington.)

CANOE-LAUNCHING SONG

Atiu

'The double canoes of Atiu', says Gill in recording this chant, 'are usually fifty feet in length, provided with a mast and mat sails. The cordage is made of the bark of the lemon hibiscus. As many as a hundred and fifty men, women, and children are often accommodated on board one of these primitive vessels. In launching them, one may still [c. 1870] hear the following song, referring to Captain Cook's visit to Atiu. It was composed somewhere about the year 1780.'

This new translation of Gill's native text owes a great deal to Mr. J. M. McEwen of Wellington, and not a little to my own recollections of an excited departure from Atiu's landing place on a certain perilously overcrowded vessel.

The reference to the guns recalls a circumstance of Cook's visit in 1777. A shore-party (including Omai) caused concern on board by being a long time returning, and guns were fired as frighteners, lest anything had gone wrong. The idea of 'sailing for Great Tahiti' is not exactly poetic licence, for the Atiuans were very much aware of Tahiti—there being several Tahitian castaways living among them at that time (much to Cook's surprise). There would naturally be even more talk of their homeland after his visit. Wooden rollers were used for launching heavy Polynesian canoes. [Gill, 59: 259–264]

BY WHOSE COMMAND?

Atiu

Impromptu poetical words spoken on an historic occasion by the paramount chief of Atiu and recorded by Gill in his account of John Williams' visit to the island in 1823. The people were all for attacking and plundering the little ship, as they could easily have done in their big canoes (see preceding note), but Rongomatane was awed by her appearance and forbade any violence, uttering, says Gill, 'the following poetical words, now become proverbial'. Mrs. Chadwick (9: 269) discusses this and other 'occasional poetry' of Polynesia. [Gill, 58: 45, 1885]

CHANT TO IO

New Zealand

More than fifty years after Christianity reached New Zealand it was suddenly disclosed by certain Maori elders that the pantheistic mythology hitherto revealed was not in fact the full story, and that according to an esoteric or 'higher' learning—withheld till then because of its sanctity—the Maori did have a single, Supreme Creator, whose name was Io.

The first reference in print to Io seems to have been made in 1876, by C. O. Davis, who said a member of the Ngapuhi tribe had told him 'that the Maoris in olden times had worshipped a Supreme Being whose name was so sacred that none but a priest might utter it at certain times and places...' (70: 32). The only complete account was given much later, in a manuscript dictated by the Maori elder Te Matorohanga and published in 1913 (Smith, 82). But both this elder and his scribe Te Whatahoro were converted to Christianity long before the manuscript was composed.

The little word 'io' or 'kio', as Buck points out in an amused survey of the principal evidence and claims (69: 526f.), can sometimes mean the squeak of a rat or bird, at other times muscular twitches of the body that were regarded as omens by the Maori. Even so, Io-Jehovah caused some excitement in an age which wished to persuade itself that primitive peoples had really been Believers all along, and His revelation soon led to further discoveries elsewhere in Polynesia—notably in the Tuamotu, where Stimson believed as late as 1933 that he had unearthed a cult of 'Kiho'. The reader, ever alert, will have noticed already that a minor deity named Io is listed among the 'progeny of Tu' in Shand's Creation myth from the Chatham Islands (p. 49) which was first published in 1894. But in view of the date he could easily have been one of the 'un-Moriori interpolations' which Shand's rival William Baucke (91: 384) asperly charges Shand with having made.

This is no place to open up the unprofitable 'Io problem'; those who wish to may pursue it in the pages of Buck or Prytz Johansen and their sources. It is enough here to say that the problem might never have become a problem at all, but for the attention commanded by the poetic quality of some of the material that came to light—of which this well-known 'Chant to Io' is the best-known sample.

It is obviously influenced by Genesis I; but it still is the product of a Polynesian mind, and is, in fact, the only piece in this book of which the English rendering is by a Polynesian. The Maori original was first published in the *Journal of the Polynesian Society* in 1907, having been given to Col. W. E. Gudgeon some years earlier by Tiwai Paraone. This rendering is by Hare Hongi (H. M. Stowell, 1859–1944), a member of the Ngapuhi tribe. It has been ably criticized by Prytz Johansen (79: 53f.), but I think the fragment earns its place here, following the pieces about ships, by showing what the Maori was able to make of Judaeo-Christian influence, and make his own, before those ships completely swamped his cultural canoe. [Paraone, 76]

REFERENCES

The references are of three kinds: 1. Source material directly drawn upon or cited, as shown in the notes to the stories and pictures and in the Introduction; 2. Comparative material indirectly drawn upon but not cited; 3. Some other works which I have found to be essential background.

A fourth category, 'items consulted but not drawn upon', would greatly enlarge this list, and a bibliography of all material relating to or purporting to be Polynesian oral literature would be immense. For a truly comprehensive view of the relevant literature the reader must turn to C. R. H. Taylor's *Pacific Bibliography* (33).

Where more than one edition of a book is shown, all references are to the later edition.

ABBREVIATIONS

Bishop Mus. Bull.: Bulletin of the Bernice Pauahi Bishop Museum, Honolulu, Hawaii. (The term disguises numerous works that are in fact large books.)

Bishop Mus. Mem.: Memoir of the same. (The 'Memoirs' were precursors of the Bulletins.)

JPS: *Journal of the Polynesian Society*, Wellington, New Zealand.

Pol. Soc. Mem.: Memoir of the same. (Often a reprint of material published serially in the *Journal*.)

GENERAL

1. Andersen, Johannes C., *Myths and Legends of the Polynesians*. Harrap, London 1928. [The stories in summary, with commentary.]
2. Beaglehole, J. C., ed., *The Endeavour Journal of Joseph Banks, 1768–1771*, vol. I. Public Library of New South Wales and Angus and Robertson, Sydney 1962.
3. ——, *The Journals of Captain Cook*, vols. 1 and 2. Cambridge University Press for the Hakluyt Society, 1955 and 1961.
4. Beckwith, Martha W., 'Polynesian Mythology,' *JPS*, 49: 19–38, 1940
5. ——, 'Polynesian Story Composition,' *JPS*, 53: 177–203, 1944.
6. Bowra, C .M., *Primitive Song*. Weidenfeld and Nicolson, London 1962.

7. Buck, P. H. (Te Rangi Hiroa), *Vikings of the Pacific*. Chicago University Press, 1959. First published as *Vikings of the Sunrise*, 1938.

8. Campbell, Joseph, *The Masks of God*: vol. 1, *Primitive Mythology*. Viking, New York 1959.

9. Chadwick, H. M. and N. K., *The Growth of Literature*, vol. 2. Cambridge University Press, 1940. [Described on pages 30–32.]

10. Chadwick, Nora K., 'Notes on Polynesian Mythology,' *Journal of the Royal Anthropological Institute*, 60: 425–446, 1930. [An important article, comparing the Kae-Tinirau stories with certain tales in the Kojiki of Japan.]

11. ——, 'The Kite, a Study in Polynesian Tradition,' *Jour. Roy. Anthrop. Inst.*, 61: 455–491, 1931.

12. Codrington, R. H., *The Melanesians: Studies in their Anthropology and Folk-Lore*. Clarendon Press, Oxford 1891.

13. Davison, D. S., 'The Pacific and Circum-Pacific Appearances of the Dart-game,' *JPS*, 45: 99–114, 119–126, 1936; *JPS*, 46: 1–23, 1937.

14. Dixon, Roland B., *The Mythology of All Races*: vol. 9, *Oceania*. Marshall Jones Co., Boston 1916.

15. Elbert, Samuel H., 'Internal Relationships of Polynesian Languages and Dialects,' *Southwestern Journal of Anthropology*, 9: 147–173, 1953.

16. Ellis, William, *Polynesian Researches*, 4 vols. Fisher, Son and Jackson, London 1839–42.

17. Finley, M. I., *The World of Odysseus*. Pelican, London 1962.

18. Forster, J. R., *Observations made during a Voyage Round the World, on Physical Geography, Natural History, and Ethic Philosophy*. G. Robinson, London 1778.

19. Golson, J., ed., *Polynesian Navigation*. Pol. Soc. Mem. 34, Wellington 1962. [A symposium of experts discussing Andrew Sharp's theory of accidental voyaging.]

20. Handy, E. S. C., *Polynesian Religion*. Bishop Mus. Bull. 34, 1927.

21. Highland, Genevieve A., R. W. Force *et al.* eds., *Polynesian Culture History: Essays in honour of Kenneth P. Emory*. Bishop Museum Special Publication No. 56, 1967. [Twenty-four essays. A conspectus of the present state of research into Polynesian origins, migrations, mythology, languages and material culture. See Introduction, page 2.]

22. Langer, Suzanne K., *Philosophy in a New Key*. Harvard University Press, Cambridge, Mass. 1942. [Contains an interesting section on Maui.]

23. Luomala, Katharine, 'Documentary Research in Polynesian Mythology,' *JPS*, 49: 175–195, 303–304, 1940.

24. ——, *Maui-of-a-Thousand-Tricks: His Oceanic and European Biographers*. Bishop Mus. Bull. 198, 1949.

25. ——, *The Menehune of Polynesia and other Little People of Oceania*. Bishop Mus. Bull. 203, 1951.

26. ——, *Voices on the Wind: Polynesian Myths and Chants*. Bishop Museum, Honolulu 1955.

27. Mackenzie, D. A., *Myths and Traditions of the South Sea Islands*. Gresham Publishing Co., London (n.d.).

28. Moerenhout, J. A., *Voyages aux Îles du Grand Océan*, 2 vols. Paris 1837.

29. Quiros, *The Voyages of Pedro Fernandez de Quiros, 1595–1606*, tr. and ed. Sir Clements Markham. Hakluyt Society, London 1904.

30. Sharp, Andrew, *Ancient Voyagers in the Pacific*. Penguin, London 1957.

31. Smith, S. Percy, *Hawaiki, the Original Home of the Maori*. Pol. Soc. Mem. 4, Auckland 1921.

32. Suggs, Robert C., *The Island Civilizations of Polynesia*. Mentor, New York 1960.

33. Taylor, C. R. H., *A Pacific Bibliography: printed matter relating to the native peoples of Polynesia, Melanesia and Micronesia*. Clarendon Press, Oxford 1965.

34. Williams, John, *A Narrative of Missionary Enterprises in the South Sea Islands*. J. Snow, London 1840.

34a. Yawata, I., and Y. H. Sinoto, eds., *Prehistoric Culture in Oceania, A Symposium* (Eleventh Pacific Science Congress, Tokyo 1966.) Bishop Museum Press, Honolulu 1968. [See Introduction, page 2.]

TAHITI (SOCIETY ISLANDS)

35. Carrington, A. H., 'A Note by Captain James Cook on the Tahiti Creation Myth,' *JPS*, 48: 30–31, 1939

36. Handy, E. S. C., *History and Culture in the Society Islands*. Bishop Mus. Bull. 79, 1930.

37. ——, *Houses, Boats and Fishing in the Society Islands*. Bishop Mus. Bull.

38. Emory, K. P., 'The Tahitian Account of Creation by Mare,' *JPS*, 47: 45–63, 1938.

39. Henry, Teuira, *Ancient Tahiti*. Bishop Mus. Bull. 48, 1928. [Described on page 27.]

40. ——, trans., 'The Legend of Honoura,' *JPS*, 4: 256–294, 1895. [Collected on Ra'iatea by John Williams.]

41. Leverd, A., trans., 'The Tahitian Version of the Story of Tafa'i,' *JPS*, 21: 1–12, 1912.

42. Monberg, Torben, 'Ta'aroa in the Creation Myths of the Society Islands,' *JPS*, 65: 253–281, 1956.

TUAMOTU (PAUMOTU) ISLANDS

43. Emory, K. P., 'Tuamotuan Concepts of Creation,' *JPS*, 49: 69–136, 1940.
44. Leverd, A., trans., 'The Paumotu Version of the Story of Rata,' *JPS*, 19: 176–194, 1910.
45. ——, 'The Paumotu Version of the Story of Tafa'i,' *JPS*, 20: 172–184, 1911.
46. Emory, K. P., 'The Tuamotuan Legend of Rongo,' *JPS*, 56: 52–4, 1947.
47. Stimson, J. Frank, *Tuamotuan Religion*. Bishop Mus. Bull. 103, 1933.
48. ——, *The Cult of Kiho-Tumu*. Bishop Mus. Bull. 111, 1933.
49. ——, *The Legends of Maui and Tahaki* (told by Fariua-a-Makitua of Fagatau). Bishop Mus. Bull. 127, 1934.
50. ——, *Tuamotuan Legends* (Island of Anaa). Bishop Mus. Bull. 148, 1937.
51. ——, *Songs and Tales of the Sea Kings: Interpretations of the Oral Literature of Polynesia*. Peabody Museum, Salem 1957.

COOK ISLANDS AND NIUE
(*See also* ATOLLS AND OUTLIERS, *below*)

52. Buck, P. H., *Material Culture of the Cook Islands*. Board of Maori Ethnological Research, Wellington 1927.
53. ——, *Mangaian Society*. Bishop Mus. Bull. 122, 1934.
54. ——, *Arts and Crafts of the Cook Islands* (Aitutaki). Bishop Mus. Bull. 179, 1944.
55. Gill, W. Wyatt, *Life in the Southern Isles*. Religious Tract Society, London 1876.
56. ——, *Myths and Songs from the South Pacific*. H. S. King, London 1876.
57. ——, *Historical Sketches of Savage Life in Polynesia*. G. Didsbury, Wellington 1880.
58. ——, *Jottings from the Pacific*. Religious Tract Society, London 1885.
59. ——, *From Darkness to Light in Polynesia*. Religious Tract Society, London 1894.
60. ——, 'Extracts from Dr. Wyatt Gill's Papers,' *JPS*, 20: 116–157, 1911; *JPS*, 21: 39–64, 120–33, 1912; *JPS*, 24: 140–155, 1915. (The 'song in favour of peace' quoted on p. 22 is in *JPS*, 21: 58.)

61. Loeb, Edwin M., *History and Traditions of Niue*. Bishop Mus. Bull. 32, 1926.

62. Low, Drury, 'Traditions of Aitutaki, Cook Islands,' *JPS*, 43: 17–24, 171–186, 258–266, 1934; *JPS*, 44: 26–31, 1935.

63. Savage, Stephen, 'The Rarotongan Version of the Story of Rata,' *JPS*, 19: 142–168, 1910.

64. ——, 'Rarotongan Legends and History: The Period of Iro and Tangiia,' *JPS*, 25: 138–149, 1916; *JPS*, 26: 10–18, 52–59, 1917.

65. ——, *A Dictionary of the Maori Language of Rarotonga*. Department of Island Territories, Wellington 1962. [Much more than a dictionary in some respects. An amateur work of great value.]

66. Te Ariki Taraare, 'History and Traditions of Rarotonga' (trans. S. Percy Smith), *JPS*, 8: 61–88 [the story of Maui]; 171–178 [the story of Tinirau], 1899.

NEW ZEALAND

67. Best, Elsdon, *Some Aspects of Maori Myth and Religion*. Dominion Museum Monograph No. 1, Wellington 1922.

68. ——, *The Maori*, 2 vols. Pol. Soc. Mem. 5, Wellington 1924.

69. Buck, P. H. (Te Rangi Hiroa), *The Coming of the Maori*. Maori Purposes Fund Board and Whitcombe & Tombs Ltd., Wellington 1949.

70. Davis, C. O., *The Life and Times of Patuone, the Celebrated Ngapuhi Chief*, Auckland 1876. [Cited by Buck, 69, and Prytz Johansen, 79.]

71. Duff, Roger S., *The Moa-Hunter Period of Maori Culture*. Canterbury Museum Bulletin No. 1, Christchurch 1950.

72. Grey, (Sir) George, *Polynesian Mythology and Ancient Traditional History of the New Zealanders, as furnished by their Chiefs and Priests*. John Murray, London 1855. Reprint, Whitcombe & Tombs, Christchurch 1961.

73. Hongi, Hare: *see* Paraone, Tiwai.

74. Maning, F. E., *Old New Zealand*. Richard Bentley & Son, London 1887.

75. Paraone, Tiwai, 'A Maori Cosmogony,' (trans. Hare Hongi), *JPS*, 16: 109–119, 1907.

76. Posinsky, S. O., 'The Death of Maui,' *Journal of the American Psychoanalytical Association*, 5: 485–489, 1957.

77. Potae, H., 'The Story of Tawhaki,' *JPS*, 37: 359–366, 1928.

78. Prytz Johansen, J., *The Maori and his Religion in its Non-Ritualistic Aspects*. Munksgaard, Copenhagen 1954.

79. ——, *Studies in Maori Rites and Myths*. Munksgaard, Copenhagen 1958.

80. Shortland, Edward, *Traditions and Superstitions of the New Zealanders*. Longmans. London 1854.

81. ——, *Maori Religion and Mythology*. Longmans, London 1882.

82. Smith, S. Percy, *The Lore of the Whare-wananga, or Teachings of Maori College*, Parts 1 and 2. Pol. Soc. Mems. 3 and 4, 1913. [Cited by Buck, 69.]

83. Taylor, Richard, *Te Ika a Maui, or New Zealand and its Inhabitants*. Wertheim and Macintosh, London 1855.

84. White, John, *The Ancient History of the Maori, his Mythology and Traditions*, 6 vols. Government Printer, Wellington 1887–90.

85. Williams, H. W., *Dictionary of the Maori Language*, 6th Edition. Government Printer, Wellington 1957.

86. Wohlers, J. F. H., 'The Mythology and Traditions of the Maori,' *Transactions of the New Zealand Institute*, 7: 3–53, 1875; 8: 108–123, 1876.

CHATHAM ISLANDS

87. Best, Elsdon, 'Maori and Maruiwi' [Moriori], *Transactions of the New Zealand Institute*, 47: 436, 1915. [Cited by Skinner, 90.]

88. Shand, Alexander, 'The Moriori People of the Chatham Islands, their Traditions and History,' *JPS*, 3: 76–92, 121–133, 187–198, 1894; *JPS*, 4: 33–46, 89–98, 161–176, 209–225, 1895; *JPS*, 5: 13–32, 73–91, 131–141, 195–211, 1896; *JPS*, 6: 11–18, 145–151, 161–168, 1897; *JPS*, 7: 73–88, 1898.

89. ——, the same, collected as Pol. Soc. Mem. 2, Wellington 1911.

90. Skinner, H. D., *The Moriories of Chatham Islands*. Bishop Mus. Mem. vol. 9, no. 1, 1923.

91. Skinner, H. D., and William Baucke, *The Moriories*. Bishop Mus. Mem. vol. 9, no. 5, 1928.

THE MARQUESAS, AND MANGAREVA

92. Buck, P. H. (Te Rangi Hiroa), *Ethnology of Mangareva*. Bishop Mus. Bull. 157, 1938.

93. Handy, E. S. C., *The Native Culture in the Marquesas*. Bishop Mus. Bull. 9, 1923.

94. ——, *Marquesan Legends*. Bishop Mus. Bull. 69, 1930.

95. Handy, Willowdean C., *Tattooing in the Marquesas*. Bishop Mus. Bull. 1, 1922.

96. ——, *Forever the Land of Men. An Account of a Visit to the Marquesas Islands*. Dodd, Mead & Company, New York 1965. [No other book has conveyed so well the 'feel' of Polynesian gift-exchange.]

97. Linton, Ralph S., *The Material Culture of the Marquesas*. Bishop Mus. Mem. vol. 8, no. 5, 1923.

98. Melville, Herman, *Typee: or a Narrative of a Four Months Residence among the Natives of a Valley of the Marquesas Islands*. John Murray, London 1846.

EASTER ISLAND

99. Métraux, Alfred, *Ethnology of Easter Island*. Bishop Mus. Bull. 160, 1940. [Reviews and synthesizes all published material on Easter Island to that date.]

100. ——, *Easter Island, A Stone-Age Civilization of the Pacific*. André Deutsch, London 1957. [Presents for the general reader the main material of the previous item, but also discusses more recent material dealing with the Easter Island 'script'.]

101. Routledge, Mrs. Scoresby, *The Mystery of Easter Island, The Story of an Expedition*. Sifton, Praed & Co., London 1919. [Valuable for its photographs and drawings.]

HAWAIIAN ISLANDS

102. Beckwith, Martha W., *Hawaiian Mythology*. Yale University Press, New Haven 1940. [Though primarily concerned with Hawaiian examples, which are copiously presented in summary, this valuable work also contains much comparative material.]

103. ——, *Kepelino's Traditions of Hawaii*. Bishop Mus. Bull. 95, 1932.

104. Bishop, Marcia B., *Hawaiian Life of the Pre-European Period ... with a Catalogue of the M. B. Bishop Collection....* Peabody Museum, Salem 1940.

105. Colum, Padraic, *Tales and Legends of Hawaii*: vol. 1, *At the Gateways of the Day*; vol. 2, *The Bright Islands*. Yale University Press, New Haven 1924 and 1925. [Colum was commissioned by the Hawaiian Legend and Folklore Commission to visit the islands and produce a collection 'primarily for the children of the Hawaiian Islands'. Interesting preface and notes.]

106. Elbert, Samuel H., ed., *Selections from Fornander's Hawaiian Antiquities and Folk-lore*. University of Hawaii Press, Honolulu 1959.

107. Ellis, William, *A Narrative of a Tour through Hawaii.* . . . Fisher, Son and Jackson, London 1826. Reprint, Honolulu 1917.

108. Emerson, J. S., 'The Myth of Hiku and Kawelu,' *Hawaiian Annual* for 1883: 36–39.

109. Emerson, Nathaniel B., *Unwritten Literature of Hawaii, Sacred Songs of the Hula*. Smithsonian Institution, Bureau of American Ethnology, Bulletin 38, Washington 1909.

110. Fornander, Abraham, *An Account of the Polynesian Race* . . ., 3 vols. Trübner & Co., London 1878–85.

111. ——, *The Fornander Collection of Hawaiian Antiquities and Folk-lore*, ed. Thos. G. Thrum. Bishop Mus. Mem. vols. 4–6, 1916–20. [See also Elbert, above.]

112. Handy, E. S. C., K. P. Emory, *et al.*, *Ancient Hawaiian Civilization*. Chas. E. Tuttle, Rutland, Vermont, and Tokyo, Japan, 1965. [Popular lectures delivered in Honolulu, collected and revised.]

113. Leib, Amos P., *Hawaiian Legends in English, an Annotated Bibliography*. University of Hawaii Press, Honolulu 1949. [An essential time-saver. Sorts out an immense quantity of published material, clearly identifying that which has any value. Excellent introduction.]

114. Malo, David, *Hawaiian Antiquities*. Bishop Museum Special Publication No. 2, Honolulu 1903.

115. Rice, William Hyde, *Hawaiian Legends*. Bishop Mus. Bull. 3, 1923.

116. Thrum, Thos. G. (compiler), *Hawaiian Folk Tales. A Collection of Native · Legends*. Various authors. A. C. McClurg & Co., Chicago 1907.

SAMOA

117. Buck, P. H. (Te Rangi Hiroa), *Samoan Material Culture*. Bishop Mus. Bull. 75, 1930.

118. Fraser, J., 'Folksongs and Myths from Samoa,' *JPS*, 1: 164–189, 1892; *JPS*, 5: 171–183, 1896; *JPS*, 6: 19–36, 67–76, 107–122, 1897; *JPS*, 7: 15–29, 1898; *JPS*, 9: 125–134, 1900.

119. Krämer, Augustin, *Die Samoa-Inseln*, 2 vols. Stuttgart 1901–2. [Citations are from the English translation, mimeographed, Government of Samoa, Apia 1942.]

120. Mead, Margaret, *Coming of Age in Samoa*. William Morrow & Co., New York 1928.

121. Schultz, E., 'The Samoan Version of the Story of Apakura,' *JPS*, 18: 139–142, 1909.

122. Stair, J. S., 'Early Samoan Voyages and Settlement,' *JPS*, 4: 99–132, 1895.

123. ——, 'Jottings on the Mythology and Spirit-Lore of Old Samoa,' *JPS*, 5: 33–58, 1896.

124. Turner, Rev. George, *Samoa a Hundred Years Ago and Long Before*. Macmillan, London 1884.

TONGA

125. Buck, P. H. (Te Rangi Hiroa), 'Material Representation of Tongan and Samoan Gods,' *JPS*, 44: 48–53, 85–96, 153–162, 1935.

126. Collocott, E. E. V., 'Legends from Tonga,' *Folklore*, 32: 45–58, 1921; *Folklore*, 35: 275–283, 372–8, 1924.

127. ——, 'Notes on Tongan Religion,' *JPS*, 30: 152–163, 227–240, 1919.

128. ——, 'A Tongan Theogony,' *Folklore*, 30: 234–8, 1919.

129. ——, *Tales and Poems of Tonga*. Bishop Mus. Bull. 46, 1928.

130. Gifford, E. W., *Tongan Myths and Tales*. Bishop Mus. Bull. 8, 1924.

131. ——, *Tongan Society*. Bishop Mus. Bull. 61, 1929.

132. Mariner, William, *An Account of the Natives of the Tonga Islands. . . .*, 2 vols. John Martin, London 1817.

ATOLLS AND OUTLIERS

133. Beaglehole, Ernest and Pearl, *Ethnology of Pukapuka*. Bishop Mus. Bull. 150, 1938.

134. Buck, P. H. (Te Rangi Hiroa), *Ethnology of Tongareva*. Bishop Mus. Bull. 92, 1932.

135. ——, *Ethnology of Manihiki and Rakahanga*. Bishop Mus. Bull. 99, 1932.

136. Burrows, William, 'Some Notes and Legends of a South Sea Island, Fakaofo, of the Tokelau Group,' *JPS*, 32: 143–173, 1923.

137. Elbert, Samuel H., 'Uta-matua and other Tales of Kapingamarangi,' *Journal of American Folklore*, 62(245): 240–246, 1949.

138. Emory, K. P., 'Myths and Tales from Kapingamarangi, a Polynesian-inhabited island in Micronesia,' *Journal of American Folklore*, 62(245): 230–239, 1949.

139. ——, *Kapingamarangi, the Social and Religious Life of a Polynesian Atoll*. Bishop Mus. Bull. 228, 1965.

140. Firth, Raymond, 'A Dart match in Tikopia,' *Oceania*, 1: 64–96, 1930.

141. ——, 'Totemism in Polynesia,' *Oceania*, 1: 291–321, 1930; 377–388, 1931.

142. ——, *The Work of the Gods in Tikopia*, 2 vols. P. Lund Humphries, London 1940.

143. ——, *History and Traditions of Tikopia*. Pol. Soc. Mem. 33, Wellington 1961. [Very important. Some basic thinking on the functions of myth.]

144. Lamont, E. H., *Wild Life Among the Pacific Islanders*. Hurst and Blackett, London 1867.

PICTORIAL

145. Archey, Gilbert, *South Sea Folk*, Handbook of Maori and Oceanic Ethnology, Auckland War Memorial Museum, 2nd ed. 1949.

146. Bühler, A., T. Barrow and C. P. Mountford, *Oceania and Australia: The Art of the South Seas*. Methuen, London 1961. [Includes 16 colour plates of Polynesian material. See note to item 167 below.]

147. Choris, Louis, *Voyage Pittoresque autour du Monde . . . par M. Louis Choris, peintre . . .* Paris . . . Firmin Didot . . . 1822. [Choris was draughtsman to the captain, Otto von Kotzebue, on this Russian expedition in the brig *Rurik*, 1815–18.]

148. [Cook, Captain James] *Plates to Cook's Voyages;* vol. 1, London 1773; vol. 2, London 1777; vol. 3, London 1784. Acquisitions 266, 267 and 268 of the Alexander Turnbull Memorial Library, Wellington. [Engravings from drawings by Sydney Parkinson, William Hodges and John Webber, artists respectively on the three voyages.]

149. *Discoveries in the Southern Hemisphere; Voyages in the Pacific; Plates; in the years 1765 to 1775.* [Binder's title.] 'Published February 1st, 1777, by Wm. Strahan . . . and Thos. Cadell . . . London.' [Contains engravings after William Hodges.]

150. Dumont-d'Urville, Jules, *Voyages de la Corvette l'Astrolabe . . . 1826–1829 sous le commandement de M. Jules Dumont-d'Urville, capitaine de vaisseau*. Atlas (*Histoire du Voyage, I*). Paris: J. Tastu . . . 1833. [Contains engravings after de Sainson.]

151. ——, (as above) *Atlas, Zoologie*.

152. Dumont-d'Urville, J., *Voyage au Pôle Sud et dans l'Océanie sur les corvettes l'Astrolabe et La Zélée . . . 1837–1840 . . . sous le commandement de M. Dumont-d'Urville, capitaine de vaisseau . . . Atlas Pittoresque*, Tome Premier. Paris, Gide et cie . . . 1846. [Contains engravings after le Breton.]

153. Edge-Partington, J., and Charles Heape, *An Album of the Weapons, Tools, Ornaments, articles of Dress etc. of the Natives of the Pacific Islands drawn and described from examples in public and private collections in England*, 3 vols. Manchester 1890–98. [Although the drawings are no pleasure to the eye, this is an important documentary source.]

154. Guiart, Jean, *The Arts of the South Pacific*. Thames & Hudson, London 1963. [461 pp., 371 photogravures, 107 colour plates, 5 maps. Mostly Melanesian material.]

155. Linton, Ralph, and P. S. Wingert, in collaboration with Renée d'Harnoncourt, *Arts of the South Seas*. Museum of Modern Art, New York 1946.

156. Oldman, W. O., *Polynesian Artifacts: The Oldman Collection*. Pol. Soc. Mem. 15, Wellington 1938. [Photographs of a large and comprehensive collection.]

157. Parkinson, Sydney, *A Journal of a Voyage to the South Seas, in His Majesty's ship, The Endeavour, faithfully transcribed from the papers of the late Sydney Parkinson, Draughtsman to Joseph Banks, Esq. . . .* London: printed for Stanfield Parkinson, the editor . . . 1773.

158. [Raper, Geo.] *Birds of Australia and South Seas: Original drawings, 1788–90*. [Binder's title.] A copy in the Alexander Turnbull Memorial Library, Wellington.

159. Steinen, K. von den, *Die Marquesaner und ihre Kunst* (3 vols). D. Reimer, Berlin 1925–28. [The standard work on this subject.]

160. Tischner, H., and Fr. Hewicker, *Oceanic Art*. Thames & Hudson, London 1954. [96 high-quality gravure plates, mainly of Melanesian material.]

161. *Voyage autour du Monde . . . 1836 et 1837 . . . sur la corvette La Bonite, commandée par M. Vaillant . . .* Paris: Arthus Bertrand . . . 1840–1866 . . . London, Akermann et cie., 96 Strand.

162. Warner, Oliver, *Captain Cook and the South Pacific*. Cassell Caravel Books, London 1964. [Contains some rare items in colour.]

163. Wingert, Paul S., *An Outline Guide to the Art of the South Pacific*. Columbia University Press, New York 1946.

164. ——, *Art of the South Pacific Islands*. Thames & Hudson, London 1953. [102 photogravures and text.]

UNPUBLISHED COLLECTIONS

165. Hodges, William: The Admiral Isaac Smith Collection in the Mitchell Library, Sydney. [Original wash drawings from which engravings

for Cook's *Voyages* were later made.]

166. Tobin, Rear Admiral George: Water-colours, Tahiti 1792, in the Mitchell Library, Sydney. [Tobin (1768–1838) was an officer on the *Providence* with Captain Bligh on the voyage to Tahiti, 1791–3.]

ADDENDUM

167. Dodd, Edward, *The Ring of Fire*: vol. 1, *Polynesian Art*. Dodd, Mead and Company, New York 1967. [Nearly 500 illustrations. Items 146 and 154 above have better reproductions and layout and a more professional text, yet this work of an enthusiast correctly claims to be 'the first comprehensive book' devoted to the arts of Polynesia, as distinct from Oceania.]

INDEX AND GLOSSARY

The meaning of Polynesian words in the text is usually made evident on their first appearance, but not when they recur. In this index translations or explanations are offered in parenthesis for a number of native words or names that appear frequently. The dialect to which a word belongs can generally be inferred from the place of origin of the story in which it appears.

Proper names have not always been indexed when they appear in headings. Figures in bold type refer to illustrations.